Emerald Anfield

Keith Falkiner is a reporter with the *Irish Daily Star Sunday*. He lives in Dublin. *Emerald Anfield* is his second book.

Emerald Anfield

Keith Falkiner

HACHETTE
BOOKS
IRELAND

Copyright © 2010 Keith Falkiner

First published in 2010 by Hachette Books Ireland

A Hachette UK Company

1

The right of Keith Falkiner to be identified as the Author of the Work has been asserted by him in accordance with the Copyright, Designs and Patents Act, 1988.

The author and publisher would like to thank the following for the use of their copyrighted material in *Emerald Anfield: The Irish and Liverpool FC*. Photo Section: Colorsport: p. 1, 2; 3, 4, 5, 6, 7; Offside: p. 2, 8; Inpho: 5; Getty: p. 4, 7

All rights reserved. No part of this publication may be reproduced, stored in a retrieval system, or transmitted, in any form or by any means without the prior written permission of the publisher, nor be otherwise circulated in any form of binding or cover other than that in which it is published and without a similar condition being imposed on the subsequent purchaser.

Some quotations have been taken from contemporary sources at the time

A CIP catalogue record for this title is available from the British Library.

ISBN 978 1 444 70101 2

Typeset in Bembo by Hachette Books Ireland
Cover and text design by Anu Design
Printed and bound in Great Britain by Mackays, Chatham, ME5 8TD

Hachette Books Ireland policy is to use papers that are natural, renewable and recyclable products and made from wood grown in sustainable forests. The logging and manufacturing processes are expected to conform to the environmental regulations of the country of origin.

Hachette Books Ireland
8 Castlecourt Centre
Castleknock
Dublin 15
Ireland

www.hachette.ie

A division of Hachette UK, 338 Euston Road, London NW1 3BH, England

To my mother Elizabeth (Betty) Falkiner.

And to the ninety-six fans who lost their lives at Hillsborough on 15 April 1989. May truth and justice prevail.

Contents

Foreword by Nicky Allt   ix

Introduction   xiii

Section 1
The Rise of a Red Giant (1892–1934)

1. Foundation of a Club   3
2. John McKenna: A Liverpool Visionary   11
3. Elisha Scott: Anfield's Belfast Boy   20

Section 2
The Slide to Relegation (1934–1959)

4. Post Elisha Scott: Liverpool Stumble   45
5. Sammy Smyth: Goals but No Glory   51

Section 3
From Second Division to European Domination (1959–1981)

6. Thank Shanks: The Reds Rise Again   59
       When Liverpool Played in Ireland   66
7. Steve Heighway on the Wing   69
       When Liverpool Played in Ireland   90
8. Kings of Europe: 1977, 1978, 1981   95

Section 4
The Great 1980s

9. Ronnie Whelan: A Midfield Maestro — 113
       When Liverpool Played in Ireland — 128
10. Kings of Europe: 1984 — 131
11. Kenny's Green Army: Aldo, Razor and Stan — 137

Section 5
Twenty Years Of Hurt

12. From Dalglish to Souness — 147
13. The Roy Evans Revolution: Babb and McAteer — 155
14. Steve Finnan: Mr Dependable — 163
15. Kings of Europe: 2005 — 169
16. Where Next for Anfield's Irish? — 179

Section 6
The Irish Reds: Half a Century of Supporting LFC

17. The Fans Speak — 187
18. Hillsborough Horror: An Irish View — 199
19. Anfield: A Home from Home — 215

Timeline — 221

Player Profiles — 225

Statistics — 289

Foreword

I'm delighted to see a book like this paying homage to the influence the Irish have had on the entire history of a great club like Liverpool FC.

Whether it is the great players from Ireland who have represented the club or the magnificent fans from all over the country who make their way across the Irish Sea for games at Anfield, the Irish have made a wonderful contribution to our club.

But the connection between the city of Liverpool and the Irish runs much deeper than just the football.

Anybody who knows the history of our city will understand the massive part played by the thousands of Irish immigrants who made Liverpool their home over the past couple of centuries.

I don't think I'm going too far when I say that without the Irish there would be no Liverpool, or certainly not the contemporary Liverpool that we see today.

From the football side of things, Liverpool FC have been very fortunate to have had some magnificent Irish players over the years.

The likes of Ronnie Whelan, John Aldridge, Steve Staunton and Ray Houghton gave great service to the club and the fans on the Kop always loved them.

The great thing about the Irish players is that they know what it means to play for a club like Liverpool, they don't have to be educated about the club or its history as they already know it.

They have that in built grit, heart and passion that Liverpool fans always look for in their players.

If there is one Irish player that sticks out in my mind above all the others it has to be Steve Heighway.

Steve was a natural footballer and a brilliant winger; if he was playing the game today he would easily be worth £30 million and I would pay that just to have a player exactly like Steve in our team now.

I can remember in the 1970s how we would be standing by the Kop wall shouting for Steve to get on the ball and stretch those long legs of his as he was a nightmare for defenders to deal with.

If a game was really tight and not going Liverpool's way, we could always depend on Steve to make a raking run down the wing to set up a goal or win us a penalty.

It's remarkable how much we took Steve Heighway for granted back then but it's only when I look back now I appreciate what a brilliant player he really was.

For over twenty years from the late 1970s through to the 1990s Liverpool had such a great conveyor belt of Irish talent coming through the ranks into the first team.

It really annoys me that the club has lost that in recent years, even though I know there are still a lot of talented young footballers in Ireland.

Friends who run schoolboy football clubs in Ireland tell me that there is a lot of talent there but that clubs like Liverpool don't take a serious look anymore.

That's sad and it's something we need to get back because of the great connection Irish people have with the club. I see it every week with all the fans who come over from Ireland for the games. They are so similar to Scousers in so many ways and, again, I think a lot of that harks back to our own Irish ancestry. Even in my own family, all my mother's side were Fagans from County Tipperary and almost everyone in Liverpool that I know can trace some part of their family back to Ireland.

Liverpool is a Celtic city and we love nothing better than to enjoy a bit of storytelling and singing songs, just like the Irish. I've been going to Liverpool games as a fan for forty years now and it's remarkable to see how many more songs the Liverpool fans have compared to other teams. Fans from opposing teams always remark how amazed they are at the range of songs we have and I don't think it's any coincidence that we have such a strong Celtic heritage. Another aspect of the Scouse character that is so similar to the Irish is our humour. We share the same wit and ability to laugh at ourselves.

I recently brought my play *One Night In Istanbul* to Dublin, the first time it had featured outside the UK, and I was concerned that the audience might not understand the strong Scouse humour in it. To my surprise, the Irish audience were laughing at all the same things in the play that we in Liverpool also find funny.

As Liverpool born and bred, I am so proud of my football club and its successful history but just as proud that so many people from outside our city in Ireland share the same passion and understanding of what the club is all about.

Liverpool FC is all the better for all the great fans, players and coaches from Ireland who have given so much to the club.

Long may it last.
Nicky Allt

Introduction

I was born in Dublin in March 1977 and the only issue I've ever had with this is that I was far too young to recall a single second from Liverpool's first European Cup triumph just two months later.

Neither, unfortunately, do I have any first-hand memories of classy Scot Kenny Dalglish's delightful Wembley chip that retained the trophy a year later.

Given that my first real vivid football memory is Northern Ireland's iconic 1–0 victory over the World Cup hosts Spain in 1982, I can safely say that I also have no recollection of Liverpool's third European Cup win in 1981.

What being born in the year of 1977 did give me, however, was the opportunity to grow up through the golden decade for Irish players at Liverpool FC.

Right from the very moment fellow Dubliner Ronnie Whelan curled a trademark beauty to win the 1983 Milk Cup final over Manchester Utd, while zany goalkeeper Bruce Grobbelaar was busy doing handstands across the Wembley pitch and legendary manager Bob Paisley got to climb the steps to collect the trophy, I have been hooked on the Reds of Liverpool.

The fact that my chosen team mopped up a trophy or two of some sort almost every season throughout the 1980s meant it wasn't exactly a chore being a Liverpool fan.

It also helped that the team was littered with some of the best Irish players to have ever graced the game of football.

Apart from midfielder Whelan, who for me was the best of them all, there was stout defender Mark Lawrenson – a player of tremendous ability and versatility – and young Waterford full-back Jim Beglin.

Later in the decade came Jack Charlton's 'Boys in Green' heroes John Aldridge, Ray Houghton and Steve Staunton.

What was great about all of the Irish Liverpool players of the 1980s was not only that each of them was good, but they all had a certain character and spirit both on and off the pitch and a will to win, for both Ireland and Liverpool, that made you admire them even more.

Because of the feats of these guys, it made so many proud to be Irish.

Of course, the Irish link with Liverpool FC didn't just start in the 1980s, it has its roots as far back as the very foundation of the club.

The Reds' first manager was County Monaghan man John McKenna and during a forty-year association with the Anfield club, McKenna put in train many of the iconic aspects of Liverpool FC which we still take for granted to this day.

Perhaps the most popular ever Irishman to play for Liverpool was long-serving Belfast goalkeeper Elisha Scott, who manned the posts at Anfield for an incredible twenty-two years from 1912 to 1934.

Such was Scott's popularity that he was even afforded the honour of addressing the Liverpool crowd from the director's box following his final game at Anfield – an honour very few players have experienced.

However, the connection between the city of Liverpool and Ireland runs much deeper than just the football.

Being a popular port city and within a hair's-breadth of Dublin, Liverpool has naturally attracted tens of thousands of Irish emigrants over the past couple of centuries. At least a third of the population of the city lays claim to Irish ancestry and our similarities with the wit and character of Liverpool natives is well established.

It is this familiarity between the people which makes each trip to Anfield for Irish fans ever more welcoming and Liverpool is often referred to by scousers as Ireland's 'real capital'.

But there is even more to Liverpool FC which has made the club so appealing to so many Irish; it is the manner in which the club has conducted itself down through the years.

The 'Liverpool Way' as it became known was an unwritten code of conduct that insisted on the players, management and fans remaining humble whenever victorious and gracious in defeat.

Although admittedly lost a bit in recent years as the club has struggled to maintain its real identity in the fast-paced modern era of football, the 'Liverpool Way' has resonated so much on these shores.

There are football fans in Ireland who scoff at the very notion of so many people from this country so fervently supporting an English team.

However, football by its very nature has been a global game from as far back as anybody can remember.

The very first team to ever represent Liverpool FC way back in 1892 was almost exclusively Scottish and, let's not forget, the many great Irish players who have graced Anfield with their presence in the Liverpool team.

Considering the domestic and continental success of Liverpool FC over the past half century and the club's global standing within the game, no country outside the UK has impacted on this success as much as the Irish.

It is for this reason above all others that I am so proud to be an Irish Liverpool FC supporter.

Keith Falkiner
July 2010

The Rise of a Red Giant
(1892–1934)

1

Foundation of a Club

In late 19th-century Britain, association football was fast becoming the game of the people.

Where cricket had once stood as the nation's overriding sporting passion, football began to take hold and revolutionise how the vast majority of working-class people enjoyed their sparse recreation time. It had grown from its origins as a diverse localised game in the 1850s to a much better organised association of clubs by the time the English FA Cup, the oldest football competition in the world, was first contested in 1872.

Towns across the country, particularly in the northern county of Lancashire, were busy putting together well-developed clubs, which, just like in the modern game, only the best footballers were given the opportunity to represent. Even before the top clubs had stumbled on the idea of creating a competitive league competition in 1888, thousands of fans would gather for friendly games between teams from opposing towns and villages. Workers and labourers who had struggled for years to obtain a half-working day on Saturdays were now using their new spare time to indulge their new passion as fans of their local football team.

And things were no different in the port city of Liverpool where, by 1888, thousands of excited dock workers made their way to the specially built stadium on the Anfield Road end of the impressive Stanley Park recreational area to cheer on their city's team.

'Anfield', as the ground was simply known, was already playing host to some special football days as the proud locals gathered to watch their team battle it out for English Football League glory. Even at this early stage the Irish had made their presence felt at the club: the name Anfield derived from the old townland Annefield in New Ross, County Wexford. The name had been bestowed on this area of Stanley Park by famous Wexford shipbuilder Robert Samuel Graves who had moved from Annefield in the 1850s to live in Liverpool. Graves was later appointed mayor of the city.

In its first season in 1888, the English Football League consisted of twelve clubs from the midlands and the northern region of the country.

The midlands was well represented by Aston Villa, Birmingham, Wolverhampton Wanderers, Derby County, Stoke City and Notts County, whilst farther north in Lancashire, the first teams to play in the English Football League included Accrington, Blackburn Rovers, Burnley and Preston.

Games at Anfield were often fast and furious with goals aplenty whenever any of these sides came to town, and the fans were always kept enthralled during those early years of competitive football. The game was already big business in the city and even local newspapers, such as the *Liverpool Echo*, dedicated special Saturday editions to football.

By 10 January 1891, in just the third year of the English League championship, excitement at Anfield reached fever pitch as the home team were just one win away from clinching the league title. Despite it being a bitterly cold winter Saturday afternoon, 15,000 fans crammed into Anfield to watch their team battle it out with English football powerhouses Preston North End, who had already won the league for the first two years of its existence.

Fifteen thousand was a huge crowd for any game of football in the English league at the time, as grounds had yet to be developed to a standard that could accommodate the type of gatherings we see at modern games.

Far from the all-seater stadium it is today, Anfield in 1891 had just the one main covered stand and two uncovered embankments to the back of each goal where fans could huddle up to watch the action.

Despite a 1–0 defeat on the day, the atmosphere around Anfield Road was electric and locals had only to wait one more week for their team to finally land what, along with the FA Cup, had become the most coveted prize in English football. In so doing, Anfield, a passionate football arena that would become synonymous with success as the home of the world-renowned Liverpool Football Club, had witnessed the first of nineteen league titles that would be won at the ground. Though, back in 1891, it was not Liverpool FC that was tasting this glory.

Liverpool FC had not yet even been formed and it was future city rivals Everton who brought the first league championship back to Anfield.

As a founder member of the English Football League, Everton had firmly established itself among the elite in the game at that time. However this successful professional club had its beginnings as a much more humble amateur football team started as a recreation club for Sunday school members of a local Methodist chapel based in the Everton area.

The team that would become known as Everton FC, and later branch off into its offshoot Liverpool FC, was instigated by Methodist minister Ben Chambers in 1878, who thought football would be a good and healthy past-time for his pupils at the St Domingo Chapel in Everton.

As the chapel's Sunday school students already had a flourishing cricket team competing in the summer months, Chambers decided that football could help to keep them fit during the winter off-season.

It was for this reason that the St Domingo Football Club was established in the winter of 1878 and the chapel's Bible class scholars congregated in the Stanley Park recreational area to play their games.

Initially, the St Domingo boys played games amongst themselves before branching out in 1879 to play other local church teams and clubs also based out of Stanley Park.

As the number of their opponents increased throughout that year, it soon became clear that St Domingo were one of the best sides playing in Stanley Park and the club began to attract players from other teams.

Before the year was out, it was decided that the club needed a new name as it was already clear that not every player on the team was from the St Domingo Chapel. In December 1879, the club unanimously agreed to change its name to Everton Football Club after the district in which most of the club's players lived.

Friendly games with other newly established clubs in the Merseyside area came thick and fast for Everton in 1880 and the club was developing at such a rate that it applied for membership to the newly formed Lancashire Football Association.

Everton's membership of the association afforded it the opportunity to play in registered cup competitions in the area, although the club mostly continued to play friendly games from its Stanley Park base.

It was whilst playing these games that the team caught the eye of successful local brewer John Houlding, whose imposing red-brick home was located close to Everton's pitch at Stanley Park.

As a highly respected businessman in the area, Houlding's interest in Everton was keenly welcomed by the club and, before the start of their 1881–1882 season of cup and friendly games, he was appointed the club's president.

Houlding took to his new role with gusto and was equally thrilled to see the thousands of people who thronged to Stanley Park each weekend to watch Everton play friendly games throughout 1882.

Eager for the club to prosper further by having its own enclosed football ground, in 1883 Houlding moved Everton across Stanley Park away from their original pitch to a field on Priory Road, where he could fence off the pitch and erect a stand from where fans would have to seek admission to the ground to watch games.

Unfortunately for Everton, their stay at Priory Road didn't last a year after the owner of the field, cattle salesman William Cruitt, railed at the disturbance being created each week by the large number of fans coming to support the team.

By the summer of 1884, Everton were on the move again and, this time, Houlding secured them a site from a friend, and fellow brewer, John Orrell, who owned a stretch of land that straddled the Walton Breck Road and Anfield Road ends of Stanley Park.

As in the previous year, Houlding fenced off a pitch on Orrell's land and erected a stand in time for Everton to embark on their annual batch of friendly games for the 1884–1885 season.

Under the stewardship of Houlding, Everton named their new ground Anfield and set off on a meteoric rise that saw the club gain membership to the exclusive twelve-team professional English Football League in 1888.

As Everton naturally became more popular with the public during this period, Houlding seized on the opportunity to make money back from the club by charging his own rent in accordance with the yearly gate receipts. Even at the very origins of the professional game, businessmen knew that there was money to be made from investing in football, and they could see that it was a game that was only going to grow. And similar to the billionaire Premier League owners of today, club presidents like Houlding were only too happy to show off their impressive projects as a sign of their wealth and business acumen.

Friends and business partners were encouraged to come to the games and they developed their own growing interest in football.

By the time Everton clinched their first English League title in 1891, football had eclipsed all other sports as the most popular for fans in the area.

However the euphoria surrounding Everton's stunning success was short lived as Houlding soon found himself at loggerheads with some club members who opposed his plans.

In early 1892, barely a year after their league triumph, proposals by Houlding to increase the annual rent which Everton would pay him did not go down well. Neither did a subsequent suggestion by him that the club should buy the Anfield ground along with a nearby patch of land which he also owned.

Fearing that Houlding's proposals were little more than an elaborate plan to gain himself some additional profit, Everton broke away from the brewer with the intentions of setting up the club at a new home ground.

Without the backing of Houlding, Everton FC successfully found a new piece of land from which to operate and, remarkably, it was located only a few hundred metres away from Anfield, across the other side of Stanley Park. It was here that Everton's new ground of Goodison Park was formed and the basis of a fierce Merseyside rivalry was born.

Far from giving up on his own dream of having a professional club playing at Anfield, Houlding set about creating a new team that he hoped could match Everton in its ambition and achievement. He already had a strong basis from which to work in that his beloved Anfield was as good as any other football ground built in England at the time.

Houlding was also helped by the fact he wasn't alone in his vision for this new club. One associate who often joined Houlding at Anfield during Everton's early glory years was none other than County Monaghan man John McKenna.

Between them this pair would create a new football club in Liverpool, one that would go on to dominate football not just in England but across Europe in the century ahead.

Liverpool/Everton Rivalry

Everton FC's move away from Anfield in 1892 and the subsequent formation of Liverpool FC at the ground by John Houlding set in train a fierce rivalry that exists to this day.

The first encounter between the two clubs came on 22 April 1893 when Liverpool defeated Everton 1–0 in the final of the amateur Liverpool Senior Cup.

The clubs' first league clash came in the 1893–1894 First Division season which Everton won 3–0 at Goodison Park.

Since then, Liverpool and Everton have met on no less than 182 occasions in the English league, with Liverpool winning seventy of those games, Everton fifty-six and with fifty-six draws.

Although Everton have generally been seen as the Catholic club in Merseyside, a religious divide has never been an issue between the supporters and both clubs have signed players of all religions and races through the years.

The city of Liverpool is statistically the most successful football city in England with Everton and Liverpool winning a combined twenty-seven league titles, eighteen for Liverpool and nine for Everton.

The two clubs have met in three major English cup finals – the 1984 Milk Cup, and the 1986 and 1989 FA Cup finals, with Liverpool winning on all three occasions.

2

John McKenna: A Liverpool Visionary

It is fair to say that when the vast majority of Liverpool football fans across the globe ponder the glorious history of their club, few ever make the link between the illustrious Merseysiders and the tiny Ulster county of Monaghan. Far from being a hotbed of soccer, Monaghan is more renowned in sporting circles for producing the talented boxer Barry McGuigan, the 'Clones Cyclone', who captured the hearts of the nation by winning the WBA Featherweight world title in 1985. Apart from Monaghan Utd's two brief stints in the League of Ireland Premier Division and former Leeds Utd midfielder Jonathan Douglas' eight senior Republic of Ireland caps, there has been little to associate the county with major achievements in the professional football ranks. Yet if it wasn't for the brave and audacious endeavours of a north Monaghan man over 100 years ago, Liverpool Football Club, and its famed Anfield ground, may never have become what it is today.

Long before flying Dublin-born winger Steve Heighway was helping the Reds to European Cup glory in the 1970s followed by Limerick man

Steve Finnan in 2005, the foundations of what Liverpool Football Club was to become and achieve were being set by a man by the name of John McKenna. In his forty-year association with Liverpool FC, which began from the first day it came into existence in 1892, visionary McKenna oversaw the club's rise from of the shadow of their near neighbours Everton FC to become one of the most successful teams in the English football game.

Off the pitch, McKenna also sowed the seeds for the development of one of the most iconic symbols of Liverpool FC and its devoted fans when he initiated construction of Anfield's Spion Kop.

Devout Protestant McKenna was born in January 1855 in the northern Monaghan parish of Donagh, the son of local couple Patrick McKenna and Jane McCrudden. Born into an Ireland still recovering from the worst ravages of the Great Famine, McKenna, like thousands of other young Irish men and women before him, left Irish shores for Liverpool at the tender age of seventeen. Over the following twenty years, McKenna's passion for the relatively new sport of association football would turn him into a legend in his adopted city.

Back in McKenna's homeland, however, an entirely different cultural and sporting phenomenon was about to take hold. In 1884, the Gaelic Athletic Association (GAA) was formed to promote declining Irish culture through the country's traditional sporting past-time of hurling and its own brand of football. The spread of the GAA in communities across Ireland naturally affected the popularity of association football in those embryonic years.

However, over in Liverpool, John McKenna had become a keen fan of the game.

The Monaghan man was a regular visitor to Anfield during the days that Everton spent establishing itself as a real force in English football. Sporting his customary black bowler hat and exquisite moustache, McKenna was an impressive figure amongst the hordes who came to cheer on the burgeoning club. McKenna had thrived in Liverpool since his arrival in 1872 and, within ten years, he was a well-respected member of the business community who could hold his own in the company of powerful businessmen such as John Houlding.

He had gained his first job in the city as an errand boy for a local shop before progressing from there to work as the vaccinations officer for the West Derby Union, the company which oversaw a number of workhouses for the poor in the Liverpool area.

It was while there that McKenna made acquaintance with John Houlding and the pair formed a strong friendship upon which the early foundations of Liverpool Football Club would be built.

McKenna's first passion had been rugby and, in 1885, during a spell as a volunteer with the Lancashire Artillery unit of the British army, he helped to establish a regimental rugby club that he himself played for.

It wasn't until Houlding had convinced him to visit Anfield to watch Everton play a few years later that his love of football was born.

After matches, the affable Irishman could be regularly spotted in the company of Houlding as they toasted the team's achievements at the club president's Sandon Hotel bar.

The Sandon, which to this day still stands as a conference centre in the shadow of Anfield and is a pre-game meeting point of many devout Kopites, acted as Everton's dressing rooms and general meeting area back then.

It was where the fans and players alike had gathered to celebrate the club's tremendous league title in 1891 and all were looking forward to what they hoped to be many more years of success for the best team in England and the pride of Liverpool.

As Houlding prepared to create a new club of his own, his old friend John McKenna stuck by him by giving up his allegiance to Everton in favour of whatever new club they could develop for Anfield.

Houlding was impressed with McKenna's loyalty and, in return, appointed him as the new secretary of the Liverpool Football Association Club, which officially came into being in April 1892.

The position of secretary equated to the modern-day manager, although much of the job was taken up with administration work rather than the day-to-day coaching of the team. McKenna would also have another man to work alongside as he attempted to mould a team worthy of carrying on Everton's successful tradition at Anfield.

Liverpool fans who remember the ill-fated Roy Evans/Gerard Houllier double act at the beginning of the 1998–1999 season may shudder at the thought that such an unusual arrangement had already been played out at the club over 100 years earlier.

In deciding who would look after the team affairs of his new club, Houlding came up with the idea of pairing McKenna with another loyal lieutenant from his Everton days, William Barclay.

Barclay was Everton's manager for the club's very first English League campaign in 1888–1889 and provided his steady football knowledge to Houlding's growing new project.

Barclay and McKenna worked well in their new roles together, although there was little doubt that it was the Ulsterman who made most of the big decisions.

Although Barclay was the man with the experience in the day-to-day running of a team, McKenna's drive and enthusiasm brought him to the fore as the senior man in the partnership. Almost all important decisions on player selections and the general direction of the club were carried out by McKenna who wasted little time in his pursuit of making Liverpool one of the best clubs in the country.

One of McKenna's first duties was to recruit players of a sufficient calibre to ensure that Liverpool could become an instant success at Anfield, and he knew exactly where to look. Using contacts he had built up in his business life amongst the Irish community in Glasgow, McKenna headed north to Scotland to head hunt the best players he could convince to come and play for Liverpool.

Glasgow was already a hotbed for football by 1892 as the city's two main clubs and bitter rivals Celtic and Rangers had helped form the inaugural Scottish Football League a year earlier.

For his part, McKenna had little trouble in enticing a number of players to move from Scotland and follow him to Merseyside.

Eight players were nabbed from Scottish clubs, including James McBride, Andrew Hannah and James Kelso from Renton, Joe McQue from Celtic, Billy McOwen from Darwen, Arthur Kelvin from Kilmarnock, Malcolm McVean from Third Lanark and John Miller from Dumbarton.

Scotsmen Duncan McClean and Tom Wyllie were also convinced to make the short trip back across Stanley Park from Everton, and McKenna

William Barclay

Englishman William Barclay cut his teeth in professional football as the first manager of Everton FC during their inaugral season in the English First Division in 1888–1889.

Everton won nine of the twenty-two games that they played under Barclay that season, but he was replaced as the club's manager for the following season by fellow Englishman Dick Molyneaux.

When Everton broke their ties with Anfield in 1892, Barclay remained loyal to the club's former chairman John Houlding, who appointed him to work alongside Irishman John McKenna as joint secretary of the new club Liverpool FC.

During their four-year partnership, Barclay and McKenna led Liverpool to two English League Second Division titles and winning eighty of the 131 games played.

Barclay also served two spells as Liverpool chairman between 1896 and 1910 and worked for the Football Association.

A widely respected and well-liked man, Barclay later became a headmaster of the Industrial Schools in Everton Crescent, Liverpool.

added further to his squad by enlisting two more Scots, John Smith from Sunderland and Jonathan Cameron from Aston Villa.

Such was the huge Scottish influence amongst McKenna's playing staff that this early Liverpool team became known as the 'team of macs'.

As he busied himself assembling this team, McKenna was also looking to Liverpool's future which he knew belonged amongst the professional English football league. As one of the club's first great visionaries,

McKenna almost instinctively knew what was best for Liverpool FC, and even though his team had yet to play a game at Anfield, he could see that the professional surrounds of the football league was the place to be.

Within a month of the club being formed, McKenna applied to the English Football League to have Liverpool elected into its ranks. His ambitious application was turned down by the football authorities, who believed the new club still had a long way to go to prove they could be anywhere near a match for English football's leading lights at the time which included Everton, Preston and Sunderland.

Liverpool FC were even overlooked for entry into the Football League's new Second Division league which had been established in 1892 to act as the second tier for English professional football – a division to which local Merseyside club Bootle and nearby Cheshire side Crewe Alexandra had managed to gain entry.

Instead, Liverpool were left to join the much smaller Lancashire League, where they would compete against the likes of local rivals Southport Central.

However the very fact that McKenna had even applied for membership of the football league showed how big his plans for Liverpool were.

If it wasn't for such bold moves in his early years at the helm at Anfield, Liverpool FC might very well have been left to languish outside the Football League and never flourished into a successful professional outfit.

Challenging the well-established might and popularity of Everton was also a brave move by both Houlding and McKenna.

Everton had already built up a strong fan base during its three years in the English Football League and it would have been difficult to predict how Liverpool could convince many of the city's football fans about the merits of their new club, which would be competing in the relative backwater of the Lancashire League.

By the time of Liverpool's first competitive outing in the Lancashire League, McKenna could even have been forgiven for questioning if they had made the right move. Playing in shirts of half white and half blue (the familiar red would not become Liverpool colours until 1894 when the club made a complete break from the Everton colours of blue and white), few fans had yet to be persuaded that following this new team would be a decent alternative to sticking with the familiarity of Everton.

Unlike the 15,000 who where there to cheer Everton on to league glory, Liverpool had mustered a paltry 200 fans.

This uncertainty surrounding the new boys on the block was perfectly summed up in the *Liverpool Echo* match report into McKenna's first league game in charge against Higher Walton on 3 September 1892. 'There was a miserable array of empty benches, not more than 200 spectators being present, the ground presenting a striking contrast to the opening Saturday of last season.'

Although for the 200 who had braved the trip to Anfield that day, any fears they had thrown their lot behind a dud was soon blown out of the water as Liverpool began life in the Lancashire League with a phenomenal bang.

Lancashire League

The Lancashire League was formed in 1889 as a competition for clubs in the northwest of England who had failed to gain entry into the professional English Football League, which had been established a year earlier.

Prime movers in the formation of the league were the officials of Bury Football Club, who had ambitions to set up a regional competition which would be a stepping stone for them and other clubs to gain a place in the Football League.

Although the majority of the clubs were based in the county of Lancashire, the league did eventually accept several clubs from neighbouring Cheshire.

The league survived for fourteen seasons until 1903 during which time many Lancashire League member clubs had taken their place in the English Football League. These included Liverpool, Bury, Crewe Alexandra, Accrington Stanley and Stockport County.

The home side hit Higher Walton for eight in a magnificent display of courageous attacking football which gave an early indication of McKenna's keen eye for a player. All the men he had recruited from Scotland blended in seamlessly at Anfield and Liverpool's 8–0 win on the opening league day, with goals from John Cameron (two), John Smith (two), Joe McQue (two), James McBride and Malcolm McVein, was just a sign of the great things to come.

Over the following month, Southport Central, Bury and West Manchester were all soundly beaten at Anfield, as McKenna's Liverpool raced to the top of the Lancashire League. Like all successful football managers, McKenna had realised that a strong spine to the team from the back through the midfield and up to the forwards was the best way to ensure consistent results.

One of his most important signings was defender Andrew Hannah, whom McKenna had installed as the first Liverpool captain. Hannah was an extremely experienced campaigner, having previously captained Everton for two years before returning to Renton in Scotland.

Eagled-eyed McKenna knew from Hannah's Everton days that he was the man to lead his new team from the back and his early judgement proved spot on, with Liverpool keeping fourteen cleans sheets in the twenty-nine league and cup games they played in their first season.

Just in front of Hannah, former Celtic player Joe McQue was another talented operator who could also get forward from his position at centre-half to score important goals. Up front, McKenna had unearthed three excellent goal getters in Jonathan Cameron, Tom Wyllie and John Miller, who notched up forty-nine goals between them at the head of the Liverpool attack. Miller was particularly prolific, scoring an incredible twenty-seven goals in twenty-eight games that season.

Just two months into the season, McKenna also added to his squad with another two great signings, brothers Matt and Hugh McQueen from Leith Athletic in Scotland. Hugh was a skilful midfielder who could chip in with the odd goal, whilst Matt was a versatile all-rounder who could play well in any position on the pitch, including goalkeeper.

In all, this meant that Liverpool were a serious proposition for the other teams in the Lancashire League and very few enjoyed their trips to Anfield.

By early December 1892, it was clear that the battle for the Lancashire League was a three-horse race between Liverpool, Bury and Blackpool – subsequently the only three teams out of the twelve in the league still operating as professional football clubs today.

Liverpool's only defeat in their first eight leagues game had been a 3–0 reverse at Blackpool in November and they looked to gain revenge against their top-of-the-table rivals when Blackpool arrived at Anfield on 17 December 1892. By then, just four months into their first competitive season, Liverpool's support had grown unbelievably with a crowd of 6,000 coming through the gates of Anfield for the clash with Blackpool, a sure sign of how success for a football team could generate added interest from the watching public.

Liverpool played well that day and had the majority of possession in the Blackpool half, but their opponents were smart operators and twice caught Liverpool on the break to score two goals. Despite McKenna's Liverpool laying siege to the Blackpool goal, they just couldn't find a response and they lost the game 2–0, a defeat which looked to be setting Blackpool on their way to the Lancashire League title.

McKenna's troops put their disappointment against Blackpool behind them, however, as they embarked on a remarkable run of ten wins in their next twelve league games.

This series of results gave Liverpool a one-point advantage over Blackpool going into the final game of the Lancashire League season on 15 April 1893.

Liverpool made the short journey through Merseyside to Scarisbrick New Road to take on Southport Central knowing that victory would give them a league title in just their first year.

Whatever nerves John McKenna and his players may have had as they made their way to Southport would surely have been increased by the chaos that ensued as they arrived for the game.

The referee who had been appointed by the Lancashire League failed to show up and, after a forty-minute delay, a local referee was eventually found so the match could go ahead.

It is hard to imagine how McKenna must have been feeling to endure such a charade before a game of such magnitude for Liverpool.

If that wasn't enough, McKenna's team also fell behind to an early goal, as Southport broke from a Liverpool corner to snatch the lead after just twelve minutes. To their great credit, Liverpool got over these early setbacks and clawed their way back into the game. They secured an equaliser through John Miller and withstood everything Southport could throw at them to gain a 1–1 draw.

The point at Southport was crucial for Liverpool as although they finished on equal points with bogey side Blackpool, the Anfielders were crowned Lancashire League champions because they had a better goal average than their rivals.

Like any good visionary, McKenna spent little time basking in this success and was already looking to the future for Liverpool. Ignoring the fact he had been knocked back the previous year, McKenna made a new application to the Football League in the hope that Liverpool's success in the Lancashire League would be looked on favourably.

Such was McKenna's eagerness to have Liverpool promoted to the Football League that he neglected to tell anybody else at the club that he had made the application.

It came as a great surprise to right-hand man William Barclay therefore when he received a message back from the Football League stating that Liverpool's application had been accepted and that the club would become part of the expanded English Second Division for the 1893–1894 season. Barclay had not been overly keen on Liverpool joining the Football League, but with their application now accepted, it was difficult for him to turn it down, meaning persistent McKenna had finally got his way.

As Liverpool prepared for their new life in the English Second Division, McKenna was again busy in the transfer market.

Liverpool's success had also garnered interest in their players from other clubs, and McKenna lost his two top forwards that summer when Tom Wyllie joined Bury and John Miller moved to English First Division outfit The Wednesday in Sheffield.

It was a blow for McKenna to lose such good forwards, but he again showed his great eye for a player when he replaced the duo with David Henderson from Kings Park and James Stott of Middlesbrough. Between them, they scored thirty goals as Liverpool became a real force in the

Second Division.

At the back, McKenna had managed to hold on to the big presence of Andrew Hannah and Joe McQue, giving his Liverpool team a very settled look at they began life in the English League.

They started the season as if they meant business with a 2–0 win away to Middlesbrough Ironopolis and followed this up with a 4–0 trouncing of Lincoln City in their first English League match at Anfield.

If Liverpool had been impressive during their first season as a football club, they were even better in their second, remarkably remaining unbeaten throughout the entire league campaign to finish a massive eight points ahead of nearest rivals Small Heath (now Birmingham City).

As the Football League had yet to devise promotion and relegation from its divisions, Liverpool were forced into a play-off with the first division's bottom side Newton Heath (who in 1902 changed their name to Manchester Utd) to decide who should play in the First Division.

One of the keys to Liverpool's amazing success in their first two years was McKenna's devotion to detail and preparation. Prior to the hugely important play-off match, which was held at Blackburn on 28 April 1894, McKenna took his players off to nearby Hightown to prepare properly for the challenge ahead.

The trip to Hightown allowed the team to dedicate more time than normal to tactical training sessions whilst also giving the players a chance to bond during their time away. As with almost everything he had done up until that point, McKenna got his tactics spot on and Liverpool steamrolled Newton Heath.

Right from the kick off, Liverpool had their First Division opponents on the back foot and secured a deserved lead through a Patrick Gordon header on twenty minutes. There was no let up to the Liverpool onslaught and they added a second goal before the break to effectively kill off the Newton Heath challenge.

The game eventually finished 2–0 in Liverpool's favour, winning them promotion to the First Division at the first time of asking and rounding off an astonishingly successful two years for John McKenna's team. McKenna himself was building a reputation as a stern but honest manager and he always tried to instil a sense of fair play and respect within his own team.

Players who had any particular problems were always welcome to discuss them with McKenna at his home in Castlewood Road, near Anfield, although he was always keen to keep an authoritative distance between himself and the players who could expect a strong rebuke from the boss if they ever stepped out of line.

The summer of 1894 was to prove another busy one for McKenna after his club's rapid promotion and he sought to bring in players who could help the club settle in the First Division. Among those he brought into the club that year was County Down forward David Hannah, who became the first ever Irishman to play for Liverpool after he was signed from Sunderland in November 1894.

However McKenna was already finding out that life in the First Division was a difficult proposition. Liverpool struggled badly to impose themselves against the higher class of opposition in the top flight, finding it almost impossible to compete with the established might of English's football's big hitters in the shape of Sunderland, Everton, Preston and Aston Villa.

They failed to win any of their first four First Division games at Anfield and were also on the receiving end of two 5–0 drubbings on their travels to West Brom and Aston Villa.

Those defeats aside, nothing was going to allay the excitement of a first Merseyside league derby between Liverpool and Everton on 13 October 1894, a sure sign to McKenna that his side had really reached the big time.

A game of such local importance was also given special treatment by the *Liverpool Football Echo* in the lead up to the Goodison Park encounter which it dubbed 'The Great Football Match' and adorned its front page with half-page portraits of both teams.

Unfortunately, despite the big build up, Liverpool were unable to match their more experienced opponents on the day and suffered a 3–0 defeat, a painful introduction into big league-derby games.

McKenna's men wouldn't have to wait long to attempt revenge on their local rivals when the second derby took place at Anfield on 17 November.

With Everton riding high at the top of the table and Liverpool languishing at the bottom of it, the *Liverpool Echo* reported that there was 'the general expectation that today's game would result in another couple of points to the Evertonians'.

Possibly buoyed on by this grim newspaper assertion and also not wanting to disappoint in front of their own fans, Liverpool ensured the first Merseyside league derby at Anfield would be one to remember, with one of the most exciting finishes ever to a game against Everton.

It started badly for the home side, however, when they fell behind to a penalty scored by Everton's Bob Kelso, before Irishman David Hannah lifted the gloom around Anfield with a stunning shot for a well-taken equaliser.

The game remained all square until the final five minutes when Everton looked to have snatched the points with a goal through Alex Latta. Not to be outdone, McKenna's troops laid siege to the Everton goal for the remaining few minutes and with the 25,000 crowd all holding their breath, Liverpool were awarded a last-minute penalty for a foul on

Liverpool in the First Division

Although Liverpool's first foray into the English First Division ended in disaster with immediate relegation in the 1894–1895 season, the club has enjoyed a number of remarkably successful stints in the division.

After regaining promotion to the division in 1896, Liverpool remained in English football's top flight for the next eight years, winning the league for the first time in 1901.

The club was relegated in 1904 but regained promotion a year later and won their second league title in 1906 and remained in the top flight for the following forty-eight years, winning another three titles in 1922, 1923 and 1947.

Following relegation to the Second Division in 1954, Liverpool remained out of the top flight for seven years.

Since they regained promotion under Bill Shankly in 1961, Liverpool have remained in the First Division and have won the league title another thirteen times, the last of which came in 1990.

John Drummond, which Jimmy Ross smashed home to send Anfield into raptures.

The glee from this derby game was soon forgotten, though, as McKenna just couldn't conjure up enough wins to keep Liverpool out of danger of being relegated from the First Division.

Their seven wins from thirty games that season just wasn't enough to save them and Liverpool sadly finished bottom of the league.

If Liverpool's poor performances in the First Division throughout 1894–1895 affected McKenna, then he certainly didn't show it as he looked to get Liverpool back on track in the Second Division.

He made another shrewd investment in the transfer market by acquiring the lethal striking skills of George Allan from Leith Athletic in Scotland. Scottish international Allan, one of Liverpool's first great goal-scoring heroes, notched up no fewer than twenty-five goals in twenty games that season, as Liverpool fought off the tough challenge of Manchester City to win their second Division Two crown in three seasons.

In all, that success marked a third league win in four years for John McKenna since Liverpool FC was established – a feat that, even today, is impressive alongside the heroics of the club's later legendary managers Bill Shankly, Bob Paisley and Kenny Dalglish.

Perhaps McKenna's greatest decision in his time at Liverpool came following this Second Division success in 1896 when he stepped aside from his position as team secretary to appoint a man whom he obviously believed was better qualified to turn the team into genuine First Division contenders. Rather than chance a second failed attempt at leading the team in English football's top division, McKenna turned to Tom Watson, the most experienced and decorated manager of his time.

Englishman Watson had guided northeast giants Sunderland to three First Division titles between 1891 and 1895 and getting him on board for Liverpool was the equivalent to snaring an Alex Ferguson or Arsene Wenger in the modern era. It is really hard to overestimate the significance of this move by McKenna as it sent a clear message throughout English football that Liverpool were now a top-class operation to be feared. And in only his first season in charge, Watson brought Liverpool to fifth place in the First Division, marking them down as potential future champions.

They were unlucky to lose out on the title by just two points after a final day defeat to rivals Aston Villa in the 1898–1899 season but, finally, landed the club's first Division One crown two years later, bringing Liverpool's first decade in football to a successful conclusion.

Once again, Liverpool had John McKenna to thank for this.

Like his brave move to back John Houlding in forming Liverpool FC and his later efforts to get the club promoted into the professional English Football League, McKenna's selfless decision to step aside in favour of Tom

Tom Watson

Englishman Tom Watson was one of English First Division's first great managers, enjoying stunning and prolonged success with both Sunderland and Liverpool.

Watson was in charge of Sunderland for six seasons from 1889–1896, during which time he led the club into the Football League.

Under his guidance, Sunderland won three league championships in 1891–1892, 1892–1893 and 1894–1895, making him the most successful manager in their history.

Watson moved to Liverpool in 1896, where he enjoyed further success before his death in 1915. During his time at Liverpool, he won the league on two occasions, in 1900–1901 and 1905–1906 and took Liverpool to their first FA Cup final in 1914, which they lost 1–0 to Burnley.

Watson in 1896 was done because it was what was best for the club.

As McKenna initially took on a role as director at the club, Watson enjoyed a nineteen-year tenure in charge of Liverpool winning two titles in 1901 and 1906. His almost two decades at the helm also makes Watson the longest serving manager in the club's history.

Despite taking this step back in 1896, John McKenna remained very much involved in the running of Liverpool. His interest in the administration of football also grew significantly and McKenna looked to expand his influence on the game beyond Liverpool FC.

McKenna's standing within the English game was confirmed when he was appointed to the Football League's management committee in 1902 and he rose up through the ranks of the governing body to become its president by 1910, a position the Ulsterman held until his death over twenty years later.

But McKenna's first love and interest always remained Liverpool FC and, in 1906, after the Reds captured their second league title under Tom Watson, both he and John Houlding made another momentous decision that still stands to the club to this day.

The pioneering pair decided it was time to expand the Anfield ground to give the club's loyal fans a better enclosure behind the goals at the Walton Breck Road end from where they could to watch the team play.

On a huge mound of ash and rubble a new towering and steep embankment was built, which was later dubbed the Spion Kop in reference to the many brave Liverpool people who died in a battle over a hill of the same name during the Boer War in South Africa.

The Kop became the citadel from where all the most vociferous and loyal Liverpool fans massed for games at Anfield and it reached the height of its popularity and fame in the 1960s and 1970s when Liverpool became a major European football force. While other grounds also had their own Kops, none became as famous as the one at Anfield and it is hard to think of another section of a football ground anywhere in the world that is as well known as the Liverpool Kop.

When the club later completely covered the Kop in 1928 – making it the largest covered terrace in an English ground at the time – John McKenna was again involved when he was invited back to Anfield in his role as vice president of the Football Association to open it.

During his later years as president of the Football League and vice president of the FA, McKenna, who became known as 'Honest John', fought a lengthy campaign to keep the game fair and free from any scandals. Wherever he went, he preached a message of fairness within the game and for clubs and players to respect the authorities.

During a local schools final clash at Anfield in 1930 after which

McKenna had been invited to make the cup presentation, he gave a speech to the young players involved that was thoroughly typical of the man he was. 'Always obey the referee. He is the autocrat on the field of play. You may not always understand his decisions. You may sometimes disagree with them. He may make mistakes and often will do. But obey his ruling at all times.'

Off the field, McKenna was equally anxious that everything remained within the spirit of the game.

Stunned by an earlier betting scandal involving Liverpool players during his time as the club's chairman in 1915, McKenna fought right up until his dying day against the growing interest in football pools and coupons which he believed threatened the very fabric of the professional game he loved. He abhorred the idea of fans betting on football results and, in 1936, in his role as Football League president, even went as far as withholding the publication of each week's fixtures until the day before the games were played.

However, in March 1936, following a special meeting of the Football League in Manchester to discuss what had become known as the 'pools war', eighty-one-year-old McKenna slipped on a railway station platform. Whilst he recovered sufficiently to attend an international football match in Scotland a week later, he was taken seriously ill on his way back to Liverpool after the game and passed away in the early hours of 22 March 1936.

Despite his advanced years, McKenna's death stunned the football world and people of all persuasions came together to mourn the loss of the one of the game's first great administrators. His honest decency made him a well-liked and respected figure with players, managers and clubs alike and his funeral through the streets of Liverpool was befitting of a man of his stature and popularity.

Members from all over the football fraternity, including European club dignitaries, gathered in the city to pay a final farewell to a man described at his moving funeral service as 'one of the greatest figures in British Association Football'. These words, spoken by Canon W.J. Sexton, vicar of the Anfield Parish, perfectly summed up the admiration reserved for John McKenna by the entire community of Liverpool.

The city was proud that one of its own, albeit an adopted Irishman, had been elevated to the very top of the English FA, whilst at Liverpool Football Club, McKenna's contribution would never be forgotten.

On the morning of his funeral, up to 100 people gathered at Anfield to pay their own respects to McKenna before his coffin was carried into the nearby St Margaret's Church, where it was followed by a number of Liverpool and Everton footballers.

John Troop, vice-president of Liverpool Football Club, led the tributes and added the sorrow which was felt at the club at his passing. 'We have lost one of our greatest friends. I cannot tell you how shocked I and other directors of Liverpool FC are at the sad news. John McKenna, although he had retired from an official connection with Liverpool, was still a faithful supporter of the club which he, more than anyone else, did so much to found. Any information we required he was always ready to give and we shall miss him very much. John McKenna rarely missed one of Liverpool's home matches and he was probably one of the most familiar figures in the directors' box at Anfield to the spectators in the paddock. He will leave a gap that we shall find very hard to fill.'

A year after McKenna's death, a plaque was unveiled in his honour at the entrance hall to Anfield by his close friend William Cuff, vice president of the Football League and chairman to Liverpool's deadliest rivals Everton. When Liverpool played Preston North End in a league game at Anfield on 13 March 1937, the match programme was also issued in honour of McKenna, containing a memorial tribute that described him as a 'great sportsman and a football genius'.

High praise for the man from County Monaghan who became the football darling of the red half of Merseyside.

3

Elisha Scott: Anfield's Belfast Boy

Name: Elisha Scott

Date of birth: 24 August 1894

Place of birth: Belfast

Position: Goalkeeper

Years at Liverpool: 1912–1934

Games played: 468

Goals scored: 0

Honours: First Division Championship (1922, 1923)

Other clubs: Linfield, Broadway United, Belfast Celtic

Every so often, a player arrives at a football club who embodies its true spirit, character and personality. Liverpool FC may or may not have known it at the time, but in September 1912, under the management of Tom Watson, they acquired such a player when a Belfast teenager arrived at the club to begin a career that would span almost quarter of a century.

The name Elisha Scott may not have meant much around the halls of Anfield in those early years of the twentieth century, but by the mid-1920s the charismatic goalkeeper had well and truly established himself as one of the club's first real legends, helping the Reds to an unprecedented back-to-back First Division titles in 1922 and 1923.

Such was Scott's influence in an era that saw Liverpool attain its foothold as one of mainstays in the English First Division, that he is now remembered in the same breadth as other early Red greats such as Billy Liddell.

Elisha Scott's success as a Liverpool goalkeeper is a story of remarkable longevity and triumph over adversity.

That adversity came in the mistaken belief from some within the game that Elisha was too small to play in goal at a professional level – but he was a man who was simply destined to be a goalkeeping great and it is to Liverpool FC's fortune that he spent almost all of his incredible playing career representing the club.

Born into a hard-working Church of Ireland family, young Elisha grew up in a row of fifteen houses on the Donegall Road in West Belfast, surrounded by his many siblings on the street that became known as 'Scott's Road' in reference to his large family of twelve.

Blessed with a God-given agility that he used to his advantage from a young age, Elisha began to make a name for himself as a goalkeeper of some talent with his local side Broadway Utd.

As a kid, it was always Elisha's dream to become a professional goalkeeper and he was helped by the fact that his older brother Billy was already carving out a career across the Irish Sea as a net-minder for Everton. Ten years older than Elisha, Billy had signed for Everton in 1904, having previously played for Belfast clubs Linfield and Cliftonville.

Billy Scott was a huge success at Everton, playing in 251 games between the sticks in an eight-year career at Goodison Park, the highlight of which included keeping a clean sheet in the FA Cup final as Everton won the trophy with a 1–0 victory over Newcastle.

As Elisha's own reputation began to grow back in Belfast, he even harboured hopes of following his brother to Goodison Park, after Billy enquired about the club taking him on as a teenager in 1912.

But like many inspiring football stories, Elisha Scott's started with a rejection.

After a trial with the Merseyside giants, it was decided that Elisha was too young and too small, and Everton manager William Cuff passed up on the chance to keep him at the club. Instead, legendary Liverpool manager Tom Watson stepped in and brought the Belfast kid to Anfield in September 1912. Although rather small for a goalkeeper at just under five foot ten inches, it was clear to everyone at Liverpool that Elisha had something special about him and Watson had him earmarked as a future first-team regular.

Scott got an early chance to stake his claim for the number one jersey after an injury to regular goalkeeper Ken Campbell gave him his debut against Newcastle on New Year's Day 1913. The youngster proved to be a safe pair of hands, keeping a clean sheet in a dour 0–0 draw, but he impressed so much that Newcastle even enquired if they could sign him up. However, the wily Watson refused to even think about letting the talented Scott go and even though it was the only game he would play that season, Liverpool were not prepared to give him up permanently.

Scott made his first appearance in goals at Anfield nine months later as he helped Liverpool to a 2–1 win over Bolton Wanderers but, again, he had to bide his time that season playing just another three games as the more experienced Campbell was still the preferred keeper.

He got his first extended run in the team in the second half of the 1914–1915 season, keeping five clean sheets during twenty-five league and cup games as the Reds finished way off the pace in thirteenth place in the First Division.

Nevertheless, all at Anfield were left in no doubt as to the quality of their new goalkeeper as 20-year-old Scott was brave and commanding in his penalty area and didn't lack in confidence when it came to dishing out instructions to his own team's defence.

Unfortunately for Scott, the outbreak of the First World War in 1914 interrupted his promising early career and he had to wait another four years to get back in the Liverpool goal after the suspension of competitive English football in 1915.

Scott returned to Belfast during the war years and enjoyed a colourful stint in goals for three clubs during that time, first signing up to play for the newly formed Belfast Utd before moving on to Linfield and finally ending at Belfast Celtic, where he went on to win an Irish League and Irish Cup winners medal.

Away from football, Scott also found the time to marry Belfast lass Alice Maud and, in 1918, the couple's only child Billy was born.

When football resumed in England in 1919, Scott and his young family moved back to Liverpool, where they lived in a one-bedroomed flat in the New Brighton area of the Wirral, twenty miles from Anfield.

Scott didn't have far to look for Irish company as his fellow Liverpool player, Wexford man Billy Lacey, lived in the same flat complex in New Brighton and the pair had struck up a firm friendship.

On the field of play, Scott's first year back at Anfield didn't exactly go according to plan as the club's new manager David Ashworth preferred to use Ken Campbell as his first-choice keeper. Meaning Scott made just nine appearances during that season, as Liverpool posted an impressive fourth place finish in the league behind eventual champions West Brom.

It wasn't until the 1920–1921 season that Scott's Liverpool career really began in earnest, when he played in twenty-six league games in which he kept nine clean sheets.

The Reds continued their decent form under Ashworth by again finishing fourth in the league and Scott proved his quality as a keeper as Liverpool conceded fewer goals than any other team in the division, including the champions of that season, Burnley.

Scott would repeat this feat for the following two seasons when he cemented his place as a Liverpool legend by helping the team to back-to-back First Division championships.

It didn't appear as if Liverpool would have title aspirations at the start of the 1921–1922 season when they were soundly beaten 3–0 in their opening game at Sunderland. But just a week later at Anfield, Scott gave an exhibition in quality goalkeeping as he kept Sunderland at bay with a string of fine saves as Liverpool ran out 2–1 winners. The exasperated Sunderland striker Charlie Buchan was consistently left scratching his head as Scott used all his cat-like agility to pull off three phenomenal saves from him – the last of which was from a point-blank header that even Buchan congratulated Scott on making by patting him on the back.

This was certainly high praise as the prolific English international Buchan was considered the top centre-forward in the First Division at the time.

Such shows of affection were not uncommon where Scott's goalkeeping was concerned and he was even once famously kissed by a fan running on the pitch after Scott produced a world-class save in a league encounter with Blackburn in 1924.

The confidence garnered from that Sunderland win saw Liverpool rack up a fourteen-game unbeaten run in which Scott kept four clean sheets and conceded just ten goals as the Reds streaked to the top of the First Division.

Fans at Anfield were now getting to see the very best of the vocal custodian who kept the Liverpool defenders on their toes and the crowd entertained by constantly barking out instructions in his colourful Belfast language.

Scott played in all but three league games that season as Liverpool comfortably won the title with six points to spare from Tottenham. The team conceded just thirty-six goals in forty-two games, a miserly record which went a long way to securing Liverpool's first league crown since 1906. If Scott's Liverpool proved they were a good side that season they went on to confirm themselves as a great one in the following campaign by retaining their title.

This time Scott played in every game in Liverpool's successful league run and let in five goals fewer than the previous season.

The run to the title that season even included a remarkable eight-game league spell by Scott in which he didn't concede a single goal. In an era when teams played virtually all-out attack this really was a sensational feat.

Not even the threat of a fire at Anfield could stop Scott during this run as he ended the eight-game streak with a shut-out in a 3–0 win over Bolton in March 1923.

During this routine home victory for Liverpool, the game was almost brought to a halt as a small fire mysteriously broke out at the Anfield Road end of the ground, near to the players' dressing rooms, just after half-time.

As smoke billowed out onto the pitch, Scott was still able to keep his cool to fling himself at a shot from Bolton's Scottish striker J.R. Smith and maintain his fantastic clean sheet record.

The only sore point for Scott throughout the entire season came on the final day of the campaign when he had to leave the field injured during a 1–0 victory over Stoke that wrapped up the title.

The unlucky keeper injured his thigh overstretching for a back pass from Liverpool defender Jock McNab and his place in goal was taken by his Irish pal Bill Lacey.

It was a bizarre injury for Scott to pick up considering he was regularly on the receiving end of heavy thumps and kicks from marauding forwards looking to find any way to get the ball past him in an era when referees turned a blind eye to fouls on the goalkeeper.

In fact one of the great secrets to Scott's unbelievable twenty-two-year tenure at Anfield was his ability to avoid major injuries by being to prepared to hit incoming forwards before they got the chance to hit him.

Scott's son Billy, who regularly went to watch his dad keep goal at Anfield throughout the 1920s and 1930s, testifies to this. Billy, now ninety-one-years-old and living back in his native Belfast, has revealed how his father's bravery saved him from crippling injuries. 'My dad used to always say to me that his motto was to 'hit first, hit hard and hit often',' Billy says. 'But it was a tough era for a goalkeeper, they could get taken out of the game by an opponent's hatchet man at any stage. They certainly weren't protected like the way they are now, so he needed to be brave to survive out on the pitch.'

Winning that second league title in the 1922–1923 season proved to be the pinnacle of Elisha Scott's career at Anfield because, although he remained with the club for another eleven years, he would not win another major honour.

He endured heartache on a number of occasions during the FA Cup but it was a competition in which Liverpool regularly failed to make an impact until they broke their hoodoo under Bill Shankly in 1965. Sadly, Scott had passed away by then, so he never got the chance to witness Liverpool win the famous trophy.

Scott would certainly have had reason to believe he was jinxed in the

FA Cup after an unfortunate goal against Newcastle in 1921 knocked Liverpool out of the competition, and left Elisha red-faced with embarrassment. During a hard-fought encounter at St James Park in January 1921, the game was decided in Newcastle's favour by an unlucky bounce of the ball off a divot which deflected it past the bemused Scott.

Later, Scott explained the bizarre goal with his typical Belfast wit. 'It was a freak goal. Someone headed in from about eighteen yards out and ball bounced six yards from me, hit a hole in the ground and shot into the top corner. Funniest thing I have ever seen. It looked that simple that naturally I got the blame. The poor goalkeeper always gets blame, but the only simple thing about it was that it made me look a bit simple.'

It was a rare mistake for the keeper, however, whose brilliance regularly outshone such mishaps and he was regarded by fellow players, coaches and the media as the best in the business.

From 1923 to 1926, Scott missed just seven league games for Liverpool through injury but the team was unable to hit the heights of their double league-winning seasons as they could finish no better than fourth place during those three years. It was still a special time for Scott though, as his young son Billy joined the hordes of his adoring Liverpool fans for games at Anfield.

Billy recalls how, as a young lad, he proudly went to see his dad play in goal for Liverpool and was astounded by the passionate atmosphere at Anfield. 'The atmosphere really was something else and it was very exciting for me as a kid as we didn't have anything to match it back in Ireland. My dad was a real favourite with the fans and you could tell that he loved to perform for them. He might have been in danger of a bit of stick from the crowd if he ever did make a mistake, but he was always able to block that out and mostly he got a great reception from the Liverpool fans.'

Billy remembers a happy childhood growing up in New Brighton and said that while his dad was vocal and committed on the football pitch, he was a very different man off it. 'My dad was always fairly quiet at home and I never remember him discussing or talking about football there. Maybe he just didn't want to be bringing his work home with him but he was able to leave whatever happened out on the pitch and away from our family life.'

During the later years of the 1920s, Scott embarked on a legendary rivalry with one of the best strikers to ever grace the English game.

As Scott kept goal for Liverpool, a world-class striker by the name of Dixie Dean emerged at Everton in 1925 and he went on to break all sorts of scoring records for the Toffees. Dean was phenomenally gifted in front of goal, even going on to score an incredible sixty league goals during the 1927–1928 season as Everton marched on to the First Division title. In all, Dean scored an incredible 349 goals in 399 games for Everton, a strike rate that is unlikely to ever be matched again.

But the one goalkeeper he found most difficult to get the better of was Elisha Scott and the two men built up a firm but healthy rivalry whilst maintaining the greatest respect for one another. In three league encounters between the pair from 1925 to 1928, Dean managed to score just the one goal in a 3–3 draw with Liverpool in February 1926 and was never on the winning side during those games.

The one time Dean did manage to score a hat-trick against the Reds at Anfield in February 1928, Scott was not available for Liverpool and the three goals were scored against the team's other net minder Arthur Riley.

Dean's overall appreciation for Scott's goalkeeping ability was summed up many years later, when he admitted the Belfast man was the best keeper he had ever come across. 'Elisha was the greatest I've ever seen. You can have Swift, Trautmann, Banks, Wilson. You can have them all. I'll take Elisha Scott,' were Dean's words.

By 1932, a full twenty years after signing for the club, Elisha Scott was still the first choice in goals for Liverpool.

During the 1932–1933 season, Scott kept goal for twenty-seven league games but, unfortunately, the team had slipped to mid-table obscurity and was just unable to repeat the heroics of a decade earlier.

Liverpool finished fourteenth in the league that season and slipped even farther down to eighteenth the following season when the evergreen Scott finally waved goodbye to Anfield.

With age catching up on him, Scott was ousted for good from the number one jersey by Arthur Riley and made his last appearance for Liverpool on 21 February 1934 in a 2–0 defeat to Chelsea at Stamford Bridge.

Scott's last game in goal at Anfield had come just four days earlier when Liverpool were dumped out of the FA Cup by Bolton in a 3–0 reverse.

He had achieved his last clean sheet for Liverpool in the Merseyside derby at Goodison Park during a 0–0 draw earlier in February 1934.

Before his eventual departure from Anfield at the end of that season, Scott caused some controversy on Merseyside as he attempted to leave for Everton.

The rivalry between the club's two sets of fans even back then made the move virtually impossible as Liverpool supporters kicked up a stink at the thought of such a legend playing for their biggest rivals.

Scott had made his plans to sign for Everton known to a local newspaper journalist, sparking protests from anguished Liverpool fans. Finally he had to relent and the move to Everton was scuppered.

In a letter to a *Liverpool Echo* journalist afterwards, Scott revealed: 'I think the loyal Anfielders are upsetting the directors more than you or me. If you know of any second or third division club wanting a goalkeeper, I am prepared to go to them.'

Scott never did find such a team in the lower divisions in England to sign for and, instead, returned home with his family to Northern Ireland to play for Belfast Celtic.

At Liverpool's final home game of the 1933–1934 season, Scott was afforded a hero's departure. Following the game with the new FA Cup winners Manchester City, Scott was called upon to address the Anfield crowd from the director's box.

During his emotional goodbye to his adoring fans, Scott said, 'We have always been the best of friends and shall always remain so. I have finished with English Association football. Last, but not least, my friends of the Kop. I cannot thank them sufficiently; they have inspired me. God bless you all.'

The fans responded with a rousing roar of 'Lisha, Lisha' as Scott departed the club amid one of Anfield's most iconic moments.

Despite his own brilliant football career, Scott always tried to steer his son Billy away from the game.

'He always told me it was no way to earn a living,' Billy says. 'Although he earned decent enough money himself during his time with Liverpool.

As far as I can recall, dad would have got a basic pay of £8 a week, plus another pound for each first-team appearance and bonuses such as £4 for a win or £3 for a draw. But the way he saw it back then was that you could get injured at any time and then your whole livelihood would be finished.'

In his crueller moments, Scott would even admonish young Billy for his poor football skills. 'I would be looking to play the game anywhere on the streets, as we all did as kids back then, but dad would always say that I was no good at it. Looking back on it now, I think it was his way of discouraging me from getting involved in the game, and I suppose it worked as I ended up getting a trade as an electrician instead.'

Although not keen for his son to get involved in the game, professional football really was in the blood of Elisha Scott and Billy says he just had a natural love for the game.

'Football was all he knew himself and he always just wanted to be involved with it. He was very dedicated when he played at Liverpool. He would socialise with the other players but he always kept himself in great shape. He liked to smoke cigarettes but, during his playing days, he rationed himself to just four a day. It wasn't until he had finally given up playing and took up management that he then became a chain smoker. He was smoking up to forty a day after that!'

If Scott's playing career at Liverpool had been one of high achievement, then his later days as manager of the now defunct Belfast Celtic were equally successful.

After playing on in goals for Celtic up to the age of forty-two, Scott progressed into management, where if anything, he had some of his greatest achievements.

Between the years 1936 to 1947, Scott led Belfast Celtic to an incredible ten Irish league titles as well as six Irish cups, and is revered as the godfather of the club, much in the same way as the legendary Bill Shankly is now at Liverpool.

Billy Scott revealed that one of his father's best traits both as a player and manager was one that has been found in all of the game's greats.

'He was always good at communicating with his team-mates as a goalkeeper, shouting at them and letting them know what needed to be done. And he continued that when managing his own players with Belfast

Celtic. Players are able respond well to somebody who has that sort of easy communication. It was something which helped Bill Shankly create his great Liverpool sides and I suppose my dad had those similar traits.'

As he continued to rack up the trophies season after season with Belfast Celtic, it is somewhat surprising that Liverpool never made the move to bring the legendary keeper back across to Anfield.

There's little doubt Scott would have been a popular figure as a Liverpool manager.

'It was just something that never came up and I'm not sure it was anything he ever really thought about,' Billy says. 'I think it was always my dad's intention to move back to Belfast when his playing days in England were over and he absolutely loved his time with Belfast Celtic. But in all his time managing the club, he always kept a close watch on how things were going over at Liverpool. He would get a copy of the *Liverpool Football Echo* sent to him by post every Saturday night and enjoyed keeping an eye on them that way.'

Despite all his success as manager of Belfast Celtic, Scott's career in football came to a shattering end in 1949 when the club pulled out of the Irish Football League amid growing political and sectarian tensions in Belfast.

Although he remained on as the club's honorary manager, Belfast Celtic would never again rejoin the league and Elisha Scott was lost to the game for good.

Almost ten years after his retreat from football, Scott passed away on 17 May 1959 following a series of strokes.

Tributes poured in for the famous Belfast son who captured the hearts of all at Liverpool, and few were more eloquently put than by the *Liverpool Echo*'s football correspondent Leslie Edwards.

Writing in his column on 19 May 1959, at a time when Liverpool languished in the Second Division, Edwards wrote:

> The death in Ireland, aged sixty-six, of the former Liverpool goalkeeper, Elisha Scott, has removed one of the most famous players in the history of Liverpool Football Club. Scott, whose face had the map of Ireland written all over it, was as famous in

his day as Billy Liddell and was the rival contemporary of Dixie Dean at a time when both our senior clubs possessed league or cup winning First Division teams the like of which we have never enjoyed since.

Scott was a goalkeeper who moved with almost instantaneous reflexes. He was also of great character, possessing an Irish brogue which fairly lashed some of his co-defenders if they were ever guilty of blocking his line of vision. He played for Ireland for many years and although not a big or tall man, was acknowledged the best goalkeeper in Britain in his era and one of a long line of wonderful men between the sticks at Anfield.

It is now almost 100 years since Elisha Scott first signed up for Liverpool but despite the passing of time, he is still regarded by fans today as one of the club's best servants.

In an online poll of Liverpool fans on the official club website in 2006, Scott was voted as number forty-one out of the club's all time top hundred players, not a bad achievement considering almost all those who voted would never have actually seen the man play.

Billy Scott obviously did and although he admits he would be biased towards his father, he has also had the benefit of seeing every other keeper at the club in the past seventy years and is sure he knows who has been the very best.

'There is no doubt Liverpool have had some great goalkeepers, such as the likes of Ray Clemence, and the current guy Pepe Reina is also very talented but I would have no hesitation is saying that my dad was the best the club ever had. He could do everything well, make great saves from point-blank shots, come to catch or punch the ball when needed and had total command of his area. And he had an agility that was just incredible. If he played the game now, I'm sure he would be up there with the very best in the world, he really was that good.'

Billy adds that he was astounded and felt emotional by the number of people who came to pay their respects to Elisha at a special ceremony arranged by the Belfast Celtic Society at the city cemetery in May 2009. The society, led by chairman and broadcaster Padraig Coyle, tracked down

Scott's burial place in the cemetery and refitted the family plot with a brand-new grey-marble headstone emblazoned with the crests of both Liverpool and Belfast Celtic. Up to 200 fans of both clubs then gathered to pay their respects to a man who had left an indelible mark on the game.

A red and white wreath of flowers, donated by the West Belfast Liverpool Supporters Club, were laid at the grave by Scott's great-grandchildren, while Billy himself unveiled the refurbished gravestone.

'It amazed me to see how many made the effort to come that day, many of them even from Liverpool,' Billy said. After such a long time since he actually played for the club, you don't expect many fans to still remember him so it is great to see that everything he did whilst playing for a great club like Liverpool hasn't been forgotten.'

The Slide to Relegation
(1934–1959)

4

Post Elisha Scott: Liverpool Stumble

The Liverpool side Elisha Scott left had become little more than an average mid-table team, far from achieving any sustained level of success in the English game. Scott's last season at the club in 1933–1934 had actually been one of the club's worst campaigns in a long time as the team narrowly avoided relegation by just four points and finishing in a lowly eighteenth place out of twenty-two teams.

One of the only bright points of that season had been the form of Irish-born striker Sam English, who had joined Liverpool in the summer of 1933 from Glasgow Rangers. English hit the back of the net twenty times during his debut season at Anfield, helping him go some way to banish the memories of a tragic event on the field when he was a Rangers player.

A tough and powerful centre-forward, Coleraine-native English had been involved in a terrible collision with Celtic goalkeeper John Thompson during an Old Firm clash on 5 September 1931. As he attempted to score a goal, English's knee clashed into Thompson's head and burst an artery in his right temple, which led to the goalkeeper's death.

English's move to Anfield two years later had allowed him to create a new career for himself and despite the fact that the team overall was struggling to make progress on the pitch, he finished Liverpool's second highest scorer in the 1933–1934 season behind South African hotshot Gordon Hodsgon.

However, despite English's goal-scoring exploits, Liverpool were still unable to recreate the brilliant back-to-back championships of the early 1920s, the club had stalled and was far off the pace been set by a trailblazing Arsenal side of the early 1930s.

Under the guidance of George Patterson, an Englishman who had joined the Liverpool coaching staff as an assistant to manager Tom Watson in 1908 and was named manager himself in 1928, Liverpool improved in the 1934–1935 season by finishing in seventh place in the First Division, but they were still a full thirteen points behind the champions Arsenal.

Unfortunately for Sam English, he fell a little out of favour with Patterson during that season as the manager decided to pair Gordon Hodsgon with Walsall-born striker Vic Wright in his forward line.

Whenever he did get in the team throughout that season, English proved he still had the ability to get goals by scoring six times in nineteen games.

It was not enough to keep him at the club, however, and Patterson let English go in July 1935.

Despite serving his managerial apprenticeship under the master Watson over twenty years earlier, Patterson was struggling to translate all he had learned into the successful running of the team as a manager himself.

Liverpool's form dipped dramatically in the 1935–1936 season and the club came perilously close to relegation to the Second Division, when they finished fourth from bottom with just three points to spare over relegated side Aston Villa. Patterson resigned from his role as manager following this scare, citing ill health, but remained on at the club as part of the backroom board.

The manager's job was passed on to former Southampton boss George Kay in August 1936, who travelled north to take on the job at Anfield after five years with the coastal club.

Manchester-born Kay, a former FA Cup finalist with West Ham Utd, also spent a number of years playing in Ireland for Belfast side Distillery, for whom he scored fourteen goals in ninety-one games between 1911 and 1914.

During his time as manager of Southampton, Kay had developed an impressive nursery system, producing a line of ready-made players for the cash-strapped Second Division outfit. It was for this reason that Kay was well respected within the game, even if Southampton regularly finished in the lower reaches of the Second Division, although this was mainly because Kay had continually to sell on his best players.

Kay's first season in charge at Liverpool did not go well, however, as the Reds were again lucky to stay in the First Division, avoiding relegation by three points as Manchester Utd dropped down a division instead.

It was a strange situation for both northwest giants to be in such trouble and it would be an unthinkable scenario for United and Liverpool to be battling relegation in the modern era.

Irish players were thin on the ground at Liverpool during this period, with only Belfast-born defender William Hood a part of the squad that began the 1937–1938 season under Kay. Former Cliftonville, defender Hood was by no means a first-team regular, however, and played just three games for Liverpool before being shipped out to Derry City after less than a year at the club.

Liverpool improved under Kay during his second season at the club, as the team finished well out of danger in seventh place.

The summer of 1938 saw Kay make one of the best signings in the history of Liverpool FC when he snapped up Scottish-born winger Billy Liddell from amateur side Loughgelly Violet. The mesmerising Liddell would go to score 228 goals for the Reds in over 500 games and is still remembered as one of the club's truly great legends.

A year later, Kay made an even more significant signing when tough Geordie half-back Bob Paisley was brought to the club from Bishop Auckland. While Paisley enjoyed a decent playing career at Anfield, even captaining the side for a period, it was as Liverpool manager in the 1970s and 1980s that he really made his name, winning countless European and domestic honours.

Unfortunately for Paisley and Liddell, their early Liverpool careers were hampered by the outbreak of the Second World War and the club played no competitive football for almost seven years until 1946.

Incredibly when George Kay regrouped his team for the 1946–1947 season, he guided Liverpool to the club's fifth First Division championship.

However, the Liverpool directors had made a fatal error the previous summer by allowing former player Matt Busby to leave the club and take up the position of manager at Manchester Utd. Busby had initially been earmarked as an assistant coach to George Kay at Liverpool, but the strong-minded Scot did not see eye-to-eye with the club's main directors over what his coaching role should be.

Busby wanted to have greater control over the playing staff at the club, but Liverpool chairman Billy McConnell would not accede to this and let Busby go. It seemed to matter little after Liverpool won the league title in the 1946–1947 season but ominously the runners-up that campaign were Busby's Manchester Utd.

As Liverpool faltered in the years following their league success, Busby's United grew stronger and by the middle of the 1950s were easily the best club in England while Liverpool floundered in the Second Division.

Liverpool's fall from grace after their initial post-war success was actually quite dramatic and they finished no better than mid-table for any of the following three seasons under Kay's stewardship.

Kay did somewhat redeem himself with a brilliant FA Cup run in 1950 which saw his Liverpool side march on to the final with a convincing 2–0 semi-final win over Merseyside rivals Everton, with both Bob Paisley and Billy Liddell getting on the scoresheet. Unfortunately, Liverpool were unable to claim the cup after a 2–0 final defeat to Arsenal.

George Kay's time as manager of Liverpool came to an end midway through the following season. Liverpool were once again struggling to keep pace at the top of the table which at the time was being dominated by Tottenham Hotspur and Manchester Utd.

Kay was replaced by former England international Don Welsh as the Reds finished in ninth place in the First Division in 1951, with Tottenham winning the league and Manchester Utd, captained by the legendary Irish defender Jackie Carey, finishing runners-up.

Welsh, who played for much of his career at Charlton Athletic, was something of a surprise choice to be Liverpool's new manager as he had spent the previous three years in charge of Brighton & Hove Albion in the

Third Division, where he had very little success, leading the team to no higher than eighth place.

Nevertheless, Liverpool began their first full season under Welsh in excellent fashion, winning six and losing just one of their first nine league games before a serious dip in form saw them drop dramatically down the table.

After a run of eight defeats in their next thirteen league games, Welsh sought the services of a Belfast-born striker to halt the team's dip in form.

Former Linfield striker Sammy Smyth was brought to Anfield at a time when Irish players were scarce at Liverpool. If anything, Manchester Utd had stolen a march on the Reds at that time by attracting the best young talent coming through from Ireland to join their ranks in the 1950s. With Dubliner Jackie Carey captaining their side, United had also managed to snap up classy Irish youngsters such as Liam Whelan, Jackie Blanchflower and Shay Brennan into their all-conquering youth side of the mid-1950s. All three would also go on to win First Division titles with Manchester Utd in 1956 and 1957 and represent the Republic of Ireland and Northern Ireland on the international stage.

5

Sammy Smyth: Goals but No Glory

With almost half of the 1952–1953 season completed, Liverpool manager Don Welsh paid fellow First Division side Stoke City £12,000 to bring their forward Sammy Smyth to Anfield in December 1952.

Free-scoring Smyth, who was born on the Shankill Road in Belfast in 1925, started his career as a seventeen-year-old with Distillery in the Irish League before also moving on to play for top Belfast club Linfield in 1945 from where he attracted the attentions of English First Division club Wolverhampton Wanderers.

Before arriving at Anfield, Smyth had enjoyed six good seasons in the English game, four of them spent with Wolves where he famously scored a cracking FA Cup final goal during a 3–1 win over Leicester City in 1949.

At eighty-four-years-old and living on the Bangor Road in north Down, Smyth remembers his time with Liverpool with some fondness and displays a sharp Irish wit when revealing how his move from Stoke City to the Merseyside club transpired. 'I can remember after training one day the Stoke manager Frank Taylor called me aside and asked if I would like to go to Liverpool,' Smyth says. 'I asked him if he was sending me home to Ireland on the boat. He looked at me strangely and said, 'No the football team over there are willing to sign you' and naturally I was delighted to make the move to Liverpool then.'

Smyth had never really settled in Stoke anyway, preferring to still live in Wolverhampton and travel the fifty-six-mile round-trip from there to the Potteries town for training and games. That all changed when he signed up for Liverpool as the Belfast lad was only too happy to live permanently in one of the more lively cities in Britain.

Smyth got his Liverpool career off to a decent start by scoring in three crucial wins which helped maintain the club's First Division status at the expense of his old club Stoke.

In all, Smyth scored seven goals in eighteen games at the head of the Liverpool attack in 1952–1953 in a team that also included legendary winger Billy Liddell.

Liddell and Smyth built up a good understanding between them and were the source of the vast majority of Liverpool's goals over the following year and a half.

Smyth said it was a pleasure to have played on the same pitch as one of the true Anfield greats, even if his time at the club didn't go so well overall.

'Billy Liddell was first and foremost a lethal finisher when he got in front of goal,' Smyth said. 'He was a right-footed player who was quite often picked to play on the left wing so that he could cut back inside onto his favourite foot and score a lot of goals that way, so it certainly worked for him. My own strength was anticipation in the box. I was probably one of the slowest running players at Liverpool at the time but what I could do well was anticipate where the ball was going to land in the box and that was where most of my goals came from.'

After settling in well at Anfield, Smyth was Liverpool's main goal-scoring threat throughout the 1953–1954 season but it proved to be a disastrous time for the club.

Despite being Liverpool's top scorer, Smyth couldn't help the club avoid relegation as they finished bottom of the First Division for only the second time in the club's history. The team won only nine league games all season and conceded a staggering ninety-seven goals as they lost seventeen of the twenty-one games played away from Anfield.

'I was our top scorer that season but only with thirteen goals, so you can tell by that tally that it was a struggle for us,' Smyth admitted. 'I don't believe it had anything to do with bad luck, we just weren't good enough over the season to remain in the First Division – it was just one of those things. It was a pity because Liverpool was a fairly well-run club at the time and they looked after us as players very well but we just didn't do the business out on the pitch. We lost far too many games away from home in particular and never really looked as if we were going to get ourselves out of it.'

However Smyth was to find that in times of trouble, the loyal Liverpool fans stood even firmer behind their team. 'I can remember every time walking out onto the pitch at Anfield, the Kop was always to your right and the roar from it would be deafening. I always got a great reception from the fans at Liverpool and they treated me well during my time there. There were a lot of Irish people living in the city so it was easy to adapt to and I got on very well there. Despite the fact that we were struggling, and did eventually get relegated, there wasn't an overall air of despondency amongst the fans or around the club, they did everything to get behind us.'

With Smyth being the top scorer during that ill-fated season for Liverpool, he had expected the club to keep him on for their following campaign in the Second Division. So it came as something of a surprise when Don Welsh informed him that his contract would not be renewed.

Initially stung by the news, Smyth made the decision to return to his native Belfast and though only twenty-seven-years-old, he ended his association with professional football by signing on as an amateur with Bangor.

Out of the game, Smyth took up a role within his father Jimmy's thriving bookmaker business in Belfast.

'I don't know why my contract was not renewed by the club, nothing serious happened between me and them, it was just a decision that was made. But I loved the year-and-a-half that I lived in the city. Liverpool was a buzzing place and a great city to be in the early 1950s. Outside of football, I had a great interest in theatre and plays and they had two great theatres there which was where I spent a lot of my spare time.'

During his time at Anfield, Smyth had also got the chance to see the early workings of the great football mind of Bob Paisley.

'Bob was the team captain at the time I was at Liverpool. He was a decent midfielder who was very good at tackling but you would never have said that he was in the top echelons of players in England at the time, although you got the feeling that he could have been. But it didn't surprise me that Bob went on to do so well as the manager of Liverpool, as he had a very good knowledge of the game and was far from stupid. I got on very well with Bob during my time at Liverpool and liked him a lot, so I was delighted to see him do so well for the club in his later career as manager.'

He may have only spent eighteen months as a player at Anfield, but Smyth's twenty goals in forty-four games – a strike rate of a goal every two games – is as good as any of the club's legendary goal scorers.

However he modestly admits that he would hardly be remembered as one of the greats at Liverpool.

'I wouldn't have said I was a particularly great striker for the club when you look down through its history. It wasn't until Bill Shankly came in and shook things up a few years after I had left that Liverpool really got going and I don't think I would have got near any of Shankly's sides. Although I do look on my whole time in English football with pride and I always still keep a look out for the results of Liverpool as they were one of just three teams I ever played the game professionally for.'

Relegation to the Second Division in 1954 really knocked the stuffing out of Liverpool. It was a dismal time as the club had seriously lost its direction since being crowned First Division champions in 1947 and there appeared to be little ambition left around Anfield.

Major signings in the summer of 1954 were few and far between and mostly consisted of picking up free bargains from non-league outfits.

The departure of Sammy Smyth also heralded in a lean period for Irish players at the club. It would be sixteen years before another Irishman would set foot on the Anfield turf in the red jersey of Liverpool, by which time the club was back at the top end of the English game.

Despite being in charge of Liverpool's disastrous relegation run, manager Don Welsh was given the opportunity to turn the club's fortunes around in the Second Division.

The first game at Anfield started brightly with Liverpool notching up a 3–2 victory over Doncaster Rovers thanks to a hat-trick from Welsh forward Tony Rowley, which included two goals from him in the last four minutes of the game. Any hopes the Reds had of a quick promotion back to the First Division were soon quashed, however, as they failed to win in any of their next six league games. The team was conceding goals for fun and was even on a receiving end of a humiliating 9–1 thrashing by Birmingham City in early December 1954.

Welsh attempted to shore up the defence when he shelled out £5,000 to bring imposing defender Alex South to the club from Brighton. But this did little to help matters and South struggled to find form at Liverpool and played in just six games as the Reds finished their first season in the Second Division in eleventh spot.

Welsh had little money to play around with in the transfer market in the summer of 1955 and apart from spending £4,500 on tough tackling full-back John Molyneaux from Chester, he again had to settle for free transfers to help bolster the squad. Nevertheless, Liverpool did manage a significant improvement that season and ran Leeds Utd close for a promotion spot.

With Sheffield Wednesday running away with the Second Division in 1955–1956, Liverpool went into the final game of the season knowing a victory over Lincoln City and defeat for Leeds at Hull would see them claim the vital second spot. But the results went the wrong way for the Anfield men as Liverpool slumped to a 2–0 defeat whilst Leeds ran out easy 4–1 winners in their game.

Failure to claim promotion spelled the end of Don Welsh's tenure in charge and Liverpool brought in Bristol-born former player Phil Taylor, who had been a legendary centre-half for the club in his eighteen-year Anfield playing career. It came as no surprise that he was given the chance to manage the club he loved.

The purse strings were opened a little for Taylor too and he splashed £9,000 to bring in Scottish international goalkeeper Tommy Younger from Hibernian. A further £9,000 was paid out for midfielder Johnny Wheeler from Bolton, bringing Taylor's spend in the transfer market to almost twice what Liverpool had spent in the three previous seasons.

Once again, Liverpool were high up the table in the Second Division in the 1956–1957 season but fell just agonisingly short of the promotion places by finishing third, one point behind second placed Nottingham Forest.

Close failure to gain promotion back into the First Division became a feature of the Liverpool team in the late 1950s as, a year later, Taylor would lead them to fourth spot, this time only two points behind Blackburn in the second promotion place.

The summer of 1958 was notable for the arrival at Anfield of young forward, Roger Hunt, who was prised from Cheshire League side Stockton Heath. Twenty-year-old Hunt didn't play a single game for Liverpool during the 1958–1959 season but would go on to establish himself as one of the best strikers to ever play in the English game.

As Hunt waited his turn, Phil Taylor yet again led Liverpool to fourth place in the Second Division as frustration began to set in at the club's continual failure to make the step up into the final promotion places.

When Liverpool made a poor start to the following season, pressure mounted on Taylor as it became apparent that the club was struggling to find a way out of the Second Division. By November 1959, Taylor had resigned and Liverpool had a desperate search for a new saviour who could drag the club back up to former glories.

From Second Division to European Domination

(1959–1981)

6

Thank Shanks: the Reds Rise Again

In the five years that Liverpool toiled in the Second Division, former player Matt Busby had transformed local rivals Manchester Utd into an English football powerhouse.

Busby's drive and visionary coaching techniques produced a line of top quality youngsters from throughout Britain and Ireland that took the English and European game by storm in the mid to late 1950s.

By 1957, as Liverpool struggled to gain promotion, United, known as the 'Busby Babes' had won back-to-back First Division titles and appeared unstoppable. However, the Busby Babes would never even get the chance to reach their full potential after eight of that talented squad were wiped out in the tragic Munich Air Disaster in February 1958 when the team plane crashed on an icy runway on the return from a successful European Cup quarter final victory in Belgrade.

Busby survived the crash and would remarkably go on to produce another brilliant side within the following decade.

The tenacious Scot's achievements could not have gone unnoticed in the Anfield boardroom when they went in search of Phil Taylor's replacement in 1959.

All eyes turned to another Scottish manager, who, like Busby, was a man stubbornly prepared to do things his own way.

Then Liverpool chairman T.V. Williams, a strong character himself, decided in December 1959 to give the job of manager to Bill Shankly.

Shankly, a former player with Preston North End, had been the manager of Huddersfield Town in the Second Division for the previous three years but had not tasted much success.

Nevertheless, Liverpool chairman Williams was sure he was getting the right man and Shankly himself believed he was finally arriving at the right club where he could make a real impact as manager.

What neither man could have known at the time, however, was that the decision to bring in Shankly would be the most significant in the history of the club since it was founded by John Houlding in 1892.

What Shankly saw when he arrived at Liverpool was potential. He was horrified at the dilapidated state that Anfield had fallen into and was equally shocked at the poor facilities he witnessed at the club's training ground in Melwood. But what Shankly had almost instantly recognised was the strong bond between the club and its fans, even if Liverpool had fallen on lean times. Despite spending much of the 1950s in the Second Division, on occasions Liverpool were still able to attract crowds of up 50,000 to Anfield. Shankly knew a club with this much backing couldn't remain in the doldrums forever and that, with a bit of hard work and belief, he could quickly turn things around.

On his appointment at the helm at Anfield, Shankly said, 'I am very pleased and proud to have been chosen as manager of Liverpool FC, a club of such great potential. It is my opinion that Liverpool have a crowd of followers which rank with the greatest in the game. They deserve success and I hope, in my own small way, I am able to do something to achieve that. I make no promises except that I shall put everything I have into the job I so willingly undertake.'

His first big challenge was to get Liverpool moving up the Second Division table and although they lost the first two games with Shankly in charge, he soon moulded the team into winning habits.

In 1960, Liverpool put together an impressive run from January through to the end of the league season in April, winning ten and drawing four of their seventeen league fixtures to finish, once again, in third place. Had it not been for the poor start to the season, 1959–1960 may well have been the year the Reds finally won back that coveted promotion spot.

Now that he was firmly in charge at Anfield, Shankly could start to push through the changes he believed would turn the club around.

He urged the boardroom to stump up the cash to completely revamp the training facilities at Melwood and introduced his own simple but incredibly successful training routine. During five-a-side training games, Shankly encouraged his players to do one thing and do it well – 'pass and move'. It was a system upon which thirty years of unparalleled success in the English and European game would be built.

Shankly was also keen to work on the psychological aspect of the game, always encouraging his players to think positively, bigging up his own team in an effort to intimidate the opposition. His idea was to make Anfield a fortress, a ground where opposition teams would fear to tread and would already feel beaten before a ball had even been kicked.

As part of this plan, Shankly introduced the iconic 'This Is Anfield' sign, which he had erected in the players' tunnel.

'It's there to remind our lads who they're playing for, and to remind the opposition who they're playing against,' Shankly said of the sign.

On top of all this, Shankly was further blessed with a talented and reliable coaching squad including former team captain Bob Paisley, Joe Fagan and his close friend Reuben Bennett.

Between them, the four enjoyed informal but instructive talks on all things football in the players' boot room at Anfield which Shankly also used as a makeshift tea room for the coaches, thus developing what became known as the Boot Room, another iconic emblem of the club's future achievements.

The success of the Shankly revolution was gradual at first with Liverpool winning fourteen of their twenty-one home games in the 1960–1961 season when, incredibly, they again finished third in the Second Division, the fourth time in six seasons that the club had missed out on promotion by one spot.

Nevertheless, things were on the move with Shankly and in the summer of 1961, he made two of his shrewdest ever signings.

He shelled out £37,500 to bring in prolific forward Ian St John from Motherwell and another £22,000 on towering central defender Ron Yeats from Dundee Utd.

With Yeats marshalling the defence and Scottish international St John forming a lethal front partnership with Roger Hunt, Anfield, in the season of 1961–1962, did indeed become a fortress.

The team remained unbeaten at home throughout the entire Second Division campaign, winning eighteen and drawing just three of the twenty-one games.

Hunt scored an incredible forty-one league goals, with the lively and experienced St John notching up another eighteen, to land Liverpool the Second Division title with eight points over nearest rivals Leyton Orient.

The success did not come as any great surprise to Ian St John, who says he was sure Shankly was on the road to becoming a great manager from the moment he signed for him.

'The first thing that really impressed me about Bill Shankly was his charisma,' St John says. 'He was also a real football man who talked a lot of sense and had succeeded in getting the directors out of the dressing room and letting him get on with the job of running the team. Everything Shankly did was in an effort to improve the club, whether that was the playing personnel, the ground or the training facilities; he was always looking for improvement.'

Veteran Merseyside sports broadcaster and journalist John Keith was one of a select few media men to witness first-hand the dramatic transformation of Liverpool under the Shankly regime.

Keith, who these days works as a match reporter for RTÉ Radio One and who wrote the highly acclaimed play *The Shankly Show*, explains what made the enigmatic Scot stand out.

'If there is one quality I believe Shankly brought to Liverpool more than anything else it was enthusiasm,' Keith says. 'He brought a whole new mindset to the job and was the first Liverpool manager in the club's history to have full control over picking the team, up until then, the directors would have a had a say. But once Bill came in that would have ended. He was obsessive about football and in the fitness of his players. I imagine the directors at the time would have been looking at each other and thinking,

What have we got here?'

On Liverpool's return to the top flight in 1962, they found that Merseyside neighbours Everton were one of the top dogs in the league.

In the two years leading up to Liverpool's promotion, Everton has finished in fifth and fourth place in the First Division as they gradually worked their way up as a championship contending side.

So while for Shankly the 1962–1963 season was all about consolidating Liverpool's place back in the top league in the land, Everton were on course to win their sixth First Division crown.

All the same, Liverpool would run Everton close in both league games between the sides as Shankly got his first big taste of what the Merseyside derby was all about.

The Scot's introduction to the derby was full of incident in an action-packed game at Goodison Park on 22 September 1962, when it took a ninetieth-minute strike from Roger Hunt to salvage a 2–2 draw for the Reds.

The return game at Anfield was a bit of a more sombre affair which finished scoreless.

However, Everton marched on successfully in the league campaign to finish first with six points to spare over Tottenham Hotspur.

For their part, Shankly's Liverpool had finished back in eighth spot which was a reasonable achievement for a team playing in the First Division for the first time in eight years.

For Shanks, however, eighth place the following season just wouldn't be tolerated, so he set about plotting the downfall of Everton.

Despite a shaky start to the 1963–1964 season, which included four defeats in the first nine league games, Shankly masterminded an important 2–1 derby win over Everton in late September 1963 which set the Reds on a run of nine wins in ten games to streak to the top of the table.

Part of the team's new-found success was Shankly's consistency in team selection with goalkeeper Tommy Lawrence, defender Ron Yeats, midfielder Ian Callaghan and the forward line of Hunt and St John playing in almost every match, giving a seriously strong spine to the side.

The players had also taken to the inspirational Shankly's 'pass and move' mantra seamlessly, mesmirising sides with their ability to keep the ball and move it quickly from defence into attack when necessary.

Both Hunt and St John, who could also move back to play in a deeper midfield role, had taken the move up to the First Division in their stride, scoring forty-four goals between them in the 1962–1963 season and an incredible fifty-two in the following campaign.

It was that pair's scoring exploits which had Liverpool on the verge of their first league title success since 1947 as they entered the spring of 1964. From late March to mid-April, Liverpool put together seven wins on the bounce, including a crucial 3–0 win over nearest rivals Man Utd to wrap the title up with three games to spare.

On a momentous day on 18 April 1964, a charged-up Liverpool trounced a talented Arsenal side 5–0 to win the league and truly herald the start of Bill Shankly's Anfield revolution.

Across Stanley Park, Everton had to make do with a third place finish with Manchester Utd coming second.

For Ian St John, the achievement was even sweeter giving that Liverpool's local rivals Everton had been lording it over them for numerous previous years.

'Everton were a really big and successful at that time but with Bill at the helm we were able to surpass them, which in itself was a great achievement considering how strong they were and where we had come from. Although he would have been looking at the previous success of Everton and desperately wanted us to overtake them, Bill was always looking for even higher goals for Liverpool. So, in some ways, I'm not sure if he ever looked at Everton as his inspiration by way of wanting to get the better of them. After all, Bill always said he wanted to turn Liverpool into the biggest club in the world, so, from that point of view, getting the better of his local rivals was only small cheese.'

If Shankly really wanted to rule the football world with Liverpool then he had to address the small matter of the club having never won the FA Cup.

The 1964–1965 season gave him not only that chance but also the opportunity to lead Liverpool out in the European Cup, the club's first ever taste of action in the continent's premier knockout competition.

As ever, Shankly took to both challenges with gusto, leading Liverpool to the 1965 FA Cup final against another reinvigorated club, Leeds Utd, and to the semi-finals of the European Cup, where they agonisingly lost 4–3 on aggregate to Italian giants Inter Milan.

Liverpool's European adventure that season also led Shankly to another one of his ground-breaking decisions – when he declared before a first-round tie with Belgian side Anderlecht that the team would look more intimidating to the opposition wearing an all-red strip.

Up until that point Liverpool had worn just a red jersey, accompanied by white shorts and socks. Shankly decided to change that, however, and to this day Liverpool have donned their famous all-red gear.

It obviously worked for Liverpool in the cup final at Wembley against Leeds as the team ran out 2–1 winners, an achievement that many Liverpool fans at the time put above the league title win a year earlier.

Striker Ian St John said winning the FA Cup was one of the biggest highlights of his career.

'Anytime you do something for the first time, it is usually always the best and that was how it was when we won the FA Cup for Liverpool in 1965, it was a huge achievement. When I signed for Liverpool I never actually knew they had never won the cup before. But on Merseyside people used to say that the Liverbirds would fly off the top of the city buildings before the Liverpool team would win it. Having said that, it was bound to happen someday and I was just so glad to be part of the team that achieved it.'

With a First Division and FA Cup under his belt, Shankly was already afforded legendary status with the fans. In 1966, he cemented his place amongst the greats in football management when he brought Liverpool to their second First Division title in three years.

Liverpool had certainly come a long way since the dark day of the Second Division just a few years earlier and, although the league title of 1966 would be the last trophy won at Anfield in the 1960s, Bill Shankly had set the foundations for a footballing dynasty.

For Ian St John, the brilliance of Shankly could be found not just in the titles he won but the way he transformed his players into world beaters.

'When I first signed for Liverpool in 1961, I was the only international player in the entire squad,' he says. 'Within ten years, every single player in the team was an international which was an extraordinary achievement. Bill signed up local young lads and turned them into international players. Nowadays, the club goes out and buys top internationals, back then he was making them.'

When Liverpool Played in Ireland

European Fairs Cup
Dundalk 0–4 Liverpool,
Oriel Park, 30 September 1969

A full decade after Bill Shankly had arrived at Liverpool, the club had progressed from its lowly Second Division status to the point that it had become well used to European football adventures.

It was no different in the 1969–1970 season when the reward for finishing runners-up in the league the season before was a place in the Inter City Fairs Cup, a competition that was later replaced by the European football authorities with the UEFA Cup.

The first-round draw threw up an intriguing tie for the Reds, and particularly their growing fan base in Ireland, when they were paired with Dundalk who had entered the Fairs Cup having finished in fourth place in the League of Ireland the previous season.

It was the first time that Liverpool would travel across the Irish Sea for a competitive football encounter.

Coached by future Republic of Ireland manager Liam Tuohy, Dundalk were one of the strongest clubs in Irish football at the time having won two league titles in the 1960s.

The League of Ireland was enjoying one of its best decades at the time, with sides such as Shamrock Rovers, Shelbourne and Waterford Utd attracting massive crowds of up to 20,000 to their games.

However Dundalk's largely part-time players were not expected to cause too much of an upset for Liverpool and, in the first-leg at Anfield which had taken place a fortnight earlier, they were subjected to a humiliating 10–0 defeat at the hands of Shankly's side.

That result went a long way to taking most of the excitement out of the second leg tie at Dundalk's Oriel Park, with just over 5,000 fans showing up for the game, half of what had initially been expected.

Despite the heavy loss in the first leg, Dundalk manager Tuohy vowed his team would attack Liverpool and do their best to put some gloss on the aggregate scoreline.

For his part, Shankly was able to rest a number of his top players, including club stalwarts Ron Yates and Ian Callaghan, but still expected his Liverpool team to play a good game. 'We have a job to do and we will do it,' Shankly said ominously as his Liverpool team arrived in Dundalk.

Shankly's players certainly took their managers words to heart as they again quickly set about dismantling the Irish side.

Dundalk began brightly enough, however, and had Liverpool under pressure in the early minutes but the young Reds goalkeeper Ray Clemence marshalled his defence well and was determined not to see it breached by the part-timers.

After that initial flurry from Dundalk, Liverpool quickly got a grip on the game and took the lead after just thirteen minutes through flying winger Peter Thompson.

Thompson evaded the challenge of his marker Frank Brennan to get a shot in on the Dundalk goal, with the ball squirming past goalkeeper Maurice Swan who really should have done better to keep it out.

It was a cruel blow for Dundalk to find themselves behind and they just didn't have the confidence to match Liverpool.

Thompson doubled the Reds' lead on thirty-two minutes, again cutting in from the left and, this time, his shot took a wicked deflection off defender Kevin Murray to give Swan no chance.

Liverpool were now playing well within themselves and could easily have added more to the tally before half-time.

Thankfully for Dundalk, they didn't and, at the half-time interval, Shankly took off their chief tormentor Thompson, although he was replaced for the second half by the equally capable Ian Callaghan.

The second half was just three minutes old when Liverpool defender Emlyn Hughes set up forward Bobby Graham to snatch Liverpool's third and kill off any hopes Dundalk had of at least getting some sort of result out of the game.

To Dundalk's credit they kept trying to put pressure on Liverpool but the brilliant Clemence clung on to his clean sheet. He pulled off two magnificent saves from Dundalk forward Turlogh O'Connor and the Irish side knew it just wasn't going to be their day.

To rub salt in their wounds, Ian Callaghan added a fourth for Liverpool in the eighty-first minute after good work from forward Phil Boersma.

That was the end of the scoring for Liverpool as the two-game tie finished in a thumping 14–0 win for the Reds.

Liverpool's run in the Fairs Cup that year didn't last much longer, however, when they were beaten on the away goals rule by Portuguese side Vitoria Setubal in the second round.

TEAMS

Dundalk: Swan, Brennan, O'Reilly, Murray, McConville, Millington, Kinsella, Turner, O'Connor, Bartley, Carroll
Subs: Stokes for Carroll, Gilmore for Kinsella

Liverpool: Clemence, Lawler, Strong, Smith, Lloyd, Hughes, Boersma, Evans, Graham, St. John, Thompson
Subs: Callaghan for Thompson, Hunt for Graham

7

Steve Heighway on the Wing

Name: Steve Heighway

Date of birth: 25 November 1947

Place of birth: Dublin

Position: Winger

Years at Liverpool: 1970–1981

Games played: 475

Goals scored: 76

Honours: First Division Championship (1973, 1976, 1977, 1979) FA Cup (1974); European Cup (1977, 1978); UEFA Cup (1973, 1976)

Other Clubs: Skelmersdale United, Minnesota Kicks

For Bill Shankly, the 1970s began with a search for new blood. Liverpool had gone four years without winning a trophy and, although they came close to claiming the league twice during that period, it was obvious that Shankly's team of the early to mid-1960s was ageing and in need of reinvention.

Scoring sensation Roger Hunt left Anfield in December 1969 in a £32,000 deal with Bolton and, over the following two years, other legends such as Yeats and St John would follow suit.

In the meantime, in May 1970, Shankly acquired the silky skills of a dashing new winger when Dublin-born Steve Heighway was brought to Anfield from local Merseyside amateur team Skelmersdale Utd.

Although born in Dublin, where he lived until he was ten years old, Heighway spent his teenage years in the UK where a career in professional football appeared to have passed him by as he entered his twenties still playing at amateur level. Despite his amateur background, Heighway was far more advanced than most young players arriving for the first time at a club like Liverpool.

He was already twenty-two-years-old and a university graduate with a degree in economics when Shankly brought him to Anfield and this maturity ensured Heighway settled in easily at the club.

Within a matter of months of joining Liverpool, he was in Shankly's first team squad and made his debut as a second half substitute in a 1–1 league draw away to West Brom in August 1970.

That thirty-minute appearance in the red shirt was already enough to earn Heighway a call up to the senior Republic of Ireland squad and he made his full debut for the Irish team in a friendly against Poland in September 1970 – before he had even been picked to start a full game for Liverpool.

The Ireland team at the time consisted of top Leeds Utd midfielder John Giles and leading striker Don Givens, but they were no match for the Poles as they fell to a 2–0 defeat at Dalymount Park.

Back at Liverpool, Heighway was just the type of player Bill Shankly had been looking for to liven up his team.

He was a natural winger, blessed with blinding pace, great ball control and a trickery which always had opposition defences on their toes. With his flowing locks and easy skill, he became one of the stars of the 1970s as Liverpool turned into one of the strongest forces in the English and

European game. Heighway also had a versatility in that he could play equally as well on the right or left wing or up front as a support striker and he became an important attacking force within Shankly's team.

It didn't take him long to work his way into the side in the 1970–1971 season and quickly endeared himself to the Kop. He scored his first goal for Liverpool in a 2–0 league win over Burnley at Anfield in October 1970 and, just a month later, he engineered one of the most remarkable Liverpool comebacks ever seen in a Merseyside derby.

With Liverpool two goals down to reigning First Division champions Everton, Heighway changed the game with little over a half an hour left when he squeezed in a goal from near the end line. Not long after, Heighway's raking run down the left flank set up newly signed Welsh striker John Toshack to head home an equaliser and Liverpool clinched victory with a late winner from free-scoring full-back Chris Lawlor.

The stunning victory that day heralded the beginning of a new Shankly side.

Toshack, bought from Cardiff City for £100,000, was a striker made for Heighway who knew he could just get to the end line and whip in a cross which the tall Welshman was either sure to put away with his head or lay something on for a fellow forward. The pair were integral to Liverpool's run for glory in both the FA Cup and European Fairs Cup in the early months of 1971.

Heighway played his part as Liverpool streaked past Aldershot, Swansea and Southampton in the FA Cup to set up a tough quarter-final tie with Tottenham.

It would take two games for Liverpool to get past Spurs after the initial tie at Anfield finished in a 0–0 draw but Heighway was on hand to hit home the vital winner in the replay at White Hart Lane.

Suddenly, Liverpool were on the march again and the victory over Spurs set up a mouth-watering semi-final clash with Everton.

Liverpool were also going strong in the European Fairs Cup and, just four days after their FA Cup quarter-final draw with Spurs at Anfield in March 1971, they tore strips off German giants Bayern Munich in a fantastic 3–0 home win that set them on their way to a mammoth semi-final with fellow English powerhouses Leeds Utd.

Fairs Cup

The Inter-City Fairs Cup was a competition set up in 1955 by European football clubs aiming to promote international trade fairs. As part of these business fairs, friendly games were regularly held between teams from cities holding the events and it is from there that the Fairs Cup evolved.

The competition was initially only open to teams from cities that hosted trade fairs and where these teams finished in their national league had no relevance. However, by 1968, the rules were changed to ensure that teams could only qualify for the Fairs Cup based on having finished high up in their league in the previous season.

In 1971, the Fairs Cup came under the auspices of UEFA and was replaced by the UEFA Cup.

While the Inter-Cities Fairs Cup is recognised as the predecessor to the UEFA Cup, it was not organised by UEFA and therefore the European football body does not consider clubs' records in the Fairs Cup to be part of their official record.

However, it was the FA Cup semi-final encounter with Everton which came up first as over 60,000 scousers made the journey to Manchester Utd's Old Trafford ground for one of the most eagerly anticipated Merseyside derbies ever.

As experts poured over who might prove a match winner between these two giants, the *Liverpool Echo* gave a glowing tribute to Heighway in the lead up to the match.

This boy has been a sensation this season and no-one looks better than he when he is in full flight up the field free of the defence. No-one can catch him. Steve is another natural scorer. He is at his most dangerous floating between centre and left side of field and if the ball is played through quickly and accurately he is ready to pounce. An exciting player who must not be underestimated.

The only great fear for Heighway in the build-up to the clash with Everton was the painful memories of losing two amateur cup semi-finals in a row with Skelmersdale in the two previous years. He certainly didn't want to make it a hat-trick of disappointments.

But he needn't have worried as Shankly's young Liverpool side outfought Everton to record a 2–1 victory and send them into the final with the recently crowned First Division champions Arsenal.

Heighway's Reds were unable to make it a double of cup finals, however, as a battle-hardened Leeds Utd side containing warriors such as his fellow Irish international John Giles scraped past them 1–0 on aggregate in the European Fairs Cup semi-final.

The European defeat to Leeds did little to dampen the excitement building up around Liverpool's FA Cup final clash with Arsenal.

Still only in his first year as a professional, Heighway could scarcely believe he was on his way to Wembley to play his part in a major cup final for Liverpool.

In the build up to the game, Heighway said, 'This will be the first time that I have set eyes on the place and I can't really say that I've ever had an ambition to go there. It will be a big thrill going to Wembley and I'm keeping my fingers crossed for a place in the team.'

Heighway got his wish when Shankly chose him to play on the wing, although it was a final in which Liverpool rarely shone in an attacking sense as the game went into extra time after a 0–0 draw.

Just two minutes into extra time, Heighway took centre stage when he scored one of the most memorable Liverpool goals in a Wembley final.

Similar to his earlier league strike against Everton at Anfield, Heighway belted in a shot from a tight angle on the left to give Liverpool the lead.

Afterwards he said of the goal, 'The ball fell right and the only thing I could do was hit it with my left foot. Nine times out of ten shots like that go anywhere. This was the tenth.'

Unfortunately for Heighway and his team-mates, Liverpool's delight was short lived as Arsenal scraped themselves back into the game with a scrappy goal. The Gunners substitute Eddie Kelly pounced on uncertainty in the Reds' defence to scramble the ball past an exposed Ray Clemence in the Liverpool goal to equalise four minutes before the end of the first half of extra time.

The goal proved to be a turning point as Arsenal showed all the experience and fortitude that had made them league champions by going on to lift the cup following a stunning twenty-five-yard strike from their forward Charlie George in the second period of extra-time.

The 2–1 defeat left nothing but a bitter taste in the mouth for Heighway. 'That makes three,' he said. 'In the last two years I've been on the losing side in semi-finals. Now I'm a loser in the final.'

Despite the defeat, Liverpool's march to the cup final laid down a strong statement of intent by Shankly for the future.

Just two days after the final, Shankly pulled off one of the club's greatest ever signings when he snapped up promising forward Kevin Keegan from Scunthorpe Utd for just £33,000.

During his seven seasons at Anfield, Keegan struck up a lethal understanding with Toshack and Heighway as Liverpool got set to enjoy a consistent run of glory.

Heighway was pretty much an ever-present for Liverpool during his second season as he played in forty of the club's forty-two league games but it would again end in heart-breaking fashion.

Liverpool lost out on the First Division title by just one point to surprise package Derby County, who beat the Reds 1–0 in their second last game of the season, a result which went a long way to losing Heighway his first league winners' medal.

Even so, Liverpool went into the final game of the season knowing a victory at Arsenal could still have won them the league but they could only muster up a 0–0 draw to finish in joint second place with Leeds.

If anything, that setback just made Liverpool even more determined to succeed in the 1972–1973 season as they set their eyes on glory in both the league and the UEFA Cup.

Liverpool's form in European competition had been patchy up to that point with just one semi-final appearance in the 1965 European Cup and a last-four meeting with Leeds Utd in the 1970 Fairs Cup to show for the previous decade.

This would be the first time that the Reds would compete in the UEFA Cup, Europe's 'consolation' competition. The early rounds saw Liverpool breeze past West German side Frankfurt and Greek outfit AEK Athens to set up a third-round tie with the East German's Dynamo Berlin in November 1972.

Liverpool made the tough trip to behind the Berlin Wall first and came back to Merseyside with a credible 0–0 draw under their belts.

In the lead-up to the second leg at Anfield, the Berlin manager Günter Schröder expressed concerns about his side playing a late evening game under floodlights for the very first time.

Liverpool had splashed out up to £50,000 just a couple of years earlier to kit Anfield out with one of the strongest sets of floodlights seen in any European ground at the time and Schröder feared the glare from the lights would upset his team.

But it was the dazzling Steve Heighway he should have been most worried about as the Irish international almost single-handedly took Dynamo Berlin apart in a 3–1 win for Liverpool.

It took Heighway just fifty-seven seconds to shatter Berlin's resistance as he set off on a mazy run down the left flank that left two defenders for dead and hit a shot which the Berlin keeper Werner Lihsa could only parry into the path of the on-rushing Liverpool forward Phil Boersma to knock into the net.

The resilient East Germans recovered from the early setback to stun Anfield with an equaliser, but Heighway's heroics were far from finished as he smashed in a deflected volley on twenty-five minutes to restore Liverpool's lead and John Toshack made sure of the victory with a third goal in the second half.

The win over Berlin ensured Liverpool a quarter-final clash with another tricky East German side the following March but they were, once again, triumphant with a 3–0 aggregate win over Dynamo Dresden to set up an all-English semi-final with Tottenham.

The UEFA Cup was far from the only piece of silverware Liverpool were chasing that season as great form in the league yet again saw them engage in a three-way battle for the title; this time with Leeds and Arsenal.

The Reds began the season in blistering fashion winning four of their first five games, including 2–0 wins over both Man Utd and Man City.

The early months of the season had also seen them crucially win 2–1 away at Leeds and pick up a precious scoreless draw at Arsenal's Highbury.

For his part, Heighway was enjoying his most prolific season, notching up six league goals in wins over Man Utd, Sheffield Utd (twice), Ipswich and Tottenham.

By late April 1973, Liverpool's season boiled down to a vital week when they travelled to Spurs for the UEFA Cup semi-final second leg just forty-eight hours after they had entertained Leeds in a vital league game at Anfield.

Liverpool had secured a precious 1–0 win over Tottenham in the first leg of their semi-final on 10 April but wobbled a bit in their bid to wrap up the First Division title with a 2–1 loss at Newcastle on Saturday, 21 April.

That defeat put massive pressure on Liverpool's home game against Leeds on the following Monday night.

The Reds went into the game top of the table with a four-point cushion over Leeds with just two league games to go, but they knew that defeat against their Anfield bogey team – Liverpool had not beaten Leeds at home in the league for six years – would not only bring Leeds back into contention but would also help Arsenal who sat just two points behind in second place.

In one of their most assured performances of the season, Liverpool brushed Leeds aside 2–0 and with Arsenal only drawing with Southampton on the same night, the league title was all but won.

However Shankly's boys had little time to rest as they made their way to London for their third game in five days against a Spurs side set for revenge for their UEFA Cup first leg defeat at Anfield.

If the Liverpool players were tired, they didn't show it as they completely outplayed Spurs in the first half at White Hart Lane, winning no less than eight corners, but failed to make their dominance count as the teams went in scoreless after the first forty-five minutes.

The Reds were made to pay just three minutes into the second half when English international forward Martin Peters put Spurs in front on the night and level on aggregate.

At that point, however, Liverpool rolled up their sleeves and really showed their class.

Within six minutes of the Spurs goal, Kevin Keegan and Heighway combined to draw Liverpool level in the game and also secure a precious European away goal.

Keegan took advantage of uncertainty in the Spurs defence to latch on to a ball in the box and he picked out a perfectly timed pass across goal for Heighway to score a simple tap-in with Spurs' Northern Irish goalkeeper Pat Jennings stranded.

Heighway's goal proved the defining moment on the night, and possibly Liverpool's season, because, although Peters scored another for Spurs, the Reds held on to go through to the final on the away goals rule.

The elation of making the UEFA Cup final made Liverpool's final league game against Leicester at Anfield just three days later a celebratory occasion.

The team may have been unable to produce a great performance on the day, having to settle for a 0–0 draw, but it was the point which secured Liverpool their third league title under Shankly and Heighway his first league winners' medal.

After their hectic week, the Liverpool team finally had a chance to rest up in time for their momentous two-legged UEFA Cup final clash with West German side Borussia Mönchengladbach a fortnight later.

With the first leg at Anfield, the Borussia coach Hennes Weisweiler ran the rule over the Liverpool side and pinpointed Heighway and Keegan as the two men he feared most.

Rather bizarrely, it was the wet Liverpool weather which actually put the dampeners on Weisweiler's men after a torrential mid-May downpour turned the pitch at Anfield into a swamp for the first-leg game.

Barely twenty-eight minutes of the game had passed when it was abandoned due to the waterlogged pitch and UEFA officials decided to put it back twenty-four hours.

It proved to be a crucial break for Shankly, who had initially started the tie with John Toshack on the bench, favouring instead to go with nippy forward Brian Hall.

However, the canny Scot had noticed that the German's defence had struggled under the high ball during the abandoned game and had no hesitation in recalling Toshack, Liverpool's master in the air, for the rescheduled match the next night.

It was a Shankly masterstroke as Toshack completely dominated the Borussia defence winning two crucial headers to set up his partner Keegan for two first-half goals.

In a game full of incident Keegan missed a penalty that would have wrapped up a first-half hat-trick, but defender Larry Lloyd headed in a third in the second half as Liverpool appeared to be cruising.

The night nearly turned to one of disaster for Heighway late on when he was adjudged to have fouled the Borussia midfielder Dietmar Danner in the box, giving the Germans a penalty.

Luckily for Heighway, goalkeeper Ray Clemence was on top form and managed to pull off a brilliant save from Borussia's forward Jupp Heynckes' shot to deny their opponents what would have been a precious away goal.

It still wasn't all plain sailing from there as Liverpool endured a torrid night in Germany two weeks later as two first-half goals from Heynckes ate away at their three-goal lead.

Despite this, Shankly's Reds kept their nerve in the second half of the game to repel Borussia and win the cup 3–2 on aggregate. Yet if it hadn't been for the Clemence save at Anfield, Heighway could have been left to regret the penalty he had conceded.

Instead it proved to be a second winners' medal for the Irish winger but far from the last he would win in a Liverpool shirt as the club embarked on an incredible period of dominance in both England and Europe.

After becoming the first English team to win the league and European trophy in the same season in 1972–1973, it proved difficult for Shankly's team to surpass or even replicate the feat a year later.

Steve Heighway played in thirty-six of the club's forty-two league games in 1973–1974, scoring five goals, but the team relinquished their First Division crown to old rivals Leeds.

Liverpool's European Cup adventure was short and sweet that season too, as they bowed out 4–2 on aggregate in the second round to crack Yugoslavian outfit Red Star Belgrade.

Heighway and his team-mates still had a whiff of glory in their nostrils, however, as they began their FA Cup run in January 1974.

It started poorly enough for the Reds and they needed two Kevin Keegan goals at Anfield just to draw with Doncaster Rovers in the third round, but Heighway settled their nerves in the replay with an early goal as Liverpool ran out 2–0 winners.

Injury kept Heighway out of the side for the following two rounds, when Liverpool again needed a replay to beat Carlisle Utd in the fourth round before they stepped it up a gear with a 2–0 win over Ipswich at Anfield in the fifth round.

Heighway returned for Liverpool's quarter-final clash with Bristol City and helped the Reds to a 1–0 win that set up a semi-final with Leicester City.

In keeping with how much of Liverpool's cup run had gone that year, the game finished in a draw before Liverpool marched on to the final with a 3–1 replay win four days later.

The win over Leicester sent Heighway on his way to Wembley for the second time in four years, where the Reds would come up against Newcastle Utd.

Despite their patchy form on their way to the final, Heighway was super confident his team would do the business this time at Wembley.

In his column with the *Liverpool Post* on the morning of the final on 4 May, Heighway brashly predicted, 'Tonight we will be celebrating with the FA Cup. That, I believe, will be the outcome of our clash with Newcastle at Wembley. A couple of months ago I had a strong feeling that this would be Liverpool's year for Wembley and in the past couple of weeks I have felt it in my bones that this time we would wind up collecting the cup.'

Heighway's confidence proved to be spot on as both he and Keegan lit up Wembley and left a shell-shocked Newcastle trailing in their wake.

After a scoreless first half, Liverpool came to life when Keegan volleyed them into the lead on fifty-seven minutes with a cracking strike. Heighway doubled the Reds advantage eighteen minutes later when he latched on to a John Toshask header to race into the box and slam a right-footed shot into the back of the net. Yet again, the Irishman had scored in a Wembley final and this time he would be on the winning side. Keegan notched his second later with a tap in as Liverpool were rampant.

Newcastle left-back Alan Kennedy was the youngest player on the Wembley pitch that day at just nineteen years of age and he certainly learned a harsh lesson at the hands of the Liverpool masters.

Kennedy would later go on to sign for Liverpool in 1978 and score one of the club's most memorable goals with the winner in the 1981 European Cup final. But, in 1974, Kennedy came up against the deadly triumvirate of Heighway, Keegan and Toshack and still marvels at the skill they showed in that Wembley final.

'Steve actually played on the left wing that day meaning it was my fellow full-back Frank Clarke who had the job of marking him and Frank certainly had a tough day,' Kennedy says. 'Steve played very well in that final, as did the whole Liverpool team, and we just couldn't live with them in the end. Little did I know then that I would be a team-mate of Steve Heighway's just a few years later when I signed for Liverpool myself. By then, Steve's career at Liverpool was coming to an end but he was still a very important player for the club and had been one of their best performers throughout the 1970s.

'Steve just glided over the ground and could beat people at ease with his quality. He summed up everything Liverpool was about back then and that was entertainment. I would say in the early to mid-1970s, there wasn't a better winger to be found anywhere in the game than Steve Heighway.'

Three winners' medals in two seasons represented a remarkable achievement for Heighway but just weeks after that famous Wembley triumph, his club was stunned when Bill Shankly announced he was resigning as manager.

The news sent shockwaves through the football world but when the dust had settled, Liverpool refused to panic and looked to continue on Shankly's winning traditions by giving the job to his right-hand man, and former Liverpool player, captain and physio, Bob Paisley.

Paisley's introduction as manager did little to upset the performances of Steve Heighway, who continued to torture opposition defences down the wings. He was one of Liverpool's most consistent performers during Paisley's first year in charge, playing in thirty-five league games as the Reds came close to regaining their title by finishing second, just two points off the eventual winners Derby County.

Liverpool's 1974 FA Cup win gained them entry into that season's European Cup Winners Cup and they began it in scintillating fashion at Anfield.

Steve Heighway played his part as he scored a goal in the club's biggest ever win as they trounced hapless Norwegian side Strømsgodset 11–0 in front of 24,000 mesmerised Kopites.

The Reds went a little easier on their part-time opponents in the second leg in Norway settling for a 1–0 win that rounded off a 12–0 aggregate scoreline.

However, Liverpool's shooting boots badly let them down in the following round when they could only muster up a 1–1 draw at Anfield with Hungarians Ferencváros. The score draw proved fatal to the Reds as Ferencváros held on for a 0–0 draw at home to put Liverpool out on the away goals rule, scuppering Heighway's hopes of adding another European medal to the UEFA Cup from two years earlier.

It proved to be a rare season of failure for Liverpool under Paisley and his only year in charge at the club when the Reds would not win a single trophy.

Things were quickly back on track the following season when Anfield, once again, saw the team charge for glory on two fronts.

Just as Shankly's team had done in 1973, Liverpool set off on a remarkable UEFA Cup run to complement a successful league-title charge.

Steve Heighway played in all but three of Liverpool's league games, scoring four goals, as Paisley's Reds trumped the challenge of London club QPR and Man Utd to claim the title. Added to that excitement was Liverpool's successful European adventures and Heighway as ever was in the thick of the action.

First Liverpool had to survive something of a scare in the first round of the UEFA Cup when it took a John Toshack hat-trick at Anfield to scrape past Scottish side Hibernian 3–2 on aggregate, following a 1–0 defeat in the first leg.

Next up was a trip to the north of Spain to take on Real Sociedad and Heighway helped settle any Reds' nerves with a twentieth-minute opener as Paisley's men produced an impressive display to win 3–1 on their travels.

With the tie in the bag, Liverpool opened up in the second leg at Anfield to hit Sociedad for six with Heighway, once again, getting on the score sheet in an amazing 9–1 aggregate romp.

Liverpool maintained the momentum in the third round by seeing off Polish opponents Slask Wroctaw 5–1 on aggregate before being paired with old foes Dynamo Dresden in the quarter-final.

Just seventy-three Liverpool fans braved the trip to East Germany for the first leg and they saw their team put in a disciplined display to hold on for a 0–0 draw before goals from Jimmy Case and Keegan saw the Reds march on with a 2–1 win at Anfield.

By then, Heighway and his team-mates had sensed UEFA Cup success and they weren't going to let the small matter of a semi-final with Barcelona get in the way of claiming the trophy.

With the first leg of the semi-final at Camp Nou in Barcelona, Liverpool struck a decisive blow by claiming a 1–0 win thanks to an early John Toshack strike. The Welshman's goal proved to be the one that would separate the sides over both legs as Liverpool looked forward to their second UEFA Cup final appearance in four years.

The Reds' opponents this time would be Belgian outfit FC Bruges and with the first leg at Anfield, everybody expected Liverpool to at least take a lead with them for the away game. The recently crowned English First Division champions did just that but their 3–2 win on the night couldn't have come in more dramatic fashion.

Anfield was stunned into silence in the first fifteen minutes of the clash as the adventurous Bruges side tore into Liverpool to gain a shock 2–0 lead through Raoul Lambert and Julien Cools – a lead which they held until half-time. Staring certain defeat in the face, Liverpool needed a big performance in the second half from their attacking players, such as Heighway, if they were to salvage anything from the first leg. As ever, Heighway duly obliged and just before the hour mark, he burst down the left wing to cut back a cross which fellow forward Ray Kennedy smashed into the roof of the net from just inside the box.

Anfield erupted and the goal gave Liverpool the impetus to go on all-out attack as FC Bruges did their best to hang on to their lead.

In the end, Liverpool's superior attacking play told as substitute Jimmy Case scored an equaliser after a Kennedy shot hit the post and then Heighway once more got involved as he was chopped down in the box for a penalty which a grateful Keegan hit home.

The vital recovery was complete but, at 3–2, the game was still very much in the balance as Liverpool travelled to Belgium for the second leg.

Once again it started badly for the Reds as Lambert smashed home a penalty to put Bruges ahead on away goals after just ten minutes but the ever reliable Keegan knocked home an equaliser just four minutes later. With the tie back in their favour, Paisley's men survived a couple of second-half scares to hold on for the precious 1–1 draw and capture their second league and UEFA Cup double.

Heighway's major medal count had now reached five but there was even more league title success to come the Irishman's way in 1977 and 1979 as Liverpool maintained their grip on dominance of the English game under Bob Paisley.

However, it wasn't all success for Heighway, and he did have to endure another day of Wembley heartache in 1977 when Liverpool were beaten 2–1 by Manchester Utd in the FA Cup final and he was also on the losing Liverpool team to Nottingham Forest in the 1978 League Cup final.

However his greatest achievements in a red shirt were to come as Liverpool transferred their dominance from England across the continent in the European Cup.

STEVE HEIGHWAY INTERVIEW

After eleven trophy-laden years as a player and another eighteen years as a youth team coach at Liverpool FC, flying Irish winger Steve Heighway is rightly regarded as one of the club's great legends.

From helping the club to its first European Cup triumph to nurturing the talents of Steven Gerrard and Jamie Carragher and winning three FA Youth Cups as a Liverpool coach, few other figures around Anfield have had as much influence on the club as Heighway.

Here, in his own words, the great man tells of the great highs of playing and coaching for one of the world's greatest clubs and of his absolute love and devotion to Liverpool Football Club.

My playing career at Liverpool started in 1970 after the then manager Bill Shankly brought me to the club from local amateur side Skelmersdale Utd. I had just finished up at university and the club had offered me a one-year professional contract and I just thought that I had to take my chances.

Bill obviously liked what he saw in me as I went straight into the first-team squad, which was a massive surprise considering I was coming from an amateur background. I don't think it could happen today that a player who almost nobody in the stadium knows could make it straight into the Liverpool first-team squad, especially if they were coming out of university or from an amateur team.

After making my debut for Liverpool, things also quickly started to move for me on the international front when I was called up to the Republic of Ireland team just a month later.

I was delighted to play for Ireland as although both my parents were actually English, I was born in Dublin and grew up there until I was ten, so I had that association with the country that I didn't have with England. I had played at underage level for Ireland on the international scene already but had also represented England in school's football but Ireland was the team that I had decided to play for, and I never had to give it anymore thought after that.

Back at Liverpool, I was so lucky that Bill Shankly had a soft spot for me and I was in the team a lot more in that first year than I would have thought.

It was great learning the game under Bill. I suppose all managers have their different styles and abilities but Bill Shankly was the best I worked with because he was so charismatic.

I was fortunate, too, that I played in an era when good wing play was really appreciated. I always considered myself, first and foremost, a left winger but over the years at Liverpool I spent as much time on the right wing and at other times even playing up front as a forward.

They really were great years as almost every season during the 1970s we were competing for trophies.

I got my first taste of an FA Cup final during my first season at the club and although we lost that day to Arsenal, I had scored during the game at Wembley and that's something that will always be with me.

Thankfully, when we got to the cup final again in 1974, I also managed to score and this time we ran out 3–0 winners over Newcastle, which made up for some of the disappointment of losing the other final to Arsenal.

One of our best achievements under Bill during my early years at the club was winning the UEFA Cup in 1973. We played in Europe pretty much every season anyway so we had a very experienced bunch of players who were growing in confidence.

Each week, we would be on the training ground and just listening out for where we would be off to next to play an European game and going on to win the UEFA Cup just brought us to that next level as we then had the belief that we could beat all these other top European teams.

As a young man, it was a great experience to enjoy such success and to play with so many great players in a team that always believed it could win.

I made so many good friends from that time as well, such as Brian Hall and Phil Boersma, and played with the great players, such as Kevin Keegan.

Perhaps the only unsettling period for any of us as players was when Bill Shankly announced he was resigning as manager in the summer of 1974. It came as a huge shock to us all as he had given no indication that he was going to quit. Then, of course, you started to fear that the new manager that would come in might not rate you and you could be out of the team.

In the end, it was Bill's right-hand man Bob Paisley who took on the role, although at first he had been a reluctant manager.

Bob was a lot quieter than Bill but he had a lot of good players in the team who helped him through his first year in the job and, after that, he really took off as a very successful manager.

One of Bob's best traits was that he had a fantastic eye for a player and, each year, he seemed to be able to improve the squad with one or two really good signings.

After we won the league under Bob in 1976, the team really felt we were ready for a proper challenge on the European Cup.

As things would turn out, we would win the trophy for the following two seasons and when I look back on my career as a player, I would have to say that winning that first European Cup in Rome in 1977 was my greatest achievement.

And we just kept winning under Bob. When Kevin Keegan left in 1977, he replaced him with the equally brilliant Kenny Dalglish and nobody at the time could match Liverpool for consistency.

Obviously as the years rolled on, my time at the club began to wind down. My last season at Anfield was the 1980–1981 campaign. By then, I was hitting thirty-four and you don't have to be a magician to understand that, at that age, I was getting fewer opportunities to play in the first team.

It wasn't a case of being dropped or anything like that, it was just more a gradual process and, eventually, I had to accept that my time was up.

I left Liverpool to go to play in the US in 1981, and I have to say that it was a real big wrench to leave the club. It was the only club I'd ever known and some players never get over the pain of leaving such a great club as Liverpool. But I was fortunate enough in that I was asked to come back to the club again as a coach in 1990 when Kenny Dalglish was the manager.

I had coached for the previous eight years in the US and had built up all my relevant badges and felt that I was ready to work at a great club like Liverpool again.

I was proud to get the opportunity to work as a youth coach as I was influencing these young guys not just as players but as all-round people and that always gave me great pleasure.

In my early years as youth coach, I got to develop the skills of some great players, such as Steve McManaman, Robbie Fowler and Michael Owen, players who you just knew were going to be brilliant professional footballers.

We had some success at youth level during the 1990s as well by winning the FA Youth Cup in 1996 and by bringing through this quality of player.

I know that during that decade the senior team didn't win as much as Liverpool had been accustomed to, but I can tell you from being at the club at the time that absolutely everybody, right from the chairman to the chief executive through to the manager and coaches worked extremely hard to try and bring that success back to Anfield.

It was just unfortunate that we never hit on the exact winning formula that Man Utd did at that time under Alex Ferguson but, even at that, it took Ferguson a long number of years and that bit of luck to start winning the league the way Liverpool had done in previous eras.

Even though Liverpool has not won the league since 1990, the club has still been successful and played in many big games and cup finals.

Liverpool FC have still played a very significant role in football over the past twenty years and although we are now facing some uncertain times, I am sure we will still be one of the world's most famous and important clubs in the future.

From my own role as youth coach at Liverpool in more recent years, the most disappointing aspect has been the changes in how big clubs now run their youth systems. There is more emphasis placed on the recruitment of players from all around the world than there is on developing players.

The way the game has gone now, clubs don't have the time to take a chance on developing their players the way they used to and that is to the detriment of local English and Irish players at a club like Liverpool.

I retired from my role as youth team coach with Liverpool in 2007 as I felt I no longer I had the influence I needed in developing the young players coming through at the club. One main issue I had at the club was that I always spoke my mind and that wasn't always appreciated, but that's just the way things go sometimes and it hasn't diluted my love or support for Liverpool.

There's no doubt that Liverpool now faces a big challenge into the future and one of the only ways the club can be sure of competing and being successful is to raise big massive amounts of cash year on year.

It is not for me to say how that club is being run at the moment, but the next four or five years are going to be really important and what happens in that time will dictate where the club will be in the future. But Liverpool FC has such a great history and is such a big global brand that I believe it will be successful.

From my own point of view, I was extremely lucky to have played in a very successful era and got such a great reception from the fans.

Even to this day, they sing my name at the ground and that is a huge honour and compliment. It helps that I still live the area as well where people are very friendly and I will always have a great connection with the fans and the club.

I've never lived off the fact that I am a former pro-footballer, mainly because I have spent many more years of my life as a youth team coach and I would consider that was my main career, but I am so proud and happy to have represented Liverpool Football Club.

It is very close to my heart, and I hope that the club will, once again, enjoy all the great success which I was so fortunate to experience.

When Liverpool Played in Ireland

European Cup

Crusaders 0–5 Liverpool,

Seaview, Belfast, 28 September 1976

Bob Paisley's reward for leading Liverpool to their first league championship success under his managerial reign in 1976 was a first round European Cup tie with Belfast side Crusaders.

As when Liverpool had been drawn to play Dundalk in the Fairs Cup seven years earlier, the draw was met with as much excitement in Ireland as it was on Merseyside. While it was seen in Liverpool as a routine first-round tie that they would be expected to canter through, against part-time opposition, for Crusaders and their fans it was a massive chance to prove themselves against one of Europe's top clubs.

Perhaps reminded of their 10–0 Anfield win over Dundalk in 1969, Liverpool's players went into the home first leg on 14 September expecting to rack up a commanding lead to take to Belfast.

It came as something of a shock, therefore, when the plucky Irish League champions more than held their own at Anfield.

Playing with an almost blanket defence, Billy Johnson's Crusaders frustrated the Reds for long periods and came away from Anfield having suffered only a 2–0 loss, with the goals for Liverpool coming from a Phil Neal penalty and a second-half strike from John Toshack.

Afterwards, Liverpool's outspoken captain Emlyn Hughes said he was ashamed of their dour performance and the Reds players promised to up their game for the return leg in Belfast.

However, prior to arriving for that second leg, Liverpool's great European Cup hopes were almost shattered by the weather.

Having obtained special dispensation through UEFA to only travel to Belfast on the day of the game due to the violent tensions in Northern Ireland during the height of the Troubles, a heavy fog which had descended on Liverpool on the morning of the game saw the Reds' squad stranded at Speake airport for a few nervous hours.

In the end, the delay caused little more than the cancellation of a pre-game reception planned for Liverpool officials in Belfast, but had the team not made it in time for the clash at Crusaders' Seaview ground they were in danger of being thrown out of the European Cup.

So it came as a massive relief to everybody when the Liverpool squad finally touched down in Belfast and made their way directly to Seaview to prepare for the Crusaders challenge.

After the drab first game, both managers promised their teams would attack, with Paisley promising Liverpool's hordes of fans in Northern Ireland that his team would put on a show.

When the game kicked off, the atmosphere inside Seaview was electric with over 12,000 fans crammed into the tiny stadium, many of them standing on outer walls and on the stadium roof just to get a glimpse of the star-studded Liverpool side.

Paisley certainly didn't hold back with his team selection, picking his strongest side with Ray Clemence in goal, Emlyn Hughes marshalling the defence, Ian Callaghan in midfield, Steve Heighway on the wing and star forward Kevin Keegan leading the Liverpool frontline.

Far from being overawed, Crusaders took the game to the Reds and twice in the first fifteen minutes came agonisingly close to taking a shock lead.

Both chances for Crusaders fell to their lively midfielder Ron McAteer, who first saw a shot hit the bar before, just a few minutes later, he burst through the Liverpool defence again and beat Clemence with a shot which this time cannoned back off the post.

An early goal for Crusaders certainly would have put it up to Liverpool and most in the 12,000 crowd couldn't believe how difficult the Reds were finding it to get a proper foothold in the game.

It eventually took the experience of captain Hughes and Callaghan to calm things down for the English champions as they began to pass and maintain possession of the ball with a greater superiority to that of Crusaders.

However with the tie still very much alive at only 2–0 on aggregate, Liverpool knew they would need to score to put an end to Crusaders' hopes. This they duly did on thirty-four minutes when the brilliant Keegan volleyed home the goal that finally settled Liverpool's nerves.

Reacting to a pass into the box by David Johnson, Keegan swivelled on the turn and hit an excellent volley past Roy McDonald in the Crusaders' goal.

With the breathing space of an away goal, Liverpool were able to relax after their shaky start and they played most of the second half at their own pace rarely allowing Crusaders to threaten them.

It was Liverpool who did most of the attacking in the second period but the Crusaders defence, marshalled by the excellent Walter McFarland, held firm until tiredness took over in the final ten minutes.

Liverpool's superior fitness meant they could take advantage of Crusaders mistakes late on in the game and they managed to score four goals in the final nine minutes to put a major gloss on the scoreline.

David Johnson got the ball rolling on eighty-one minutes when he reacted quickest after Steve Heighway had a twenty-yard shot parried by McDonald to knock the rebound home.

A 2–0 scoreline at that stage was probably a fair reflection on how the game had gone but Crusaders were hit with cruel luck as Liverpool piled on the pressure.

Three minutes after the Johnson goal, substitute Terry McDermott got on the score sheet when he cut in from the left and drilled a trademark shot past McDonald into the corner of the net.

Irishman Heighway was next to play his part when he got on the end of another rebound off McDonald to notch Liverpool's fourth on eighty-seven minutes and there was still time for David Johnson to score his second of the night and cap off what had actually been a hard-fought 5–0 victory for Liverpool.

Although crestfallen at the harsh final result, Crusaders could later take comfort from the fact that Paisley's Liverpool would go on to conquer Europe that season by lifting the European Cup.

TEAMS

Crusaders: McDonald, Strain, Gorman, McFarland, Gillespie, McPolin, Lennox, McAteer, Kirk, Cooke, McCann
Subs: Collins for McCann, McQuillan for Lennox

Liverpool: Clemence, Neal, Jones, Smith, Kennedy, Hughes, Keegan, Johnson, Heighway, Case, Callaghan
Subs: McDermott for Case

8

Kings of Europe: 1977, 1978, 1981

After helping Liverpool past the challenge of Crusaders in a first-round encounter in 1976, Steve Heighway was very much a regular on the wings as the Reds upped their challenge for a genuine shot at the European Cup crown.

The second round draw threw up an interesting tie with Turkish champions Trabzonspor, a team that Liverpool manager Bob Paisley admitted they should have beaten with ease.

Heighway, Keegan and Toshack were all in the Liverpool side as they travelled to Turkey for the first leg of the tie on 20 October 1976.

Paisley revealed his side would be on the defensive for the early part of the away game and would call on the attacking talents of the likes of Heighway to try to win the game in the latter stages. As it transpired it was the Turks who took a shock advantage to Anfield when a debatable second-half penalty sealed a 1–0 win for the home side.

Liverpool captain Emlyn Hughes was harshly adjudged to have fouled Turkish forward Alikemal and Trabzonspor's defender Cemel Cooly slotted home the spot kick on sixty-five minutes to send the Reds crashing to defeat.

Afterwards, a livid Paisley said the ball used for the game was not up to standard for a major European Cup clash.

'It was not good enough for blow football,' Paisley blasted. 'It was a pig's bladder and teams in the Durham Mining League would not play with such a bad ball. It was not new and it was impossible to make it flow around as we normally do.'

Paisley vowed that his Liverpool side would make amends at Anfield a fortnight later and, once again, his bullish prediction came to fruition as the Reds blew Trabzonspor off the pitch with an exhilarating first-half display.

From the first whistle, Liverpool were on their game, biting into tackles and laying siege to the Trabzonspor goal. Steve Heighway was in inspired form and took little more than eight minutes to draw Liverpool level on aggregate when he beat his marker Turgay to a headed flick-on in the box from Kevin Keegan to tap home the opener past Trabzonspor keeper Senol.

The Turkish outfit barely had time to catch their breath when Liverpool were in again on ten minutes, this time, forward David Johnson finished off a slick move as Anfield erupted.

Under strict orders from Paisley to keep the pressure up, Liverpool killed off the tie with a third goal from Keegan on nineteen minutes and the victorious Reds simply strolled through the rest of the game with the 3–0 scoreline intact.

Afterwards, the Trabzonspor manager Ahmet Suat admitted Liverpool had been the better side. 'Liverpool were just too strong for us, particularly Callaghan, Keegan, Heighway and Kennedy,' he said.

The victory sent Liverpool into the quarter-finals of the European Cup for only the second time in the club's history and a charged-up Paisley could already sense his team was preparing for an assault on the trophy.

Although the Crusaders and Trabzonspor ties were games Liverpool were expected to win easily, the same could not be said for their quarter-final clash against classy French champions Saint-Étienne the following March.

Under their coach, Robert Herbin, Saint-Étienne had been one of the best sides in France throughout the 1970s winning three league titles in a row from 1974–1976 and losing the 1976 European Cup final to German giants Bayern Munich.

Once again, Liverpool would face up to the away leg first and travelled, with some trepidation, to Saint-Étienne's Stade Geoffroy-Guichard ground where the Frenchmen had been almost unbeatable in European competition.

But as reigning UEFA Cup champions, Liverpool were no slouches on the European stage themselves and they relished the challenge put in front of them by their French opponents.

Far from being fazed by the feverous atmosphere inside the stadium, Liverpool took the game to Saint-Étienne at every available opportunity and Steve Heighway was, once again, at the forefront of Liverpool's attacking display.

The Reds should have taken the lead after just ten minutes when Heighway, who took some serious stick from his full-back Janvion all night, beat his marker and struck a right foot shot which Saint-Étienne keeper Jurkovic had to tip over the bar. From the resultant corner, defender Phil Thompson had a free header on goal but it flew over the bar.

There was further frustration in the second half when Heighway was denied a dream goal as he surged forward from the halfway line with the ball, beat his marker and chipped the ball past the Saint-Étienne keeper only to have it cannon back off the post.

Saint-Étienne showed the clinical mark of champions to soak up this pressure and catch Liverpool late on with a killer winning goal when midfielder Dominique Bathenay drove the ball past Clemence following a corner.

Despite the defeat, manager Paisley was pleased with how his team had performed in the pressure-cooker atmosphere. 'We did very well, except that we did not put our chances away. In a game like this, you may only get one chance and your finishing has to be lethal.'

With Liverpool looking to overturn the deficit at Anfield on 16 March 1977, Paisley predicted the second leg would be a 'cracker'.

His description would turn out to be something of an understatement as Anfield witnessed possibly the most iconic European game ever played at the stadium.

As they had done against Trabzonspor, Liverpool tore into Saint-Étienne from the off, and got their noses in front after just two minutes. The goal was somewhat fortuitous as what appeared to be an in-swinging cross from Kevin Keegan from out on the left flew over the head of the Saint-Étienne keeper Jurkovic to tie up the score on aggregate.

The early goal set the tempo for a game in which both sides attacked each other at will.

Ray Clemence was on top of his game during the first half as Saint-Étienne piled forward, and he beat out a number of attempts from the French as Liverpool hung on to their lead right up to half-time.

Anfield was stunned early in the second half, however, when Bathenay struck again, this time with an unstoppable twenty-yard volley that looked to be sending Saint-Étienne on their way to the semi-finals.

Roared on by a defiant crowd, Liverpool refused to give up and recovered from the Bathenay shock to regain the lead on fifty-nine minutes when Ray Kennedy smashed a low right-foot shot into the net in front of the Kop.

The game was on a knife edge as it entered the final twenty minutes, when Paisley delivered one of his most astute substitution moves by replacing John Toshack with energetic forward David Fairclough.

With Liverpool chasing a third goal that would win the tie, supersub Fairclough duly obliged with just six minutes left on the clock when he outpaced the Saint-Étienne defender Christian Lopez to a through ball and kept his nerve to slip the ball past Jurkovic to spark off some of the wildest scenes of celebrations ever at Anfield.

A jubilant Paisley couldn't compliment his team enough for pulling off one of their best achievements by reaching the semi-finals of Europe's premier cup competition. 'I thought my lads showed tremendous character when those two goals were needed,' Paisley enthused.

With Saint-Étienne out of the way, Liverpool's route to the final proved somewhat easier when they were drawn against Swiss outfit FC Zürich in the last four.

Zürich had done extremely well to make it as far as the semi-finals by beating Scottish champions Rangers in the first round and East German's

Dynamo Dresden in their quarter-final, but they were to be no match for Paisley's men.

Liverpool travelled to Switzerland on 6 April for the first leg and pretty much wrapped up their cup final place with an impressive 3–1 win in Zürich's Letzigrund stadium.

Steve Heighway had one of his best displays ever in a Red shirt as he made life hell for the Zürich defence throughout the ninety minutes.

However, Liverpool did have to recover from an early shock when Zürich took the lead after five minutes when their playmaker Risi struck home a penalty, but, from then on, it was the Heighway show.

Liverpool levelled on fourteen minutes when full-back Phil Neal took down a Kennedy free kick in the box and smashed it home. Two minutes into the second half, Heighway grabbed a killer second goal for Liverpool with a typically strong run to beat off two tackles and place a right foot shot past the Zürich goalkeeper Grob.

The Zürich defence just couldn't keep Heighway in check and it was no surprise when the Irishman was again the central figure for Liverpool's third goal.

Heighway had made a darting run into the box to gather a perfect David Fairclough pass and, just as he was about to score his second of the night, Zürich defender Chapuisat took his feet from under him with a foul and Phil Neal gladly knocked home the penalty.

It made the second leg at Anfield on 20 April fairly academic, but Liverpool still put in a very professional performance to sweep Zürich aside 3–0 with a brace of goals from Jimmy Case and another from Keegan to send them on their way to their first European Cup final, where they would take on old German foes Borussia Mönchengladbach in Rome.

The Germans had squeezed past top Soviet side Dynamo Kiev 2–1 on aggregate in their semi-final and really fancied their chances of avenging the UEFA Cup final defeat to Liverpool in 1973.

Borussia's main worry in the lead up to the final on 25 May 1977 was how they would handle the twin threat of Keegan and Heighway. Their coach Udo Lattek was unsure which of the two he would order his best defender Berti Vogts to mark throughout the game.

In the end, Lattek decided that man-marker Vogts should pick up

Keegan leaving Heighway free to run amok against his marker Hans Klinkhammer.

As in the semi-final win over FC Zürich, Heighway proved to be one of Liverpool's most effective players during the highly charged final, evading the close attention of Klinkhammer to spark numerous attacks on the Borussia goal.

Heighway's most incisive move came on twenty-eight minutes when he collected an Ian Callaghan pass on the right wing and cut inside, before splitting the German's defence with a perfect pass for on-rushing midfielder Terry McDermott to run on to and slot home to give Liverpool a first-half lead.

Borussia were by no means out of the game, however, and had Liverpool on the rack in the early stages of the second half when they found an equaliser through their star forward Allan Simonsen, the 1977 European Player of the Year.

Simonsen had capitalised on a slack back pass from Jimmy Case to hammer the ball into the top corner of the net for the Borussia equaliser. Clemence was then called on to pull off an excellent save with his feet from Borussia's Stielike as Liverpool's opponents were turning the screw.

As ever though, Paisley's men withstood the pressure and hit back.

A Heighway corner on sixty-five minutes was met by the head of legendary Reds' defender Tommy Smith and, to the delight of the 20,000 Liverpool fans that had made the trip to Rome, the ball nestled in the back of the net.

Smith's goal proved a hammer blow for Borussia, and Liverpool took complete control when Keegan was brought down in the box by Vogts on eighty-one minutes and Phil Neal stepped up to strike home the penalty.

There was simply no way back for Borussia after that as Bob Paisley and his men got set to celebrate their greatest ever achievement.

Afterwards, Paisley revealed that Heighway had played for much of the game with a slight injury after taking a kick from Klinkhammer early in the first half, although he said he never thought of substituting the Irishman. 'There was no way Steve was going to come off. How could I bring any of them off? They were all magnificent. I am proud of every one of them and the part they played.'

Heighway himself described it as 'the greatest night of my career'.

As the triumphant Liverpool team returned to a jubilant Merseyside to parade the European Cup trophy in front of a staggering 750,000 fans, Heighway wondered if he would ever achieve anything as good again.

'Where do we go from here?' he asked.

The answer was simply another European Cup final within a year, when Steve Heighway would again play his part in one more incredible Liverpool success story.

Liverpool's defence of their European Cup crown didn't begin until the second round of the tournament the following season after earning a bye through the first-round draw.

It meant European action didn't return to Anfield until late October when East German side Dynamo Dresden made the trip to Merseyside to take on Bob Paisley's all-conquering outfit.

Kevin Keegan, the hero of the 1977 triumph, had already departed Liverpool for Hamburg but in his place Paisley has secured the sublime skills of Scottish international forward Kenny Dalglish.

Dalglish had been drafted in from Glasgow Celtic, where he had been the club's main frontman scoring well over 100 league goals as the Hoops won four Scottish titles in the six years.

With the usual suspects of Heighway, Callaghan, Ray Kennedy and Toshack still in the Liverpool side alongside Dalglish they began the defence of their crown in style by demolishing Dresden 5–1 in what Paisley described as his team's best performance that season.

Heighway and Toshack in particular caused the Dresden defence all sorts of problems and it was that pair who combined from a corner in the lead-up to Liverpool's opening goal, scored by the head of young Scottish defender Alan Hansen after just twelve minutes.

The Liverpool pressure on the Dresden goal was simply relentless all night and it was no surprise they notched up two more goals by half-time through the tireless Jimmy Case and yet another Phil Neal penalty.

It didn't get any better for the East Germans in the second half when Case scored again and Ray Kennedy added an extra gloss on the scoreline with the Reds fifth goal in just the sixty-fifth minute.

Despite the massive four-goal lead, Liverpool manager Paisley was at pains to stress the danger Dresden still posed as they travelled to East Germany for the second leg on 2 November.

And Dresden's display on their home patch proved Paisley was right to be cautious, as their fluent passing game kept Liverpool on the rack for much of a nervous second leg.

Dresden attacked Liverpool at every available opportunity and it was only through good defending and solid goalkeeping from Ray Clemence that the game remained scoreless at half-time. However the impressive Dresden stepped it up a notch in the second half and were so far in control that Liverpool appeared, at one point, as if they were on the verge of completely relinquishing their huge lead.

Just a minute into the second half, Dresden took a deserved lead when their skilful forward Peter Kotte broke through the Liverpool defence to ram an unstoppable shot past Clemence. As if that wasn't enough, Kotte came at Liverpool again just five minutes later, this time barging down the right before delivering a pinpoint cross for Hartmud Schade to head into the net.

Suddenly Liverpool's advantage was down to just two goals and the East German's grew in confidence as they plotted an incredible comeback.

Not for the first time, Liverpool relied on the goal-scoring skills of Steve Heighway to get them out of jail.

With Dresden pushing forward in numbers, Liverpool caught them out with a rare counter-attack on sixty-seven minutes as Heighway snatched a fortuitous goal which finally put the tie beyond their opponent's reach.

The Irishman took advantage of a collision in the air between the Dresden goalkeeper Claus Boden and defender Hans Dorner to knock the ball into an empty net as the pair struggled to get back to their feet.

It was the lucky break Liverpool required, and try as they may Dresden were unable to pull back any more goals as the Reds left East Germany grateful to be in the hat for the quarter-final draw.

Paisley admitted his relief at avoiding a complete disaster.

'Dresden are one of the greatest teams we've met in Europe,' he said. 'I'm glad we had those four goals. I'd have been very worried if we had only taken a two-goal lead to Dresden.'

The quarter-final draw pitted Liverpool against tough Portuguese outfit

Benfica although, once again, the Reds outlined their superb European credentials with two brilliant performances.

In a torrential downpour in Lisbon on 2 March 1978, Liverpool came from a goal down to beat Benfica 2–1 and inflict a first defeat on the Portuguese champions in forty-seven games.

The win was even more remarkable as Paisley's men had to come from a goal down to silence the massive 80,000 home crowd at Lisbon's legendary Stadium of Light after Benfica striker Nente had raced on to a long clearance to fire his team in front after just eighteen minutes.

As ever, Liverpool just used their vast experience of these tricky European situations by taking the sting out of Benfica and slowly taking control of the match.

There was no hint of panic as Callaghan, Case and McDermott kept probing in midfield as Liverpool patiently looked for a way back into the game. It eventually arrived on thirty-eight minutes when the ever-willing Dalglish was fouled just outside the Benfica box.

Case stood up and belted a well-hit shot over the Benfica wall and just hard enough to beat goalkeeper Bento who, despite getting a hand to the shot, couldn't keep it out.

The goal was a welcome boost for the Reds and manager Paisley's half-time team talk was a lot easier now that they had secured a precious away goal.

Liverpool began the second half under siege from Benfica and Clemence had to be on his guard to keep out two good efforts from Celso and Sheu but as the game wore on, the home side became more desperate as Liverpool grew in confidence.

The Reds struck a killer blow seventeen minutes from time when a cross from defender Emlyn Hughes deceived Bento in the Benfica goal and landed in the net.

The 2–1 win was more than Liverpool could have wished for and thoughts already began to wander towards the semi-final as it was considered highly unlikely Benfica would overturn the deficit at Anfield during the second leg on 15 March.

Indeed the Reds made absolutely sure there was little hope of that happening as they blitzed Benfica early on at Anfield with goals from Ian

Callaghan and Kenny Dalglish in the first seventeen minutes to stretch their aggregate lead to 4–1.

Terry McDermott and Phil Neal completed the rout with late second-half goals to finish Benfica off 4–1 at Anfield and a commanding 6–2 win on aggregate.

Liverpool's semi-final reward for impressively putting Benfica to the sword was a repeat of the previous year's final when they were again drawn to play Udo Lattek's Borussia Mönchengladbach.

Wary that the West German side would be eager for revenge, Paisley heaped praise on them ahead of the first leg clash in Germany on 29 March.

'Mönchengladbach are the best team we have faced this season, there are no arguments about that,' he said. 'We respect Gladbach very much. I look on them as the Liverpool of West German football.'

Gladbach lived up to Paisley's billing during the first leg as they conjured up an important 2–1 win to give them an advantage heading to Anfield.

In a game in which Liverpool's patient build-up play stifled Borussia, the Reds rarely looked in trouble even though they fell behind on twenty-eight minutes. The German's lead goal had a touch of fortune about it after they were awarded a corner kick when the referee adjudged Reds' defender Tommy Smith to have put the ball out over the end line when it was clear it had actually come off Gladbach player Ewald Lienen.

From the resultant corner, centre-back Hannes hit an instant shot past the stunned Clemence.

Needless to say, Liverpool had to ride their luck on occasions in the second half as Mönchengladbach went in search of more goals to take with them to Anfield.

Their top striker Jupp Heynckes came closest to doubling the home side's lead when he cracked a header off the post.

Liverpool responded late on by grabbing a priceless away goal through substitute David Johnson when he finished off an impressive twelve-pass move by heading home a Kenny Dalglish cross in the eighty-eighth minute.

With a very credible 1–1 draw in the bag, Liverpool somehow managed to let it slip at the death when German midfielder Bonhoff struck a fabulous twenty-two-yard free kick that flew past Clemence.

The second leg at Anfield was a completely different affair, however, as Liverpool clinically took Monchengladbach apart to record an exemplary 3–0 win.

As they had done in their previous European games that season, Liverpool scored early, this time through Ray Kennedy after six minutes, and never really let up. Heighway, Dalglish and Kennedy attacked the Germans at will and it was no surprise when Dalglish doubled Liverpool's lead on thirty-five minutes. Heighway in particular was enjoying another sparkling performance as he gave marker Berti Vogts a torrid evening.

Gladbach's challenge effectively wilted after Liverpool's second goal and Jimmy Case rounded off a magnificent 3–0 win that sent Liverpool on the way to Wembley for the 1978 European Cup final against Belgians FC Bruges.

The build-up to the final with Bruges was dominated by two major issues – an injury to Steve Heighway and the lack of tickets available for the game for the tens of thousands of Liverpool fans hoping to make the trip to London.

The English FA had provided Liverpool with no more than 23,000 tickets for the final, even though they expected to bring at least double that to the game. In the end most Reds fans, including those from all over Ireland and Northern Ireland were forced to pay way over the odds for tickets on the black market.

Of more pressing concern for Steve Heighway was a troublesome injury he had picked up in a league game against Ipswich which he had failed to shake in the final few weeks of the season.

In his absence, twenty-one-year-old forward David Fairclough impressed manager Paisley as he scored four goals in three wins over Norwich, West Ham and Arsenal.

Although Heighway proved his fitness before the final, Paisley decided to go with the youth and speed of Fairclough on the day of the game, leaving the disappointed Irishman to take his place on the substitutes bench.

It meant that Fairclough led the Liverpool frontline alongside Kenny Dalglish in a game which Liverpool dominated but consistently failed to break through a tough Bruges rearguard.

With the game still scoreless just after the hour mark, Paisley decided to spring Heighway from the bench in place of Jimmy Case.

Heighway was barely on the pitch a minute when Liverpool made the vital breakthrough as Kenny Dalglish raced on to a brilliant through ball from his fellow Scottish international Graeme Souness and kept his nerve to gleefully chip the ball past the advancing Bruges goalkeeper.

Liverpool were in complete command of the final after this and, apart from a late scare when Phil Thompson had to clear off the line, the Reds made it two European Cups in a row.

Afterwards Paisley declared he was right to keep Heighway on the bench. 'I have no doubt I did the right thing but when Steve did come on they were looking at him and it distracted them a bit.'

And with another European Cup winners medal in his back pocket Heighway was unlikely to argue with his boss's decision either.

Age and injuries may have been taking their toll on Steve Heighway as Liverpool entered a new decade in the early 1980s but he was still able to play some small part in yet another magnificent Liverpool run to European Cup glory.

As Heighway's star began to wane after a decade as one of the club's top attacking talents, manager Bob Paisley was increasingly calling on the services of the younger David Fairclough and David Johnson whilst new Welsh signing Ian Rush was also just starting to settle in at Anfield.

Having won the league title under Paisley for a fourth time in 1980, Liverpool re-entered the European Cup in September of that year and began with a comprehensive 11–2 aggregate victory over Finnish part-timers Oulu Palloseura.

Steve Heighway played no part in either that or a second-round victory over Scottish champions Aberdeen which Liverpool again won easily enough by 5–0 over the two legs.

The Irishman was involved, however, when Liverpool embarked on a successful quarter-final clash with CSKA Sofia in March 1981, as he partnered Kenny Dalglish up front in an impressive 5–1 first leg win at

Anfield over the Bulgarians which included a hat-trick from midfielder Graeme Souness.

Defying his age, thirty-three-year-old Heighway rolled back the years during this Anfield romp. After a first half in which Liverpool failed to capitalise on an eighteenth-minute lead through Graeme Souness, Heighway took centre stage in the early minutes of the second period to destroy the Sofia defence and lay on two goals.

Firstly, the Sofia rear guard failed to deal with his dangerous cross from the right and midfielder Sammy Lee was on hand to score and then, five minutes later, Heighway ghosted past two men in the box to set Souness up for a simple finish for Liverpool's third goal.

Liverpool suffered a minor fright when Sofia forward Yonchez pulled a goal back, but midfielders McDermott and Souness made sure of the victory with two more sweet strikes for the Reds.

Heighway was on the bench when Liverpool travelled to Sofia a fortnight later but was a first-half replacement for the injured David Johnson who had already managed to score a tenth-minute goal which wrapped up a 6–1 aggregate win for Liverpool.

Next up for the Reds was an intriguing semi-final with West German champions Bayern Munich in April 1981 but by then Heighway had already agreed his departure from Liverpool as he planned a new career in the United States.

However, a chronic injury list for manager Paisley ensured Heighway put his move to the US on hold temporarily so that he could help the Reds in their quest for more European glory.

In a tight encounter with Munich at Anfield, Heighway was a second-half substitute for Terry McDermott although he failed to ignite another famous Liverpool win as the game finished scoreless.

Afterwards, Heighway said he would be only too happy to stay and help Liverpool overcome Munich in the second leg as he still felt his team had the ability to beat the German side. But, in the end, Heighway's services were not needed as Liverpool secured a crucial 1–1 draw in Munich courtesy of a late Ray Kennedy goal which put them into the final on the away goals rule.

The final against Real Madrid in Paris on 27 May 1981 proved to be every bit as tight, with Liverpool eventually coming out on top with full-back Alan Kennedy popping up nine minutes from time to give a 1–0 scoreline.

Steve Heighway's last appearance in a Liverpool shirt had been in the semi-final first-leg clash with Bayern Munich, ensuring his career ended on just as successful a note as it had started eleven years previously.

Liverpool in the League 1977–1981

Although the brilliant feat of winning back-to-back European Cups in the late 1970s brought Liverpool to an even greater level of achievement, the Reds never forgot the bread-and-butter of challenging for the domestic league title as well.

Indeed, just as they were on their way to winning the club's first ever European Cup crown in 1976–1977, Liverpool maintained their position as champions of England by fighting off the determined challenge of Manchester City.

Thanks to the goals of Kevin Keegan and Steve Heighway, the Reds won the title by a point from City in 1977 and had it not been for defeat to Manchester Utd in the FA Cup, they would have rounded off a remarkable treble.

By 1978, however, Liverpool had a serious new adversary in the shape of Brian Clough's Nottingham Forest who not only won the league that year with seven points to spare over the Reds, but would go on to emulate Bob Paisley's men by winning back-to-back European Cups in 1979 and 1980.

As Clough sent Forest on the road to European glory, which included a first-round defeat of European champions Liverpool in September 1978, Paisley's team regained their composure in the league in the 1978–1979 season to wrestle the title back from Forest with an incredible run of nineteen wins from twenty-one home games in a season when they remained undefeated at Anfield.

If that wasn't enough, Liverpool were back on the winners' rostrum again a year later, this time beating off the close attentions of Manchester Utd to claim their fourth league title in five years.

The Great 1980s

9

Ronnie Whelan: a Midfield Maestro

Name: Ronnie Whelan

Date of birth: 25 September 1961

Place of birth: Dublin

Position: Midfield

Years at Liverpool: 1979–1994

Games played: 493

Goals scored: 73

Honours: First Division (1982, 1983, 1984, 1986, 1988, 1990); European Cup (1984); FA Cup (1986, 1988, 1992); League Cup (1982, 1983, 1984)

Other clubs: Home Farm, Southend

Steve Heighway's mesmerising Liverpool career may have been winding to a close in 1981 but it didn't take long before another talented Irishman burst on the scene to make the left midfield berth his own.

Never one to rest on his laurels, manager Bob Paisley was constantly seeking out new additions to his Anfield squad even when his Reds team were already in the throes of capturing numerous league titles and European Cups.

Acting on the advice of trusted League of Ireland manager Jim McLaughlin, Paisley wasted little time in snapping up one of the hottest young teenage prospects in the Irish game in September 1978, when dynamic midfielder Ronnie Whelan was brought from Dublin club Home Farm to Merseyside under the noses of arch rivals Manchester Utd.

At just eighteen years of age, the capture of Whelan represented not only the future of Liverpool but the crafty forward thinking of Paisley who was not adverse to bringing in players whom he knew could help smooth the gradual process of changing his successful team whenever he deemed it to be necessary.

In Whelan's case, his time at Anfield would come over three years after first being signed up at Anfield when Paisley introduced him in an end-of-season league game as his Liverpool team was preparing for their challenge on the European Cup crown.

Whelan had all the attributes to become a top-class Liverpool midfielder; he possessed plenty of energy and guile, could pick a pass, could tackle and also chip in with the odd important and spectacular goal.

He got his first chance to impress in a Liverpool shirt in an Anfield encounter with Stoke on 3 April 1981, a game which meant little in the way of the league championship as, for once under Paisley, Liverpool were way off the pace in fifth place with just six games to go.

With the pressure of a league title challenge off the agenda, Liverpool manager Paisley was able to play around with his squad as he prepared for a vital European Cup semi-final clash with German champions Bayern Munich.

Nineteen-year-old Whelan was one player to benefit from this as he was given his Anfield debut in a low-key league game, just four days before the first leg with Munich.

Playing on the left side of midfield, a position normally filled by the experienced English international Ray Kennedy, Whelan grasped his opportunity with both hands by putting in a scintillating debut performance that helped the Reds coast past Stoke in an easy 3–0 win.

114 EMERALD ANFIELD

With little riding on the game, teenager Whelan had more to prove than most and it certainly showed in his performance as he attacked the Stoke defence at every available opportunity. The young debutante's energy certainly paid off on twenty-seven minutes when he raced on to a through ball from fellow midfielder Sammy Lee to steer the ball past Stoke goalkeeper Peter Fox.

In less than half an hour of football in a red shirt, Whelan had left Liverpool fans in no doubt that they had a new star in the making.

Similar to Steve Heighway a decade earlier, Whelan's introduction to the Liverpool first team earned him a call up to the senior Republic of Ireland squad in the same month as he made his Reds debut, when he played in the green shirt against Czechoslovakia. He enjoyed a winning debut with the Irish as they defeated the Czechs 3–1 in a friendly as the team, which included the skills of defender David O'Leary, classy midfielder Liam Brady and striker Frank Stapleton, prepared for the final round of games as they pushed to qualify for the 1982 World Cup in Spain.

Tragically Whelan and his Irish team-mates just fell short of qualifying in their group behind Belgium and France, the latter of whom would go on to make the semi-finals of the tournament.

Back at Anfield, the Stoke game was the only one Whelan was involved in that season as Liverpool finished fifth in the league but they more than made up for that by clinching the European Cup to go with a League Cup success.

The two trophies capped off another stunning season of success for Paisley but he would no doubt have still been stung by Liverpool's fifth place finish in the league in 1981, the club's worst league position in ten years. With this is mind, Paisley was already on the road to rebuilding his team.

Towards the end of the 1980–1981 campaign, Paisley acquired the services of Craig Johnson, an exciting Australian midfielder, and Bruce Grobbelaar, a stylish Zimbabwean goalkeeper.

In the summer of 1981, he added Irish international defender Mark Lawrenson and young Scottish full-back Steve Nicol to his growing squad.

Paisley had beaten off rivals Man Utd and Arsenal to gain the signature of Lawrenson in a £900,000 deal with Preston – a massive fee for a defender at the time but Lawrenson would go on to prove he was worth every penny. Although born in England, Lawrenson qualified to play for the Republic of Ireland through his mother Theresa and he would go on to be one of the country's best international players for a decade after making his Irish debut at the tender age of nineteen in 1977.

All the new faces around Anfield gave a fresh impetus to the Liverpool side as they began the season determined to win back their First Division crown.

They didn't make the greatest of starts, however, winning just two of their first seven league games before Ronnie Whelan entered the fray for only his second ever start at Anfield in a 2–2 draw with Swansea on 3 October.

Whelan's presence in the team brought the number of Irishmen in Paisley's squad to three as talented defender Lawrenson had already cemented a first-team place and midfielder Kevin Sheedy, who had been signed from Hereford in 1978 and had battled through the Liverpool reserve team to make it into the first-team squad, was also vying for a spot.

Liverpool's next match was a home Milk (League) Cup tie with Exeter. Whelan remained in the side and rounded off a comfortable 5–0 win for the Reds with Liverpool's fifth goal, a sign of things to come for the midfielder in a competition that was to prove especially lucky for him.

Liverpool followed up their League Cup win over Exeter by also knocking Middlesbrough, Arsenal and Barnsley out of the competition to set up a semi-final clash with Bobby Robson's talented Ipswich side. Ipswich had been going great guns in the league and by early 1982 were one of the favourites to secure a shock First Division title.

Paisley's Liverpool had other ideas though and got the chance to strike a psychological blow against Ipswich when forced to play them in three successive games in February 1982. First up was the first leg in the League Cup semi-final at Ipswich's Portman Road which the Reds, including Irishmen Whelan in midfield and Lawrenson at the back, won comfortably 2–0 to set themselves up for an easier second leg at Anfield. Sandwiched between those two games was a crucial league encounter when Whelan managed to get himself on the score sheet in a crushing 4–0 win before the Reds completed their League Cup semi-final job with a 2–2 draw at Anfield against a deflated Ipswich.

Liverpool's success over Ipswich gave them the impetus to push on in the league and Ronnie Whelan played an important part on the left of a Reds midfield also containing the substantial talents of Graeme Souness,

Milk Cup

In 1960, the English football league introduced a midweek cup competition open to all teams in its four divisions, known simply as the 'League Cup'.

Since 1982, the League Cup has been named after its sponsor which, at the time, was the Milk Marketing Board in England, earning it the title of the Milk Cup.

During its first three years of existence, it appeared as if the Milk Cup would permanently reside in the Anfield trophy cabinet as Liverpool won it on all three occasions to add to their League Cup win of 1981, meaning the Reds had actually won the competition an impressive and unprecedented four years on the trot.

It wasn't until 1985 that the competition had a different winner when Norwich City managed to prise the trophy from the Reds with a 1–0 final win over Sunderland.

Oxford Utd became Milk Cup champions in 1986 before the competition changed its title to the Littlewoods Cup a year later with Arsenal beating Liverpool 2–1 in the final.

The League Cup has since gone under a number of different names as it has changed sponsors and is currently known as the Carling Cup.

Liverpool have won the trophy a record seven times and also have the most final appearances at ten.

Terry McDermott, Sammy Lee and Craig Johnson.

In what was just his first full season in the team, Whelan played in thirty-two league games as the Reds got over their rocky start to mount an unstoppable late charge to the title. The Dubliner proved a particularly lucky charm, scoring ten goals in nine league games, all of which were victories. His stunning form earned Whelan the accolade of the

Professional Football Association (PFA) Young Player of the Year and a glittering Anfield career still lay ahead for him.

Whelan's success came as little surprise to the man he played in front of on the left wing during that debut season. Liverpool's left-back Alan Kennedy, an experienced pro who played for nine years for Liverpool and was capped twice at international level for England, said Whelan's raw natural ability often took his breath away. 'The one thing that really stood out with Ronnie Whelan when he came into what was an experienced Liverpool team at such a young age was his confidence,' Kennedy says. 'Ronnie was never afraid to try something different in a game whether it was a volley on goal or a fancy pass, even if there was a chance it might make him look silly if it didn't come off. He wasn't afraid to make mistakes although with his ability that didn't happen too often anyway.'

Although prolific during the league campaign that season, Whelan saved his best for Wembley when Liverpool took on a talented Tottenham Hotspur side in the League Cup final. In a tight game in which Liverpool had put pressure on Spurs without finding a way past their own former keeper Ray Clemence, the Reds looked to be on their way to defeat as they trailed 1–0 to a Steve Archibald goal with just three minutes left on the clock.

If ever there was a moment Liverpool needed a cup final hero to step forward this was it and it was the brilliant young Whelan who did the honours.

Whelan powered into the Spurs box to latch on to a low cross from Craig Johnson and smashed a crisply hit, right-foot shot into the bottom right-hand corner of Clemence's net to rescue the Reds at the death.

The goal set Whelan off on a wild celebration jig as the Liverpool fans were in raptures at their team's late reprieve. Afterwards Whelan revealed how he didn't fully understand how close Liverpool had come to defeat in the final. 'I didn't realise that my equaliser came so late in the game,' he said.

Whelan's goal sent the game into extra time and with Spurs deflated at conceding so late on, Liverpool looked the stronger side.

Whelan hammered this home in the second period of the extra time when he belted in his second goal of the game from close range before striker Ian Rush wrapped up a 3–1 win with another goal in the final minute.

Whelan, who was dubbed the 'Milk Cup Kid' following his exploits, was absolutely beaming at the success of his first major Wembley experience. 'Just getting into the first team was great, but to score two goals on your Wembley debut is something you can only dream about,' he said at the time.

Manager Bob Paisley was also gushing in his praise for the young Dubliner. 'If he continues to perform like that then he will be back at Wembley many times in the future,' Paisley predicted. And using a quick-witted turn of phrase reminiscent of his old boss Shankly, a delighted Paisley added that he had endured sour milk for most of the final before enjoying the cream after the extra time.

Paisley's declaration that Ronnie Whelan would enjoy further Wembley finals proved spot on as, just twelve months after the victory over Spurs, Liverpool were back in their third Milk Cup final in a row.

They began the defence of the trophy with a 4–1 aggregate win over Ipswich which included a 2–0 victory at Anfield with the goals coming from the Irish boots of Whelan and Lawrenson, before further wins over Rotherham Utd, Norwich, West Ham and Burnley set the Reds up for a glamour final against Manchester Utd on 26 March 1983.

The Wembley occasion once again appeared to inspire Whelan as he curled home an absolute beauty to win the game for Liverpool in a hard fought 2–1 victory against their Lancashire rivals.

As with the previous final against Spurs, Liverpool fell behind to a first-half goal to United with Norman Whiteside blasting them in front, before the Reds full-back Alan Kennedy ensured extra time with a long-range shot fifteen minutes from the end.

The game was set up for Whelan to steal the show again in the first period of extra time when he out-foxed his fellow Irish international Frank Stapleton to bend home a right foot shot from the edge of the Man Utd box.

'When the ball came back to me off Frank Stapleton's legs I tried to bend it into the corner and it paid off,' Whelan said afterwards. 'I think I feel even better about scoring this year because it was the winner.'

That Wembley occasion was also notable for the fact it would be the last time Bob Paisley would manage Liverpool in a major final as he had already decided he would be calling it a day at the end of the 1982–1983 season.

As a mark of respect to the popular Geordie, club captain Graeme Souness decided to let Paisley lead the team up the Wembley steps to collect the trophy and the roar from the Liverpool fans as the great man held it aloft has rarely been equalled.

Paisley's final league campaign that season also proved to be one of his best as Liverpool cantered to the title with eleven points to spare over nearest challengers Watford. Ronnie Whelan played in twenty-eight of Liverpool's forty-two league games that season and chipped in with two goals in a 5–0 rout of Southampton which extended his remarkable run of winning in every league game he scored in since his debut two seasons earlier.

Of course Ronnie Whelan wasn't the only Irishman making a name for himself at Anfield during that period, with Mark Lawrenson also shining as one of the most accomplished defenders in the English game.

Since arriving at Anfield in 1981, Lawrenson fitted seamlessly into the Liverpool set up. He was blessed with a brilliant football brain which allowed him to play in a number of key positions for the Reds, whether it be as left-back or central-midfielder. However Lawrenson's main role at Liverpool was as a central defender where he formed one of the best centre-back partnerships in the history of Liverpool FC alongside Scottish international Alan Hansen.

Meanwhile, with Bob Paisley gone and new manager Joe Fagan plucked from the Liverpool back-room staff to take charge for the 1983–1984 season, Ronnie Whelan and Mark Lawrenson had little to worry about as they were now vital cogs in the Reds juggernaut.

Just as when iconic manager Bill Shankly had retired almost a decade earlier, Liverpool continued on their winning ways even without Paisley at the helm.

Fagan still had the basis of an exceptionally strong spine to the team when he took over, with Lawrenson and Hansen at the back, a midfield marshalled by titanic captain Graeme Souness and the lethal forward line of Ian Rush and Kenny Dalglish. Fagan still added to his squad, however, when he made his first major signings in the transfer market to get Scottish defender Gary Gillespie from Coventry and Irish international forward Michael Robinson from Brighton.

Fagan's tenure got off to the worst possible start when Liverpool were soundly beaten 2–0 by Manchester Utd at Wembley in the Charity Shield, but when the serious business of the league and European Cup games came around, they were back to winning ways.

The early months of the 1983–1984 season proved frustrating for Ronnie Whelan as a pelvic injury kept him out of the side until a 1–1 draw away to Ipswich in a league match in late November.

His next start came in a 4–0 humbling by Coventry in early December and Whelan's season didn't really get off the ground until 1 February 1984 when he scored in a 3–0 win over Watford at Anfield.

Six days later, the Irishman grabbed both goals as Liverpool struggled to a shock 2–2 draw at home to Walsall in the first leg of the semi-final of the Milk Cup, which the Reds were hoping to capture for an unprecedented fourth time in a row.

He remained an ever present in the side after that as Liverpool chased glory on three fronts in the league, League Cup and European Cup.

Despite the home draw with Walsall, Whelan ensured Liverpool made no mistake in the away second leg as he and Ian Rush scored in a 2–0 win to book yet another Wembley appearance for the Merseysiders.

The final was given an added spice as Liverpool's fierce local rivals Everton made it through the other half of the draw to set up the first ever major final between the clubs at Wembley.

Under the leadership of manager Howard Kendall, Everton were an emerging force again in the English game and would do battle with Liverpool as the two strongest sides in the country over the following six years.

The final on 25 March certainly proved a very tight and tense affair with neither side able to get on top and the game finished in a disappointing 0–0 draw.

The replay at Manchester City's Maine Road ground just four days later saw Liverpool edge out on top with the only goal of the game coming early through Graeme Souness.

As on the previous two seasons, Liverpool were also on their way to winning the league by the time the Milk Cup was safely stored in the Anfield trophy cabinet.

Ronnie Whelan did his bit by scoring in vital wins over Tottenham and West Ham and also in a 3–3 draw with Leicester as Joe Fagan's men wrapped up the title ahead of challengers Southampton, Nottingham Forest and Manchester Utd.

Perhaps Whelan's most important goals that season, however, were two he scored in a highly impressive 4–1 win away to Benfica in their quarter-final of the European Cup as the Reds marched on to a fantastic treble by winning the tournament in Rome.

For Liverpool and Whelan, it appeared as if little could go wrong as they simply continued to mop up the major trophies. They began the 1984–1985 season as strong favourites in the league yet again and were also a good bet to at least make it to the latter stages of the European Cup.

Ronnie Whelan enjoyed his longest run of league games yet for Liverpool as he missed just five of their forty-two encounters that season but for once the Dubliner had to settle for a runners-up spot as Howard Kendall's Everton played up to their potential to take the title by a full thirteen points over Liverpool.

The Reds were also denied a shot at the FA Cup final when they lost a semi-final replay 2–1 to Manchester Utd. The replay loss at Manchester City's Maine Road followed on from a cracking original semi-final game in which Whelan shone by hitting home a stunning late equaliser to bring the game to extra time where Liverpool also needed a last-minute goal from forward Paul Walsh to force the replay in a brilliant 2–2 draw.

The disappointment of losing out on both the league and FA Cup would have mattered little to Liverpool if they had been able to retain their European Cup crown.

Liverpool's European Cup campaign also heralded the beginning of an Anfield career for another young Irishman, when Waterford full-back Jim Beglin burst onto the scene in a big way.

A £20,000 signing from League of Ireland side Shamrock Rovers in 1983, twenty-two-year-old Beglin gradually began to work his way into the Liverpool first team throughout the 1984–1985 season as regular left-back Alan Kennedy was coming towards the end of his Anfield career.

Beglin remarkably made his European Cup debut for Liverpool in a crunch semi-final with Greek Panathinaikos at Anfield and even managed to get on the scoresheet with a bullet header as the Reds won 4–0.

Whelan himself played in every game in the European Cup that season as Liverpool defeated Lech Posnan, Benfica, Austria Vienna and Panathinaikos to set up a mouth-watering final clash with Giovanni

Trapattoni's Juventus on 29 May 1985. Like Liverpool, Italian's Juventus were a serious European outfit at the time, having appeared in the 1983 European Cup final, won the 1984 European Cup Winners Cup and beaten Liverpool 2–0 in the European Super Cup in January 1985. That win had made Juventus slight favourites going into the final, although Liverpool were still hugely confident of winning, especially as they had captured the cup a year earlier, against the odds, by beating Roma in their own home ground.

This time there would at least be a neutral venue in Heysel, although the final itself in the ageing Belgian ground will now always be remembered for all the wrong reasons. Just an hour before kick-off rising tensions between rival fans ignited as Liverpool supporters surged towards a section of Juventus fans in the centre of the ground. As the Juve fans attempted to flee from the on-rushing Liverpool mob, a wall came crumbling down on top of them killing a total of thirty-nine people, thirty-two of whom were Juventus fans.

Despite the tragedy, and the fact that angry Juventus fans were later embroiled in a major riot inside the ground with the Belgian police, UEFA officials decided to continue with the final, which kicked off almost two hours late.

For the players on both sides, the idea of playing the game just didn't seem right.

In an interview afterwards, Ronnie Whelan said he would rather have been anywhere than on the pitch that night after what had happened. 'We were obviously aware something had gone on but not to the extent it had. Nobody wanted to play,' Whelan said. 'We went out because we were told to but it was horrible. Yet even at that stage we didn't really know the precise details.'

In a low-key game, Juventus came out on top thanks to a penalty from their star playmaker Michel Platini, even though the foul committed by Liverpool defender Gary Gillespie on Juve forward Zbigniew Boniek was later shown to have been outside the box. Liverpool players have since said they knew it wasn't a penalty but just didn't have the heart in them to dispute the decision.

Later, Ronnie Whelan said the full scale of the destruction and tragedy of Heysel hit home. 'The terraces were a mess and you could see the shoes and the bits of clothing strewn all over the place. It was only then the full horror of what had gone on started to sink in.'

Within weeks of the Heysel tragedy, English football clubs had been banned from European competitions for five years with Liverpool struck down with a further year's ban for their fans' involvement.

The tragedy and pain of Heysel proved a sad ending for manager Joe Fagan who had decided beforehand that the European Cup final would be his last in charge of Liverpool. Yet again Liverpool made their new appointment from within the club, this time targeting long-standing player Kenny Dalglish to take up the reigns as the Red's first ever player-manager. It was a lot for the inexperienced Dalglish to take on but he still had plenty of help in the guise of former manager Bob Paisley and in the wealth of knowledge gained from his back-room staff of coaches including Ronnie Moran and Roy Evans.

Just as when Fagan had taken over from Paisley, the team Dalglish took over in 1985 needed very little in the way of restructuring, although he did add combative midfielder Steve McMahon to his squad in a £350,000 transfer from Aston Villa. Given that it was Dalglish's first year as a manager and the emergence of powerful Everton and Manchester Utd sides around that time, the general consensus was that Liverpool would most likely need a year or two to become as dominant as they had been for the early part of the 1980s.

Yet Liverpool continued to confound the football world by carrying on under Dalglish just as they had done with Shankly, Paisley and Fagan — by winning major trophies. As he had when he was their team-mate, boss Dalglish found that he could put his trust in the usual suspects of Grobbelaar, Johnson, Lawrenson, Hansen, Whelan and Rush to produce the goods when necessary as Liverpool put it up to their neighbours Everton in the battle for supremacy in the First Division title race in the 1985–1986 season.

For a long stretch of the season, it looked as is if Everton would retain their title – in February 1986 they were thirteen points ahead of Liverpool – before a customary late surge from the Reds kept the pressure on into the closing weeks of the campaign.

Whelan was even enjoying his most profitable campaign in front of goal in five seasons, notching up ten strikes in the league, including a double in a 2–0 win over Nottingham Forest and an excellent hat-trick in a vital 5–0 drubbing of Coventry.

Such was Liverpool's outstanding late-season form that they went in to the final league game, an away match at Stamford Bridge against Chelsea, knowing a victory would secure them the title.

The Bridge was hardly the easiest of places to go needing a win but as they had done in tough European away matches in previous years, Liverpool did what was necessary by bagging a hard fought 1–0 victory – and, of course, it was none other than Dalglish himself who provided the goal with a clinically taken volley after being set up by Waterford man Jim Beglin.

Liverpool had also taken their great league form into the FA Cup. Ronnie Whelan was on target as the Reds trounced Norwich City 5–0 in the third round at Anfield before Mark Lawrenson helped himself to a goal in a tight 2–1 win over Chelsea in the following round.

Liverpool struggled in the fifth round to shake off lower division York City, needing a Jan Molby penalty to draw 1–1 and extra time at Anfield in the replay to eventually squeeze through to the quarter finals with a 3–1 win.

The Reds required another stroke of good fortune to see off Watford in the last eight after the Londoners held them to a 0–0 draw at Anfield. In the replay at Watford's Vicarage Road, Liverpool just managed to bring the game to extra time with an eighty-sixth-minute penalty from Molby before Rush sent them into the semi-finals with a clinical winner.

For the third time in a row, Liverpool needed extra time during their semi-final to see off Southhampton 2–0 thanks once again to goals from ace striker Ian Rush which set up a fantastic Wembley final date with Everton.

The 1986 final would be Everton's second in a row after they had just missed out on the league and cup double a year previously when Man Utd beat them in the final. Journalist John Keith remembers the era as the best for football on Merseyside.

'A lot of people look at the 1960s as the most exciting time for football in Liverpool but I have to say I thought the mid-1980s was even better because we had two brilliant teams in the city competing against each other. Both Everton and Liverpool were two of the best sides in Europe at the time, it was wonderful for Merseyside and something that will probably be difficult to replicate again in the future.'

The build-up to the FA Cup final, which took place on 10 May, was dominated for Liverpool over who would partner captain Alan Hansen in the centre of the Reds' defence.

Manager Dalglish had a choice between the imperious Mark Lawrenson and the equally capable Scottish international Gary Gillespie.

Even the Republic of Ireland manager Jack Charlton got involved in the pre-match debate, urging Dalglish to go with his international defender Lawrenson.

Charlton said, 'There is no comparison between Mark and Gary Gillespie. They are not in the same class. Mark is a world-class player and Liverpool cannot afford to go into that match without him.'

In the end, an illness to Gillespie on the day of the final made the decision easier for Dalglish as he paired Lawrenson with Hansen.

The rest of the team almost picked itself with Grobbelaar in goal, full-backs Steve Nichol and Jim Beglin, a central-midfield partnership of Whelan and Jan Molby flanked by wingers Craig Johnson and Kevin MacDonald, with Dalglish up front alongside Rush.

Facing them was an equally fearsome Everton side, including the talents of Peter Reid, ex-Red Kevin Sheedy and forwards Graeme Sharp and Gary Lineker.

In a pulsating game, Everton drew first blood when their ace marksman Lineker raced on to a sublime through ball from Reid to beat Grobbelaar at the second time of asking in the twenty-sixth minute. It was a lead Everton held until ten minutes into the second half when Liverpool took over.

As always, it was the deadly striking skills of Ian Rush who brought them back into the game after Molby emulated Reid with a brilliant pass into the box for Rush to run on to and round Everton keeper Bobby Mimms to slip into the net.

The equaliser invigorated Liverpool and within six minutes they had taken the lead when Craig Johnson blasted home at the back post from a MacDonald cross. Johnson's goal set up an exciting finish as Everton poured forward in search of the equaliser but left themselves exposed to a Liverpool counter-attack which they did with deadly accuracy six minutes from time.

An exchange of passes in the Liverpool half between Whelan, Johnson, Rush and Molby set Whelan cantering towards the Everton box whose midfield was totally stretched. Whelan kept his composure to play a beautiful right-foot pass in the path of Rush just inside the Everton box and he took one touch before ramming home the killer third goal. The defeat really hit some of the Everton players hard. Irish international Kevin Sheedy said he just couldn't muster up the willpower to do a lap of honour around Wembley, particularly as it was the second year in a row that Everton had lost the final.

'I remember last year when it was more a lap of dishonour,' Sheedy said. 'I didn't like the sensation and couldn't bring myself to repeat it.'

A day later, when both teams were paraded through the streets of Liverpool, Everton captain, and proud scouser, Peter Reid, was conspicuous by his absence from his team's bus. He later revealed he was just too devastated to show his face having lost the final to his team's closest rivals. Of course for the Liverpool players, there were no such worries and the club's Irish contingent really soaked up the atmosphere.

Mark Lawrenson was particularly moved by the occasion, 'I've never seen so many people. The scenes are fantastic and football can only be the winner. Liverpool did the double and will be the name in the record books but it could just as easily have been Everton.'

The joy of the club's first, and only, League and Cup double subsided somewhat for the fans soon after when it emerged early into the following season that Italian giants Juventus were on the verge of signing the Reds goal-scoring hero Ian Rush. It was, indeed, agreed between the two clubs that Rush would be moving to Italy in £3 million move but not until the summer of 1987 after he had completed another season at Anfield.

However despite Rush's imminent departure, Ronnie Whelan would go to enjoy even more success in a Red shirt and he would have a number of other fellow Irish internationals to share in his joy at Anfield.

When Liverpool Played in Ireland

European Cup
Dundalk 1–4 Liverpool,
Oriel Park, 14 September 1982

When Dundalk won the League of Ireland title for the seventh time in 1982, the one team they would have been hoping to draw in the first round of the following season's European Cup was reigning English champions Liverpool.

Dundalk manager Jim McLaughlin was the Liverpool scout in Ireland at the time and with Reds' fans dotted all over the Louth town and surrounding counties, the Merseysiders really were the plum draw.

So it was with great excitement when Dundalk's name did indeed come out alongside that of Liverpool, who were hoping to regain the European Cup crown they had won three times in the previous five years.

It would also be the second time that Liverpool would make the trip to Dundalk following their Fairs Cup clash in 1969 but, with the first leg this time in Ireland, there was greater anticipation that the Irish part-timers could cause at least a momentary upset.

Certainly the pressure was all on Bob Paisley's Liverpool side who were expected not only to win the tie but also score a few goals in the process.

Liverpool fans from all over Ireland descended on Dundalk where they expected their side, including the likes of Irish hero Ronnie Whelan, star striker Ian Rush and Scottish legend Kenny Dalglish, to put on a show.

A crowd of 16,000 crammed into Oriel Park on the night and they were not to be disappointed as a thoroughly professional Liverpool side played with a speed and passion that tore Dundalk apart.

The League of Ireland side began brightly enough when their leading scorer Mark Fairclough attempted to burst Liverpool's defence in the fifth minute. However Fairclough's advances were snubbed out by a timely tackle from Liverpool full-back Phil Neal and, despite home shouts for a penalty as Fairclough went to the ground, the English champions survived the scare and took control of the match from there.

Passing the ball crisply and with confidence, every Liverpool player was on top form, but none more so that the energetic Ronnie Whelan who made the biggest impact on the night with two well-taken first-half strikes.

Whelan, whom Jim McLaughlin had recommended to Liverpool just a couple of years earlier, broke Dundalk hearts as early as the sixth minute when he latched on to an astute pass from Dalglish to beat two defenders and slam the ball past goalkeeper Blackmore.

The early goal gave Liverpool the impetus to keep attacking and they pressed Dundalk and despite some good performances from the home team, most notably from Barry Keogh and Noel King, they found it difficult to hold on to possession and Liverpool pounced on every ball.

With the Reds dominating, a second goal always looked likely and, again, it was Whelan who obliged as he collected a pass from Hodgson in the twenty-sixth minute and slipped the ball past Blackmore for the strike that effectively killed off the tie.

Rather than sit back, Liverpool decided to give their loyal Irish fans something to shout about as they went in search of more goals and deadly marksman Ian Rush made sure he got his name on the score sheet with a clinically taken third just five minutes later.

Dundalk managed to survive until half-time without conceding another goal but after such a chastening experience in that opening forty-five minutes, they were probably glad to get to the sanctuary of their dressing room and catch a rest.

Just as in the first half, Dundalk began the second period on the front foot when Barry Keogh broke clear down the left but despite knocking the ball past Bruce Grobbelaar in the Liverpool goal, he was denied a dream goal as the Reds' Scottish defender Alan Hansen tracked back to clear the ball before it hit the net.

Liverpool responded to this scare by, once again, taking control of the game and David Hodgson rounded off an impressive display by bagging his side's fourth goal in the seventy-fifth minute.

Despite the thumping, Dundalk managed to keep their spirit and pegged Liverpool back in the closing stages in the hope of claiming at least a consolation goal.

They got their opportunity late on when Leo Flanagan smashed home a free kick after Grobbelaar was penalised for taking too many steps with the ball.

It would be the only bright spot for Dundalk, however, and afterwards their manager McLaughlin marvelled at how Liverpool had played. 'I've never seen in my life a team who put you under so much pressure,' he said. 'They played as though they were fighting for their lives and there was nothing a team like ours could do about it.'

TEAMS

Dundalk: Blackmore , Gregg, Dunning, McConville, Lawlor, Byrne, Flanagan, King, Kehoe, Fairclough, Crawley
Subs: Ralph for Crawley, Archibold for Byrne

Liverpool: Grobbelaar, Neal, Kennedy, Hansen, Thompson, Lee, Souness, Whelan, Dalglish, Hodgson, Rush

10

Kings of Europe: 1984

When Bob Paisley stepped down as Liverpool manager in 1983, he warned their rivals that the man to follow him into the Anfield hot seat was even hungrier than he had been during his trophy-laden nine years in charge.

And new manager Joe Fagan proved Paisley was true to his word when he set Liverpool off on a trail for a unique treble during his first season in charge.

It had been over two years since Liverpool tasted glory in the European Cup when Fagan took over and he quickly set about putting that right with a strong showing in the early rounds of the 1983–1984 season.

With Irishman Mark Lawrenson marshalling the back and Michael Robinson spearheading the frontline with Ian Rush, Fagan's Liverpool began their European Cup campaign with a low key 1–0 victory away to Danish side Odense on 14 September 1983, thanks to an early goal from Kenny Dalglish.

The return leg two weeks later gave Liverpool the perfect opportunity to really open up on their opponents and for Irish international striker

Michael Robinson, in particular, it proved to be a fruitful evening as he bagged two goals in a 5–0 romp for the Reds.

Robinson had failed to find the net since his move to Anfield from QPR just a couple of months earlier so the opportunity for him to bang in a brace in a top European game proved a definite confidence booster.

The tall striker opened the scoring after just fourteen minutes as he reacted sharply to a rebound off the Odense keeper from a Ray Kennedy shot to hit home his first goal in a Liverpool shirt.

The result of the first round tie was never really in much doubt after Kenny Dalglish doubled Liverpool's lead on the night in the thirty-second minute and the brilliant Scot soon made it 3–0 with another strike just before half-time. Liverpool continued to lay siege on the Odense goal in the second half with both Robinson and captain Graeme Souness hitting the post but the pressure finally told on Odense when defender Frank Olsen scored a cruel own goal on sixty-five minutes. Robinson was in no mood to lay off the Danish side as he hit Liverpool's fifth seven minutes later to round off the scoring in an impressive first-round performance by Fagan's men.

If that tie had been easy, then Liverpool knew they were in for a much sterner test in the second round after they were paired with Spanish champions Athletic Bilbao.

The first-leg clash at Anfield on 19 October proved to be a close and nervy encounter with neither side able to make a breakthrough as Bilbao's tough defence earned them a credible scoreless draw to bring back to Spain.

Liverpool knew that they would really need to up their performance for the second leg in Bilbao and true to form they put on one of their best and most gritty European displays to see off the Basque battlers.

With the game still tied at 0–0 midway through the second half, Welsh scoring sensation Ian Rush notched up one of his most important goals when he headed home a pinpoint cross from full-back Alan Kennedy.

The away goal meant Bilbao then needed to score twice in the remaining quarter of the match but Liverpool were in no mood to let their lead slip and held on for a crucial 1–0 victory which sent them on their way to another European Cup quarter-final.

Afterwards, Irish international Mark Lawrenson, who played in midfield that night, revealed how he had a feeling Liverpool were going to pull the win out of the bag. 'It's funny, but sometimes you can sense that the lads are going to do well. A lot of people had come to see us go out of the European Cup and we were determined to prove them wrong.'

Next for Liverpool was a quarter-final clash with Portuguese champions Benfica, a team they had beaten twice before in the competition.

By the time of the quarter-final first leg in March 1984, midfielder Ronnie Whelan had shaken off his troublesome pelvic injury and had regained his place in the team alongside fellow Irishmen Lawrenson and Robinson.

Just as they had done against Bilbao in the previous round, Liverpool struggled to find a way through the tough Benfica rearguard at Anfield. However, on this occasion, their patience did pay off as Ian Rush proved to be the match-winning hero with a single strike in the sixty-seventh minute to send Liverpool to Lisbon with a lead to protect.

Far from being on the defensive in the second leg, Fagan's Liverpool stunned Benfica with a clinical counter-attacking display.

Ronnie Whelan was on fire as he nodded Liverpool into the lead as early as the eighth minute, although the Benfica goalkeeper Bento probably should have saved the header from the Irishman.

With an away goal in the bag so early, Liverpool could relax into the clash, inviting Benfica on to them while catching them with quick-fire counters.

Such tactics paid off handsomely when another Liverpool breakaway on thirty-three minutes saw Craig Johnson hit home a second and effectively kill off any challenge from Benfica. The Portuguese side attempted to save face in the second half when they pulled a goal back through midfielder Nene but that only seemed to spark Liverpool back into life in the later stages of the game as sharpshooter Rush got in on the act with a third for the Reds before Whelan capped off an excellent personal display with his second of the night two minutes from time.

Liverpool's stunning 4–1 win on Benfica's home patch sent out a serious message that they were ready to claim back the European Cup.

With Scottish side Dundee Utd joining the Reds alongside Italian's Roma and Romanian champions Dinamo Bucharest in the last four, the only concerns for manager Fagan was the fact that the final was to be held at Roma's home ground the Stadio Olimpico.

With that in mind, Fagan had hoped Liverpool would draw Roma in the semi-finals to at least give his side a two-legged chance to beat them.

He eventually had to settle for being paired with Bucharest in a tie which most people around Anfield were confident the English champions could easily negotiate.

For the first leg at Anfield on 11 April, Fagan chose to go with Dalglish and Rush up front, with Irishman Robinson relegated to the bench, although Whelan took his place on the left of midfield with Mark Lawrenson as ever marshalling the defence alongside Alan Hansen.

The tie proved to be a tight and ill-tempered affair with Bucharest attempting to knock Liverpool off their stride, although the Merseysiders kept calm to register a 1–0 win thanks to a twenty-fifth minute goal from diminutive midfielder Sammy Lee.

Afterwards, the Romanian side cried foul with midfielder Lica Movila claiming Liverpool captain Graeme Souness had broken his jaw off the ball. Liverpool shrugged off the allegations but the second leg in Romania was set to be an even feistier affair.

Just as they had proven in Bilbao in the second round, Liverpool showed they had the battling attributes needed to overcome the Bucharest cauldron.

They took the game to their hosts in a bid to get a crucial early away goal and it arrived after just twelve minutes as lethal marksman Ian Rush again proved his worth with a close-range strike. The tie was now heavily in Liverpool's favour as Bucharest needed three goals to win against a Reds side who were masters at sitting back and soaking up the pressure.

The home side did give themselves a lifeline just before half-time when Costal Orac breached the Liverpool rearguard to make it 1–1.

It ensured a nervy second half for Liverpool but with the imperious Mark Lawrenson at his best at the back, they frustrated Bucharest. As the Romanians poured forward in search of the two goals they needed to make the final, Liverpool caught them with a late break as Rush notched his second of the night to spark wild celebrations amongst the Liverpool fans who could look forward to their team's fourth European Cup final in eight seasons.

Just as boss Joe Fagan had feared, Liverpool were to be pitted against Roma in their own back yard for the final after the Italian champions came from 2–0 down to beat a shattered Dundee Utd 3–2 on aggregate in their semi-final.

Despite his earlier reservations about the home advantage for Roma, when his Liverpool side arrived in Italy ahead of the final on 30 May, Fagan chose to play it down, instead pouring tributes on his team's opponents.

Roma certainly had quality in abundance through their Brazilian midfield playmaker Falcao and a forward line containing Italian internationals Bruno Conti and Francesco Graziani.

Fagan told the Italian press, 'I believe it will be a classic contest because both sides have so many outstanding individuals. We are here to win, make no mistake about it but if we are beaten, it will be because Roma are the better side.'

Unfazed by the massive noisy support for the home side and strong first few minutes from Roma in the Stadio Olimpico, Liverpool played with the same confidence and verve which had seen them win every other away game they played in the European Cup that year.

After soaking up the early bit of pressure, they stunned Roma with the opening goal on twelve minutes. Ronnie Whelan played his part as he ghosted in at the back post to a nod a looping Craig Johnson cross back into the Roma box and after a bit of a scramble Phil Neal was on hand to plant the ball into the net.

Having gained the upper hand, Liverpool went in search of a killer second goal and almost got it when Ian Rush turned the Roma defence and struck a shot which keeper Franco Tancredi did well to keep out.

Roma's top-notch attacking players were always a danger however, particularly Conti who could conjure up something out of nothing. It was from his cross on forty-two minutes that Roma grabbed their equaliser with striker Roberto Pruzzo powering a header past Grobbelaar.

Such a bitter blow just before half-time could have ended the challenge of many lesser sides but Liverpool were not about to let Roma boss the second half.

If anything the Reds had the best chance to win the game when Kenny Dalglish sent his fellow Scot Steve Nicol through on goal with five minutes to go but Tancredi was again down to make the save.

With neither side able to make another vital break through the game spilled over into a nerve shredding extra-time period but still no winning goal could be found, meaning it was left to the lottery of a penalty shoot-out to decide the outcome of a European Cup final for the first time.

Despite Steve Nicol missing Liverpool's first spot kick, a surprising miss from Conti kept the Reds in with a shout as strikes from Neal, Souness and Rush gave them a 3–2 lead as Graziani came forward for Roma's fourth penalty. As the Italian forward placed the ball on the spot, he was faced with dramatic antics from Bruce Grobbelaar in the Liverpool goal who started wobbling his legs on the line in the effort to put off his opponent.

Grobbelaar's trick worked as Graziani blazed his shot off the top of the crossbar leaving Alan Kennedy with the honour of shooting home Liverpool's winning penalty to spark wild scenes of celebration amongst the players and fans who had braved the trip to Rome.

11

Kenny's Green Army: Aldo, Razor and Stan

With the knowledge that Ian Rush would be leaving Liverpool by the end of the 1986–1987 season, manager Kenny Dalglish began preparing for his replacement early when he shelled out £700,000 to lure Irish international striker John Aldridge to Liverpool in January 1987.

A fervent Liverpool fan, Aldridge would prove an ideal replacement for Rush in the long term, although he could do little to help the club retain its league title from the previous season as Everton again took charge.

Ronnie Whelan was one of Liverpool's most prominent players during the campaign, starting in thirty-nine of their forty-two league games, but they could finish no better than runners-up this time as Everton impressively took the title by nine points. Perhaps the highlight of Whelan's season came in the semi-final of the League Cup when he scored in a 3–0 second-leg win over Southampton at Anfield as the Reds marched on to a Wembley final against Arsenal.

Despite all their big-game experience, Whelan and Liverpool were, for once, turned over in that final on 4 April 1987 when a second-half brace from Arsenal striker Charlie Nicholas overturned an Ian Rush goal to give the Londoners the cup.

Having won no trophies and having lost their star striker, the summer of 1987 proved particularly sore for Liverpool, although Dalglish went a long way to healing the wounds with a sensational summer spending spree, using the cash earned from the sale of Rush to bring in Watford's wing wizard John Barnes and mercurial Newcastle forward Peter Beardsley.

The pair struck up an incredible understanding with permanent new front man John Aldridge as Liverpool embarked on a brilliant winning run at the beginning of the 1987–1988 season. The Reds won eight and drew one of their first nine league games playing an unbeatable brand of attacking football that had them earmarked as champions from as early as three months into the season.

Aldridge, in particular, was on fire, banging in eleven goals in the first nine league games to become a real fans' favourite.

A tough, hard-working and all-action centre-forward, John Aldridge had come through the professional football ranks the hard way, first earning his corn with lowly Welsh side Newport County before finally making his name as a lethal marksman in the First Division with Oxford Utd.

His move to Liverpool completed Aldridge's boyhood dream to play in front of the Kop, and he certainly took the opportunity with both hands by scoring freely in front of his adoring Reds fans.

Despite his team's brilliant start to the season, boss Dalglish was always looking for that little bit extra and went back into the transfer market in late October 1987 to acquire classy Irish right midfielder Ray Houghton from Oxford Utd for £825,000.

Houghton, who was born in Glasgow but qualified to play for Ireland through his County Donegal dad, had been a professional footballer for eight years before Liverpool came calling, playing for London clubs West Ham and Fulham before enjoying two great years in the First Division with Oxford.

With the team sitting pretty at the top of the table, Houghton, known by the nickname Razor, said it was a dream come true to arrive at Anfield during such a glorious period. 'It was an easy decision to come and play for Liverpool as they were such a good side at the time and playing with such a high-quality team was obviously going to make it more enjoyable and easier. The only main worry I had upon signing was that with so much quality already in their squad I might at first have found it difficult to get into the team. There were guys there of the quality of Paul Walsh and Jan Molby who were struggling to get a game at the time, the strength and depth of the squad was unbelievable. Thankfully, I was picked for my first game, a 1–0 win away to Luton, just a week after signing and I never really looked back.'

Liverpool would incredibly go another twenty games unbeaten in the league following Houghton's signing until Everton ended their record run with a 1–0 win in the Merseyside derby at Goodison Park.

Ronnie Whelan, by now well established as a central midfielder alongside battler Steve McMahon, was a respected leader in the side who could curb his natural inclination to attack to just knit everything together in front of Liverpool's defence. But it was the new signings of Aldridge, Beardsley, Barnes and Houghton that were really making all the headlines.

Houghton says, 'It was strange how it panned out but in most games you would find that Peter often looked to link up with John Barnes, whilst myself and Aldo, having played together with both Oxford and Ireland, had a great understanding on the other side of the pitch. It was just one of those things but it obviously worked for the team as a whole as we were flying in the league.'

Liverpool weren't doing too badly in the FA Cup either, disposing of Stoke City and Aston Villa to set up a massive all-Merseyside fifth-round clash with Everton at Goodison Park.

The game was a tight and nervous affair but thankfully for Liverpool, Houghton was in the right spot to score a precious second-half winner.

He recalls, 'It had been a poor enough game against Everton that day and it always looked as though one goal might win it for either side. My memory of the goal has changed a bit over the years but I do know John Barnes made a run down the left wing and whipped in a cross. I just managed to get to the ball first in the box and steered it past Neville Southall with my head. That was special as it always took something good to get past big Nev and thankfully it was the goal that won us that Merseyside cup game.'

With the league already in the bag, Liverpool looked to capture their second double in two seasons and they rolled past Manchester City and Nottingham Forest to set up an FA Cup final clash against unfancied underdogs Wimbledon.

Unfortunately for Ronnie Whelan, injury kept him out of the final on 14 May 1988 but apart from that, Kenny Dalglish was able to pick all his strongest stars in a game Liverpool were expected to coast.

Nobody outside of Wimbledon manager Bobby Gould believed his side had a chance of upsetting the odds in beating Liverpool but just as Coventry had done a year earlier by shocking Tottenham in the final, Wimbledon caused a massive stir by winning the game 1–0.

To compound matters for Liverpool, top scorer John Aldridge, who found the net twenty-six times that season, became the first man to miss a penalty in the FA Cup final when he had his spot kick saved by Wimbledon keeper Dave Beasant midway through the second half.

Despite the hurtful defeat, Ray Houghton still refuses to be too downhearted when looking back on his debut campaign in the red shirt.

'I know we might have lost to Wimbledon in the cup final which was a huge disappointment but there were so many great games we played that year that it would be wrong to just dwell on that one negative moment. I am very proud of how well the team played that season, at times we were unstoppable and it was such a pleasure to be involved in it all. Of course it would have been nice to have capped the season off with the double by beating Wimbledon, but it was just one of those games that wasn't going to go our way.'

If the pain of losing out on the double by the shock defeat to Wimbledon had been hard to take for the players, then the manner in which they just missed out on it again a year later was far worse.

After shaking off his previous season's injury, Ronnie Whelan played in all but one of Liverpool's league games in 1988–1989 as he acquired the club captaincy from injured defender Alan Hansen. Whelan even had a new young Irishman to welcome into the squad as talented young Drogheda full-back Steve 'Stan' Staunton became a fixture in the Liverpool defence.

Making his debut against Spurs at the tender age of just nineteen in September 1988, Staunton never really looked back after that as he helped Liverpool on to further success over the following three years. Staunton had been brought to Merseyside from Dundalk just two years earlier and, like fellow left-back Jim Beglin before him, he made the jump from a League of Ireland club to the Liverpool first team with the minimum of fuss.

His Reds side, who had signed striker Ian Rush back from Juventus to compete with John Aldridge for the main striking slot, appeared to be going along fine in the 1988–1989 season until the absolute horror of an FA Cup semi-final clash with Nottingham Forest on 15 April 1989 plunged the club into anguish and turmoil.

A horrific crush at Hillsborough ground in Sheffield where the game was taking place led to the deaths of ninety-six Liverpool fans, a tragedy which shook the foundations of the tight-knit Liverpool club and city.

Somehow, the Liverpool players found the strength of character to come back from the tragedy to lead Liverpool to the cup final with neighbours Everton. In one of the proudest moments of his career, Ronnie Whelan led the Liverpool side out at Wembley as captain in possibly the most emotional FA Cup final ever staged at the famous old stadium.

John Aldridge also managed to banish the ghosts of his previous year's penalty miss by banging Liverpool in front with his first attempt on goal after just four minutes. In a tight and nervy affair, Aldridge's early goal appeared as if it would prove the winner until Everton midfielder Stuart McCall broke Liverpool hearts with a last-minute equaliser to send the game into extra time.

In a scintillating first period of extra time, there was more drama in fifteen minutes than there had been in the previous ninety as both teams opened up and went for it.

It was Liverpool who struck first when substitute Ian Rush swivelled in the Everton box on ninety-five minutes to smash home a fantastic goal, but Everton came storming back again through with McCall, with the Scotsman volleying home a cracking equaliser from twenty-five yards just seven minutes after Rush had given Liverpool back their lead.

The fans of both sides barely had time to catch their breath when Rush was in again just two minutes later, this time nodding the ball past his fellow Welshman Neville Southall to regain the lead for Liverpool for the third time.

The Reds weren't going to let it slip this time and saw out the second period of extra-time to win a pulsating final 3–2, giving Ronnie Whelan his lifetime's ambition of climbing the Wembley steps to hold aloft the FA Cup as the winning captain.

However the backlog of games created by the Hillsborough Disaster meant Liverpool were back in action just three days after that draining final in a home league game against West Ham which was to be followed up with a final and deciding encounter with their championship rivals Arsenal three days later.

Liverpool began the double-header with a convincing 5–1 victory over West Ham, with Houghton notching up two goals in one of their most impressive displays of the season.

That resounding win meant Liverpool only needed to avoid defeat by two clear goals against Arsenal in a late Friday night fixture at Anfield on 26 May 1989. The Reds appeared to be on target to do just that as the game remained scoreless going into the second half before Arsenal striker Alan Smith upped the pressure when he headed his side in front from a corner.

Despite going a goal down, Liverpool still appeared to be in control of their destiny until a disastrous final few seconds of the game when Arsenal midfielder Michael Thomas somehow managed to burst through the Reds' defence and loft an unbelievable league-winning goal past the despairing reach of Bruce Grobbelaar.

Anfield had never witnessed such scenes before as, for once, it was the away fans who were celebrating a breathtaking success.

Naturally devastated by such a cruel loss, Ray Houghton still doesn't offer up any excuses in his assessment of how Liverpool had yet again messed up the chance to win the league and cup double. 'I don't believe it was necessarily tiredness that cost us the game that night, it was just the fact that we didn't exactly know how to go about the game. If we had needed to win or even get a draw I think it would have been better for us but to be in the situation where all we had to do was avoid a 2–0 defeat left us not knowing exactly what to do.

'Not a lot had happened in the game as it was but then Arsenal, as they tended to do under George Graham, just got their noses in front. But even after that they didn't exactly put us under an awful lot of pressure and we just got caught cold right at the end. It was heartbreaking but, again, I think we could look back and say that we did very well that season, we came so close to winning the double.'

The only way for Liverpool to banish the bad memories of the Arsenal debacle was to regain the First Division title and they began the following season in clinical fashion by remaining unbeaten in their first eight games which included an incredible 9–0 drubbing of Crystal Palace at Anfield on 12 December 1989.

The Palace game was equally notable for the fact it would be the last game in a red shirt for local hero John Alrdridge who was brought off the bench to slam home a penalty before his surprising transfer to Spanish side Real Sociedad.

With Aldridge gone, Ian Rush regained the mantle as Liverpool's main targetman and, with top-scoring winger John Barnes, notched up forty league goals as the Reds battled for the title with Aston Villa and Arsenal.

Ronnie Whelan was, as ever, a strong presence in the midfield as he played in thirty-four league games and it again took a late surge for Liverpool to emerge on top.

The team overcame a sticky patch to remarkably remain unbeaten in their final twenty-three league games to win the title with ten points to spare over Villa and hand Whelan his sixth First Division winners medal.

Similar to the two previous seasons, Liverpool were also going equally as strong in the FA Cup.

Whelan was on the scoresheet as they trounced Swansea 8–0 in a third-round replay at Anfield – after the initial tie had finished in a scoreless draw – before a replay in the next round also saw them edge past Norwich City 3–1. The Reds negotiated tricky ties with Southampton and QPR to land a semi-final against Crystal Palace as thoughts again began to wander towards that elusive second double under Kenny Dalglish.

However the double jinx struck again for the Reds in that semi-final with Palace, who avenged their earlier 9–0 hammering in the league, to beat Liverpool 4–3 in one of the most incredible last four games ever played in the FA Cup.

The semi-final loss was a minor aberration in what had been another exquisite league-winning campaign for Liverpool, who began the 1990s just how they had finished the 1960s, 1970s and 1980s – at the very top of the English game.

As they moved forward with confidence under Kenny Dalglish, few people at the time would have bet against Ronnie Whelan and his Liverpool team-mates continuing their dominance right through another new decade.

Monaghan man John McKenna pictured in 1922 during his time as Liverpool chairman. McKenna previously held the role as the club's first team manager from 1892 to 1896.

The inimitable Elisha Scott between the posts at Anfield. The Belfast-born goalkeeper spent twenty-two years at Liverpool from 1912 to 1934, winning two league titles.

Belfast striker Sammy Smyth, who played for Liverpool from 1952 to 1954, was Liverpool's top scorer during the 1953-54 season.

Wing-wizard Steve Heighway in the 1977 European Cup final against Borussia Mönchengladbach. Dublin-born Heighway was one of the best wingers in the game during the 1970s, helping Liverpool to numerous domestic and European honours.

Midfielder Ronnie Whelan celebrates his winning goal against Tottenham in the 1982 League Cup final at Wembley with team mates Ian Rush and Alan Kennedy.

John Aldridge wins a header as his team mate Ray Houghton looks on in a First Division match against Wimbledon in 1989.

Drogheda full-back Steve Staunton had two spells as a Liverpool player between 1988-1991 and 1998-2000, winning an FA Cup and First Division title along the way.

Defender Phil Babb battles with fellow Irish international Roy Keane of Manchester United during a Premiership clash at Old Trafford in October 1995. The game ended in a 2-2 draw.

Midfielder Jason McAteer in action against Leeds United in the Carlsberg Trophy which was held at Lansdowne Road in Dublin from 31 July to 1 August 1999.

Dependable full-back Steve Finnan wins the ball during Liverpool's tense and dramatic FA Cup final against West Ham in 2006. The incredible game finished in a 3-3 draw before Liverpool won the trophy on penalties.

Robbie Keane celebrates his first goal for Liverpool, scored during the UEFA Cup Champions League in October 2008.

Devestated Juventus fans inspect the scene of the 1985 European Cup final in the Heysel Stadium in Belgium when a wall collapsed and killed thirty-nine Juventus supporters.

Desperate Liverpool fans are pulled out of the Leppings Lane terrace at the Hillsborough stadium in Sheffield during the FA Cup semi-final against Nottingham Forest on 15 April 1989. Ninety-six Liverpool supporters were killed in the crush.

Legendary manager Bob Paisley congratulates Mark Lawrenson (left) and Kenny Dalglish after Liverpool's victory over Manchester United in the Milk Cup final in 1983. Liverpool won 2-1 after extra time in Paisley's last major final as manager.

Delighted Harry Kewell lifts the Champions League trophy as the whole Liverpool team, including Limerick man Steve Finnan celebrate behind him. Liverpool won the trophy following a dramatic three-goal comeback and penalty shoot-out victory over Italians AC Milan in 2005.

The Liverpool team, including Irish stars Mark Lawrenson, Jim Beglin and Ronnie Whelan, celebrate their FA Cup final victory over Everton in 1986. The win gave Liverpool their first English league and FA Cup double.

Twenty Years of Hurt

12

From Dalglish to Souness

After securing their eighteenth First Division title in 1990, Liverpool began the following season in familiar winning fashion.

Irish internationals Ray Houghton, Steve Staunton and Ronnie Whelan had returned to Anfield from the high of their country's first World Cup final appearance in Italy, which had been a resounding success with the team reaching the quarter-finals before being knocked out in a 1–0 defeat by the home nation.

Their spirits were still on the up as Liverpool embarked on an eight-game winning streak at the start of the new league season and it already appeared that championship number nineteen would be on its way to Merseyside.

Liverpool made it to December unbeaten in the league but ominously fell to a shattering 3–0 defeat to their nearest rivals at the top Arsenal at Highbury.

Before the year was out, Liverpool had lost again, this time away to Crystal Palace and as Arsenal grew in stature, Kenny Dalglish's Reds were beginning to feel the pressure of maintaining the standards they had set themselves throughout the previous five years.

In an FA Cup clash with Second Division Blackburn Rovers on 5 January 1991 – a game Liverpool were expected to win with ease – the Reds needed a fortuitous last-minute own goal from unlucky Mark Atkins to force a replay.

Although Dalglish's men made sure of their progress with a 3–0 replay win at Anfield, thanks to goals from Ray Houghton and Steve Staunton, their form in the league continued to stutter with three draws in a row which allowed Arsenal take control at the top of the table by February.

In a bid to inject life into his team's flagging campaign, Dalglish brought in tigerish Coventry City striker David Speedie in a £675,000 deal. However at thirty years old, and never really a target for any of the top clubs previous to that, Speedie's signing smacked a little of panic by the Reds' boss. Although the move did pay quick dividends as Speedie scored an incredible brace of goals in a morale boosting 3–1 Merseyside derby win over Everton at Goodison Park on 9 February 1991.

It wasn't the last Liverpool heard from their near neighbours, however, as they were down to play them again eight days later in a fifth-round FA Cup tie at Anfield. Speedie was unable to repeat his heroics as Everton upped their game and Liverpool were lucky to survive the tie with a scoreless draw.

It all meant that the Merseyside giants would meet for the third successive game three days later when the sterile 0–0 draw at Anfield was replaced with possibly the most amazing derby game between the pair.

In a Goodison Park match that had everything, including extra time, Liverpool took the lead on no less than four occasions only for Everton to come storming back each time to force an unbelievable 4–4 draw.

The drama on the night paled in comparison to the bombshell news which emerged out of Anfield just a day later when Kenny Dalglish announced he was retiring as manager. The news was met with utter dismay and astonishment across not only the red half of Merseyside but from Liverpool fans all over Ireland who sensed an end of an era with 'King Kenny' gone from the dugout. If Dalglish's sudden resignation stunned the fans, it absolutely flabbergasted the players who had no idea he was thinking of moving on from the club.

Ray Houghton recalls an air of utter astonishment when they were told the news. 'We had just come in from training the day after the Everton game and it was our coach Ronnie Moran who announced to us that Kenny had quit. You could have knocked us all down with a feather as not one of us had seen that coming.

'It was a massive surprise but then none of us really knew how much pressure Kenny was really under at the time. He had been such a big hero as a player for the club and he then continued on with that as a huge success as manager but each year the pressure increased on him to continue being successful and maybe that told on him in the end.'

Houghton also admitted that although the team were still in with a shout of winning the league and FA Cup at the time Kenny quit, he could sense the team was beginning to slide. 'Perhaps if Kenny looks back, he will acknowledge he didn't make some changes to his squad in certain areas as he began to lose important players. Top guys like Mark Lawrenson were already gone and other mainstays like Alan Hansen were coming to the end of their careers and maybe we hadn't really replaced that type of player properly.'

The slide Houghton sensed certainly set in after Dalglish left. With long-serving coach Ronnie Moran in caretaker charge, a shell-shocked Liverpool were well beaten 3–1 at Luton in the league before Everton dumped them out of the cup with a 1–0 win in the second replay thanks to a winning header from their centre-half Dave Watson.

To make matters worse, Liverpool's next opponents were Arsenal at Anfield and the Reds lost 1–0 again, effectively handing the title impetus to the Gunners who moved three points clear with twelve games to play.

In fairness to Moran, Liverpool didn't play all that badly in either defeat to Everton and Arsenal, with the victors in both cases having to thank their goalkeepers Neville Southall and David Seaman respectively for keeping the Reds at bay.

Moran did ignite an upsurge in form for the team as they recorded wins over Man City, Sunderland and an excellent 7–1 win away at Derby to keep their title hopes very much alive. However, with Arsenal losing only once all season, Liverpool couldn't afford any slip-ups on the run-in but fell to almost fatal back-to-back defeats to QPR and Southampton.

As Arsenal continued on their relentless run towards a second league title in three years, Liverpool looked for some inspiration and believed they had found it when appointing former captain Graeme Souness as the club's permanent new manager in place of Dalglish on 16 April 1991.

Souness had enjoyed brilliant success as manager of Glasgow giants Rangers winning three Scottish League titles in the previous four years and many viewed his appointment at Liverpool as a master stroke.

He certainly managed to keep Liverpool on the coat-tails of Arsenal with two successive 3–0 wins over Norwich and Crystal Palace but with just three games left to play after that the Reds simply ran out of steam. Defeats to Chelsea and Nottingham Forest handed the title to Arsenal as Liverpool finished the season seven points back in second place.

The summer of 1991 was the first real acid test for the new Souness reign as he entered the transfer market in a bid to stamp his own impression on the team.

He certainly didn't hold back with the cheque book, spending just over £5 million on defender Mark Wright and striker Dean Saunders from Derby County and a further £1.25 million to bring in winger Mark Walters from his old club Rangers. Midfielder Michael Thomas was later snapped up from Arsenal in December 1991 whilst exciting home-grown youngsters Steve McManaman and Don Hutchinson were elevated into the first team squad by Souness.

To make room for the new players, Souness spent little time getting rid of some of Liverpool's top players under the Dalglish reign, controversially selling Peter Beardsley to Everton for £1 million and also surprisingly offloading Steve Staunton to Aston Villa for £1.1 million. It was a gamble by Souness to sell on two popular championship-winning players and it became particularly pronounced as Liverpool slipped down the table during his first full year in charge.

The Reds won just six of their first seventeen league games as they struggled badly to keep up with the top of the table pace-setters Leeds and Man Utd and their poor form in the league was compounded by a fifth-round exit from the League Cup to lowly Peterborough Utd.

A rare bright spot during those grim early months of Souness' reign came in the UEFA Cup – Liverpool's first venture back into Europe following their Heysel ban.

In a clash at Anfield against French side Auxerre, Liverpool rolled back the years with a scintillating display to win 3–0 and overcome a two-goal deficit from the first leg.

Liverpool's season improved somewhat during the second half of the campaign as they progressed to the quarter-finals of the UEFA Cup and began an exciting FA Cup run.

Near neighbours Crewe Alexandra were the first to fall to Souness' men as John Barnes ripped them apart with a hat-trick in a 4–0 win for the Reds at Gresty Road.

Liverpool needed a replay in the fourth round to see off Bristol Rovers 2–1 at Anfield and marched on to a quarter-final clash with Aston Villa after squeezing past Second Division Ipswich Town 3–2 in extra time of a replay.

Villa represented Liverpool's toughest challenge so far in the cup but the Reds moved past them with a 1–0 win thanks to a second-half goal from Michael Thomas.

Unfortunately for Souness, there would be no cup double challenge for Liverpool as they were dumped out of the UEFA Cup by Italian side Genoa just a few weeks before their FA Cup semi-final clash with Second Division Portsmouth.

In a hard fought and tight game with Portsmouth, Liverpool required the calm head of experienced Irishman Ronnie Whelan to keep their cup hopes alive as the Dubliner tapped home a vital extra-time equaliser to bring the game to a replay.

Liverpool looked dead and buried after Portsmouth winger Darren Anderton had given his side a deserved lead in extra time, but Whelan scored one of his most important Reds' goals ever just three minutes from the end when he followed up an exquisite John Barnes free-kick that hit the bar to knock the ball home.

Prior to the semi-final, Liverpool had been rocked by the news that manager Souness was in need of triple heart by-pass surgery and, given his condition, the boss was probably lucky to have missed the heart-stropping replay at Villa Park on 13 April 1992 when the Reds needed the drama of a penalty shoot-out to make it to the final against Sunderland.

Under strict doctors' orders, Souness didn't return to the Liverpool dugout until the day of the Wembley final on 9 May but he made a generous gesture by allowing long-serving club coach Ronnie Moran the pre-match honour of leading the side out onto the pitch.

In one of their better performances of the entire season, Liverpool broke Sunderland hearts with a clinical display, including a man-of-the-match performance from Steve McManaman.

After a goalless first half, Liverpool burst into life just two minutes into the second period when Michael Thomas belted a superb right-foot shot into the top corner and Ian Rush made sure of the victory seventeen minutes later with his fifth FA Cup final goal to spark wild scenes of celebration from a recuperating Souness.

The cup win was a welcome boost after a challenging first full league campaign for Souness with Liverpool finishing no better than sixth, the club's worst position in years.

On a personal note for Ray Houghton, the season had been one of his best and his inspired performances throughout the year earned him a nomination for the PFA Player of the Year award. It came as a massive shock, therefore, when Houghton was put up for sale in the summer of 1992 and was forced out of Liverpool as Aston Villa snapped him up in a £825,000 deal.

Despite enjoying an excellent four years with Villa, Houghton admits he was bitter at being let go by Souness as he loved every minute of playing at Liverpool.

'I had just had one of my best ever seasons for the club, mainly because I was well settled and used to playing an Anfield. But when the summer came I sat down to talk to Graeme about a new contract and we had a disagreement about what that should be. I felt I wasn't being offered what I deserved, especially in comparison to what some of the other players were earning. I knew then that he obviously didn't really want me to stay and an agreement was made with Aston Villa. Don't get me wrong I had a very enjoyable time at Aston Villa, we had a very good side there and came close to winning the league in 1993, but, if I'm honest, I was bitter to be let go from such a great club like Liverpool.'

With Ray Houghton gone, Ronnie Whelan was the only Irishman left at the club, but with injuries and age starting to take their toll on the legendary midfielder, his influence over the side began to wane and he played in just seventeen games throughout the 1992–1993 season.

Souness once again spent big in the transfer market, paying £1 million for promising goalkeeper David James from Watford and £2.3 million on Tottenham's English midfielder Paul Stewart.

However, Souness struggled to get the right results for the money he'd spent as Liverpool endured another sorry league campaign, again finishing sixth as bitter rivals Manchester Utd won their first league title for twenty-six years.

The cups offered little relief either, as Liverpool crashed out of the European Cup Winners Cup in the second round to Spartak Moscow and were dumped out of the League Cup in the fourth round to Crystal Palace. But the most damaging defeat of all came in the third round of the FA Cup when the Reds were embarrassed 2–0 in a home replay to Second Division Bolton Wanderers.

Nevertheless, Souness still had the backing of the Liverpool board as he went on another spending spree in the summer of 1993, splashing £2.5 million on centre-back Neil Ruddock and £2.25 million on attacking midfielder Nigel Clough.

The Reds started the 1993–1994 season on fire, winning four of their first five games, but they soon ran out of steam and alarmingly began to spiral down the table. By the turn of the year, Liverpool had already lost six league games and were well off the leading sides Manchester Utd and Blackburn.

A penalty shoot-out defeat to Wimbledon in the fourth round of the League Cup piled the pressure on Souness in the early weeks of 1994 as the FA Cup, yet again, became the club's only realistic possibility of success.

The Reds received a favourable third-round draw against lower division Bristol City and looked set to progress after etching out a 1–1 draw to bring the replay back to Anfield. Fatally for Souness, however, a disheartened Liverpool meekly lost the Anfield replay 1–0. It was one defeat too many for the proud Souness and he left the club by mutual consent just a day later.

Looking on from his new home in Birmingham with Aston Villa, Ray Houghton said he was not surprised that Souness struggled to make the right impact at Anfield.

'I know certain changes to the squad hadn't been made coming near the end of Kenny's time but, if anything, when Graeme took over he tried to change things too quickly. He allowed the likes of Peter Beardsley to leave far too early. Peter was still a class player with a lot to offer the side and he showed that by going on to have a great career not only with Everton but even Newcastle after that. He also let Steve Staunton go as a very young man and brought in the likes of Julian Dicks. I don't think anyone could tell me that Dicks was a better player than Staunton, a guy who played over a hundred times for his country. Maybe Graeme doesn't agree but I just believe that he allowed certain players to leave Liverpool too early and replaced them with players who just weren't as good.'

Liverpool wasted little time in replacing Souness as they again went within their old boot-room staff to appoint coach Roy Evans as new boss in time for their next game against Norwich, following that Bristol defeat.

13

The Roy Evans Revolution: Babb and McAteer

The Reds hardly set the world alight during the remainder of the season under Evans, winning just six of their sixteen league games and finishing way back in eighth place.

However, Evans' term in charge began in earnest the following season as Liverpool slowly but surely regained some of their confidence and style under the long-serving coach, who had been a coach with Liverpool right through from the Shankly era.

One thing in Evans' favour was the emergence of classy home-grown players such as Steve McManaman, midfielder Jamie Redknapp and lethal scouse striker Robbie Fowler. With such attacking talents already in his squad, Evans concentrated on getting his defence in order when he shelled out a record-breaking sum of £3.6 million for Irish international defender Phil Babb and £3.5 million on Wimbledon centre-back John Scales.

As Ronnie Whelan's best years were firmly behind him, Evans allowed the Irishman to leave the club he had served with distinction for almost 500 games over thirteen years in September 1994.

Whelan left on a free transfer to Southend, having accomplished everything a footballer could have wished for during his time with the Reds.

With Whelan gone, Phil Babb became the only Irish representative within Evans' squad and after enjoying an excellent World Cup alongside Paul McGrath in the centre of the Ireland defence at USA 1994, Babb appeared to have a great Anfield career ahead of him.

Playing with an unorthodox line-up of three centre-backs and three in the centre of midfield flanked by two wing-backs, Liverpool began their first full season under Evans on fire, smashing eleven goals past Crystal Palace, Arsenal and Southampton to streak to the top of the table.

The Reds came crashing back down to earth, though, when champions Manchester Utd beat them 2–0 at Old Trafford and they struggled after that to maintain a proper challenge for the league title. Nevertheless, Liverpool were making strides under Evans, playing a nice brand of attacking and passing football that was pleasant on the eye.

Phil Babb had settled into the Liverpool side, using his pace to earn a spot in the Liverpool rear-guard alongside Neil Ruddock and John Scales. He played in thirty-four of Liverpool's forty-two league games and was also a prominent feature as the Reds searched for cup glory in 1995.

They made strong progress through both domestic cup competitions, setting up a League Cup semi-final against Crystal Palace and a home FA Cup quarter-final with Tottenham by early March 1995.

The Reds made hard work of their Palace semi-final, relying on a last-minute winner from Robbie Fowler at Anfield to send them down to London with a 1–0 lead where Fowler was on hand again to score as they made it to the final with a 2–0 aggregate win.

Any thoughts of a cup double were snuffed out just three days after the Palace win when Spurs snatched a precious 2–1 FA Cup win with a last-gasp winner from their own star striker Jurgen Klinsmann.

Despite the cruel defeat to Spurs, Liverpool still embarked on a big Wembley outing against Second Division Bolton Wanderers in the Coca Cola Cup (League Cup) final on 2 April. Phil Babb took his place in the three-man Liverpool central defence alongside Scales and Ruddock but it was roaming midfielder Steve McManaman who stole the show as his two goals downed plucky Bolton in a 2–1 win for Roy Evans' men.

Playing in the Bolton midfield that day was future Red and talented Irish international Jason McAteer.

A boyhood Liverpool fan McAteer had been making headlines as he helped Bolton to the League Cup final that year and also promotion out of the Second Division through the play-offs, sparking rumours that he would be a target at Anfield.

McAteer now says he felt that the League Cup final at Wembley was like a Liverpool trial for him. 'Because there had been a bit of talk of Liverpool being interested in me it did kind of feel that way. Luckily enough, I played well during the game, as I felt the whole Bolton team did and although we fell 2–0 behind we did manage to pull a goal back and put pressure on Liverpool. With a bit of luck we could have even got an equaliser and sent the game into extra time.'

If the Wembley clash was indeed a trial for McAteer, then he suitably impressed boss Roy Evans. Just weeks into the following campaign, Evans splashed out £4.5 million to bring McAteer in from Bolton and round off a whirlwind couple of years for the diehard Reds' fan.

McAteer said, 'When I was a kid playing football in the parks all I thought about was playing for Liverpool and being like Kenny Dalglish. I had trials with Everton and Man Utd when I was a teenager but that never worked out and, to be honest, I thought my chance to become a professional footballer had passed me by when I went to college to study art.'

Luckily for Liverpool-born McAteer, he got one more chance to reach the big time in football when, playing for non-league Merseyside club Marine and working as a barman, he was spotted by Bolton Wanderers scouts and was snapped up by them as a twenty-year-old in 1991.

After impressing as a midfielder with Bolton, McAteer, who qualified to play for the Republic of Ireland through his grandfather Patrick, a barber from Newry in County Down, was selected to join Jack Charlton's Irish squad for the World Cup finals in 1994.

His subsequent transfer to boyhood heroes Liverpool capped it all off for McAteer. 'It was strange when I first arrived at Liverpool looking around at all their top players at the time such as John Barnes, Jamie Redknapp, Robbie Fowler and Steve McManaman, and all I wanted to do was try to fit in but, somehow, still feeling that I didn't really belong amongst such good players,' he says. 'Thankfully as I was more or less the same age as most of the other players, it didn't take me long to settle in with the squad.'

It helped that McAteer's first full start with Liverpool came in an impressive 2–2 draw away to Manchester Utd in October 1995.

After that, he was pretty much an ever present in the side, impressing with his energetic displays as the right wing-back in a side that could play some scintillating football.

Liverpool's best form during McAteer's debut season came in the FA Cup, when they simply scored goals for fun to march on to a Wembley final date with Manchester Utd.

McAteer helped Liverpool on their way with a goal in an impressive 7–0 trouncing of Rochdale in the third round and another nine goals saw them advance past Shrewsbury, Charlton and Leeds Utd to set up a tough semi-final encounter with Brian Little's Aston Villa.

The semi-final on 31 March 1996, was all Liverpool's as an early Robbie Fowler goal gave them a lead they never relinquished. Fowler added another with four minutes to play before Jason McAteer rounded off a complete Reds' performance with a third goal in the final minute of the match.

Although Man Utd had wrapped up the league title before the cup final on 11 May, such had been Liverpool's form in the cup that many backed them to win it. With both team's capable of great attacking play, the final turned out to be a major disappointment with few attacks or attempts on goal.

'It was just one of those games were everybody seemed to cancel each other out,' McAteer rememebers. 'I was marking Ryan Giggs on the day and neither he or I did anything special and it was the same all over the pitch, so it didn't make for a great spectacle for the fans.'

However, with five minutes remaining, and the game still tied at 0–0, disaster struck for Liverpool when a half-cleared Man Utd corner fell to the boot of their mercurial French striker Eric Cantona who volleyed a fabulous shot into the roof of the net to win the cup for United.

'I was absolutely devastated afterwards and don't mind admitting that I cried for a few hours,' Jason McAteer says. 'Trust Eric Cantona to do that with just a few minutes remaining on the clock. Losing to Man Utd in an FA Cup final was a dreadful feeling.'

The Reds had little time to feel sorry for themselves, however, as boss Roy Evans began to plan a way ahead for his team to win a Premier League title for the first time since the team's First Division win in 1990.

In his first two full years in charge, Liverpool had finished fourth and third respectively and everyone at Anfield was expecting the next step under Evans was to win a championship.

Czech international Patrick Berger was the one major signing for Evans in the summer of 1996 when he was bought from Borussia Dortmund for £3.25 million to add extra fire power to a squad already containing the attacking talents of Robbie Fowler, Stan Collymore and Steve McManaman.

Liverpool began the 1996–1997 season in assured fashion, winning six and drawing two of their first eight games to streak to the top of the table before old foes Man Utd beat them again with a 1–0 win at Old Trafford.

Nevertheless, Liverpool maintained their form throughout the first five months of the season and turned in to 1997 at the top of the table. The team was also making progress in the European Cup Winners Cup, beating My-Pa 47, Sion and Brann Bergen to make it as far as the semi-finals.

By early April 1997, a league title and European trophy double was not out of the question as Roy Evans looked to match the feats of previous managers Bill Shankly and Bob Paisley.

However, the wheels came off the wagon in a big way for Liverpool late on in the season as they threw away their chance of glory.

'We went into a home league game against Coventry at Anfield in early April, knowing that victory would put us clear of Man Utd at the top,' McAteer remembers. 'We battered Coventry for the first sixty minutes as Robbie Fowler gave us a 1–0 lead but we failed to put them away and Coventry came back to win the game 2–1 with two late headers from corners. We were absolutely devastated in the dressing room afterwards; it was so frustrating as we knew we should have won the game and all the defeat did was hand the initiative back to Man Utd.'

The defeat to Coventry was followed by a disastrous semi-final first leg of the Cup Winners Cup away to reigning cup holders Paris St Germain.

Some defensive lapses and dreadful goalkeeping from David James handed the Frenchmen three goals as Liverpool slumped to a 3–0 defeat.

'To be fair Paris St Germain were a very good side at the time, although we didn't give ourselves much of a chance that night,' McAteer says. 'Losing 3–0 was terrible and pretty much ended any hopes we had of making it to the final.'

Worse was to come for the Reds when Man Utd arrived at Anfield just nine days later and grabbed a crucial 3–1 win which all but wrapped up the title and left Liverpool to rue yet another missed opportunity.

At least Roy Evans' men restored some pride with a resounding second-leg performance against St Germain at Anfield as they tore into the Frenchmen to pull two goals back, but sadly fell just short and lost the semi-final 3–2 on aggregate.

Crestfallen at yet another season without a trophy, Liverpool actually slumped back to finish in fourth place in the league, on the same points total but with a worse goal difference than Newcastle and Arsenal.

McAteer admits the team had gained a reputation as 'nearly men' but says that they also came in for some unfair criticism.

'With Liverpool's previous history of success, we started every year under serious pressure to win the league and it could be difficult to deal with, both for the manager and players as every game became a must-win situation. But in all fairness we didn't do all that badly, the worst part was that we always just seemed to fall short of Man Utd and the national press loved to give Liverpool stick for some reason.

'We were called the 'Spice Boys' because there was the perception that we were always out on the town and in clubs but the funny thing is that there was many times when we would bump into Man Utd players when we were out but because they were winning they didn't get the same tag. We really weren't all that far off Manchester Utd. Perhaps we were a bit naïve in some of the games we lost and we didn't always buy strong enough players in the transfer market. United's manager Alex Ferguson had the recipe for success at the time and unfortunately for us at Liverpool we just kept falling short of that.'

In a bid to bolster his squad with more experienced pros in the summer of 1997, Roy Evans brought in former Man Utd midfielder Paul Ince,

German international forward Karl-Heinze Riedle and Norwegian Øyvind Leonhardsen from Wimbledon. It did little to dissipate the nearly-men tag as Liverpool went yet another season empty handed as they finished third in the league and lost in the semi-final of the League Cup to Middlesbrough.

As the Liverpool board began to lose patience with the lack of trophy success under Roy Evans, who was nevertheless still a very popular figure amongst the fans and players, they brought in respected French coach Gerard Houllier to work alongside him in the summer of 1998.

Ostensibly the pair were to work as equal co-managers but the strange arrangement was doomed to failure from the very start, and Evans always looked like the man who would lose out in the long run.

14

Steve Finnan: Mr Dependable

After a disappointing start to the 1998–1999 season under the Roy Evans-Gerard Houllier partnership, Evans decided that his time as Liverpool manager was up in November 1998 and he departed the club, leaving Houllier the sole man in charge of the team.

For many, it had appeared only a matter of time before the Frenchman took the reigns to begin a new era in the history of Liverpool FC.

However Jason McAteer feels Roy Evans was given a raw deal near the end of his time at the club.

'I don't think Roy was treated with the respect he deserved,' he says. 'It was obvious from the moment that Houllier came in that Roy was going to be shunted aside and that is eventually what happened. I think France winning the World Cup in the summer of 1998 had a big bearing on things as suddenly everything about the French became fashionable. It was even fashionable to do your pre-game stretching like a Frenchman, and Liverpool bought into it by bringing in Gerard Houllier.'

McAteer reveals that he didn't always see eye to eye with the stern

Frenchman and left the club for Blackburn in a £4 million deal just two months after he had taken full control of team affairs.

'I didn't like Gerard's style of management, I thought he was quite harsh and didn't have very good man-management skills with the players. I don't think he realised the quality he had in the squad, which was not far off from winning a league title, but he decided to ship a lot of them out. That said, I could have stayed at the club myself but didn't fancy sitting on the bench outside the team and picking up a pay cheque at the end of the week. I also had to think of my future with the Republic of Ireland team which wouldn't have been helped if I was not playing club football regularly and that was another reason why I chose to leave Liverpool when I did.'

McAteer's departure left just two Irish players at the club – Phil Babb and Steve Staunton – to play under Houllier.

Defender Steve Staunton, who was brought back for a second stint at Anfield by Roy Evans in July 1998, featured strongly in Houllier's side as Liverpool finished the 1998–1999 season back in a disappointing seventh place.

The team did start to make steady progress under Houllier over the following season but Staunton found himself mostly out of favour and he played in just twelve games as the Reds improved their league position to finish fourth in 2000.

That summer Phil Babb ended his six years at Anfield with a free transfer to Portuguese side Sporting Lisbon and he was soon followed out of Merseyside by Steve Staunton in December 2000 after he was allowed to return to Aston Villa.

The departure of Babb and Staunton left the Liverpool first-team squad bereft of any Irish representation until Limerick born full-back Steve Finnan arrived at the club in 2003. By then, Houllier had enjoyed some great cup successes with the Reds, memorably winning a magnificent treble of League Cup, FA Cup and UEFA Cup in 2001.

When Liverpool finished runners up to Arsenal in the league a year later, fans began to dream that Houllier would be the man to finally land them that coveted league title. However, just like Roy Evans before him, Houllier found it impossible to make that final step and the Reds actually went backwards under him over the following two years.

Another League Cup success in 2003, with a brilliant 2–0 final win over Manchester Utd, couldn't paper over the fact that Liverpool were struggling to make an impact in the league and Houllier came under increasing pressure by the start of the 2003–2004 season.

In a final attempt to mould a league-title-winning side, Houllier splashed out £3 million on Irish international Steve Finnan from Fulham as part of a summer spending spree that also saw Australian winger Harry Kewell come from Leeds Utd alongside talented French youngsters Anthony la Tallec and Florence Sinama Pongolle from Le Harve.

Finnan was a popular signing amongst the Liverpool fans who appreciated his consistent form and ability to play equally as well either at right or left full-back.

Although born in Limerick, Finnan moved with his family to Chelmsford, England, when he was still only a young boy and he began his football career in London club Wimbledon's youth system. From there, he moved around a number of clubs including Birmingham and Notts County before landing at Fulham in 1998, where he would go on to enjoy five great seasons.

During his time with the Londoners, Finnan helped Fulham win promotion through two divisions from the English League Second Division right through to the Premier League, earning himself a call-up to the Republic of Ireland squad in the process as he appeared in all of his country's four games at the 2002 World Cup finals.

It was no surprise, therefore, that a club as big as Liverpool would come looking for Finnan's services and he seemed to fit right in at Anfield.

However a poor start to the 2003–2004 season saw Liverpool win just five of their first thirteen league games as the pressure on Houllier really began to mount.

Defeats to Bolton in the League Cup and Portsmouth in the FA Cup added further misery and Houllier's fate was effectively sealed when his team failed to make it further than the fourth round of the UEFA Cup, where they were beaten 3–2 on aggregate by Marseille.

Steve Finnan's debut season at Anfield had been blighted by injury but he still managed to play in twenty-two league games as the Reds captured a coveted fourth place spot in the league, which guaranteed them a qualifying slot for the following season's Champions League.

Despite this feat, Gerard Houllier's inability to win the league with Liverpool inevitably cost him his job as the board at Anfield went in search of success under Spaniard Rafael Benitez, who had won the Spanish league twice in the previous three years with Valencia.

Tough-talking Benitez came in with the vow that he could turn Liverpool into champions just like the Valencia side he had left behind and, naturally, brought in a number of Spanish signings. Tricky winger Luis Garcia arrived at Anfield in a £6 million deal from Barcelona and on the same day in August 2004 Benitez made one of his best Liverpool signings when splashing £10 million on Real Sociedad midfielder Xabi Alonso.

Despite this influx of new players, dependable Steve Finnan became a fixture in the Benitez regime, nailing down a permanent place in the team with his confident displays from right full-back.

Only two players – centre-back Jamie Carragher and left-back John Arne Riise – played more games than Finnan during Benitez's first season in charge, but it was a difficult league campaign for the Spaniard who was struggling to find his feet in the English game.

Liverpool slumped to an embarrassing eleven away defeats that saw them struggle to catch neighbours Everton in the battle for a Champions League place.

While Liverpool finished the season behind Everton in fifth place, Steve Finnan helped them on their way to an appearance in the final of the League Cup with victories over Millwall, Middlesbrough, Tottenham and Watford.

Finnan was a starter in the Liverpool side that took on Chelsea in the final at the Millennium Stadium in Cardiff but despite taking a first-minute lead, Benitez's men eventually slumped to a 3–2 defeat in extra time.

Whatever his troubles in the league, Benitez was finding it a lot easier to get results with Liverpool on the continent as they embarked on possibly their most exciting European campaign in the Champions League, culminating in victory over AC Milan in the final. The Reds comeback from three goals down to beat the Italian giants on penalties in that European decider is regarded as one of the club's greatest feats and ensured Benitez's legendary status amongst the fans.

Victory in Europe meant Liverpool were really expected to push on under Benitez in the Premier League and they did show signs of improvement in 2005–2006, losing just once at home all season as they finished in third place behind Manchester Utd and league champions Chelsea.

The Reds complemented their stronger league showing with an excellent FA Cup run which included victories over Luton Town, Portsmouth, Man Utd, Birmingham and Chelsea to set up a cup final date with West Ham at Cardiff on 13 May 2006.

In a pulsating game, the Reds took an early lead before later falling behind twice and needing an incredible thirty-yard last-minute strike by captain Steven Gerrard to save a 3–3 draw and drag the game into extra time.

After a nerve jangling extra thirty minutes, the game entered the dreaded penalty shoot-out when Liverpool's new Spanish stopper Jose Reina came out the hero, just like Jerzy Dudek, as Liverpool captured another cup on penalties.

Steve Finnan played another significant role in this success, playing in no less than fifty-two games for Liverpool throughout the 2005–2006 season and he was still an important player in Benitez's plans as the manager plotted another monumental European campaign in 2006–2007.

Mimicking their miraculous 2005 success, Liverpool once again made it all the way to the final of the Champions League against AC Milan, having beaten Chelsea in the semi-final, but this time the Italians would exact revenge with a 2–1 victory.

Steve Finnan's appearance in his second Champions League final in three years marked him out as one of an elite group of just four Irish players to have starred in more than one final of Europe's premier cup competition – the others being ex-Reds Steve Heighway, Ronnie Whelan and Mark Lawrenson. Nottingham Forest's Derry-born midfielder Martin O'Neill was also part of his teams squad for their European Cup triumphs in 1979 and 1980 but had been an unused sub in their 1979 win over Swedish side Malmo.

Two Champions League finals in three seasons was also a serious achievement from Benitez, although as Liverpool started their new campaign in 2007–2008, there was still the lingering belief that the club should be getting closer to winning the Premier League title.

Despite the star signing of Spanish striking-sensation Fernando Torres, Liverpool actually slipped back to finish no better than fourth place in the league in 2008, piling the pressure on Benitez in much the same way as it had built up on Roy Evans and Gerard Houllier before him.

That season also proved to be the last for Steve Finnan at Anfield who, although he made twenty-four appearances in the league, and another seven in the Champions League as they made it as far as the semi-finals, found his position under threat from new Spanish signing Alvaro Arbeloa.

In the summer of 2008, Benitez allowed Finnan to leave Liverpool for Spanish side Espanyol but made another significant Irish signing for the club when he splashed out £20 million to lure star striker Robbie Keane from Tottenham.

Although put up their strongest league title challenge under Benitez in the 2008-2009 season, Robbie Keane struggled to make any impact under the Spanish boss and was shipped back out to Tottenham after just five months, in which time he had scored seven goals in twenty-one games in a Red shirt.

Despite this sorry sagas with Robbie Keane, Liverpool maintained their challenge right up into the final few games, but a number of frustrating draws earlier in the season had cost the Reds some vital points and they eventually finished second behind Man Utd by four points.

If that strong title challenge was meant to be the precursor to a genuine championship win in the 2009-2010 season, then sadly for Liverpool it just didn't work out that way.

A poor start to the season saw the Reds really lose their way under Benitez. Twenty years after their last title success, Reds fans have been left to wonder how much longer they will have to wait to experience another title success. Whenever that is, it will not be under the leadership of Rafa Benitez after the Spanish tactician negotiated his departure from Anfield after six eventful years. There is no doubt that new manager Roy Hodgson will be under the same pressure to win the league. It's pressure all Liverpool fans will hope he can handle.

15

Kings of Europe: 2005

Spaniard Rafael Benitez may have only arrived as manager of Liverpool in the summer of 2004 but he had to hit the ground running as his first competitive match in charge of the Reds was a hugely important European Champions League qualifier in Austria.

The Anfield men had been drawn to play the Austrian champions Graz AK in the final round of qualifiers and an away first leg on 8 August would be a first test for Benitez, whose reputation on the continent was strong, having won the previous year's UEFA Cup with Valencia.

Dependable Irishman Steve Finnan was selected in Benitez's first starting eleven on the right side of the Liverpool midfield and he put in a no-nonsense display in a very measured performance from the Merseysiders.

With experienced German international Dietmar Hamann patrolling the centre of midfield alongside local star Steven Gerrard, Liverpool owned the ball for large periods of the match, played at the brilliantly named Arnold Schwarzenegger stadium, and it came as no surprise when star midfielder Gerrard blasted a shot into the Graz net after just twenty-three minutes for a crucial away goal.

Liverpool could have doubled their lead just a few minutes later as Finnan got in on the action by releasing pacey striker Milan Baros free on the right but his dangerous cross was just missed by his French strike partner Djibril Cisse. The Reds kept up the pressure on the Austrians in the second half and were rewarded for their dominance when Gerrard scored his second of the night in the eightieth minute to all but wrap up the tie.

With just six minutes left on the clock, Benitez was even able to replace Steve Finnan with another Irishman, when Darren Potter came on for his competitive debut in a Liverpool shirt as his team held on for a richly deserved 2–0 win. Potter kept his place in the Liverpool side for the return leg two weeks later at Anfield, when Liverpool almost threw away their two-goal advantage with a nervy display in front of their own fans. Despite owning the ball for large spells of the second leg, Liverpool, with four changes made to the team from the first game, were unable to add to their aggregate lead and were made pay for it nine minutes into the second half when Graz's Mario Tokic smashed a twenty-yard shot past Jerzy Dudek in the Liverpool goal.

Suddenly, Graz were back in a tie they had looked dead and buried in but, apart from the odd scare, Liverpool held on to reach the coveted group stages of the Champions League.

Afterwards Darren Potter admitted it had been a nervous display from the team. 'The result was disappointing and the mood in the dressing room was one of relief at the end,' he said. 'It was a bit nervous late in the game when Graz pushed forward but thankfully we held on. It's great for the club to be back in the Champions League, and hopefully I can play a part in it.'

Unfortunately for nineteen-year-old Potter, his only other involvement in the Champions League that season were appearances on the bench as wily Benitez began to plot an exciting European run.

The group stages saw Liverpool drawn against French side Monaco, tough Spanish outfit Deportivo la Coruna and Greek's Olympiacos.

The opening group game against Monaco at Anfield couldn't have gone much better as newly signed Spanish midfielder Xabi Alonso dictated play in an assured Liverpool performance that slayed the French side 2–0 thanks to goals from strike duo Cisse and Baros.

With three points already safely secured in the group, Liverpool travelled to Olympiacos in high spirits for the second game but came unstuck in the noisy Greek cauldron. Playing in their new Georgios Karaiskakis stadium in Athens, Olympiacos had Liverpool under pressure from early on and deservedly took the lead through Ieroklis Stoltidis on just seventeen minutes.

A lacklustre Liverpool, with Steve Finnan again playing on the right of midfield, were incapable of pulling back the deficit, falling to a 1–0 defeat, their first ever against a Greek side.

It had been a drab performance which Benitez made no excuses for. 'When you lose like that it is always very disappointing,' he said after the game. 'We gave away a lot of possession; we had plenty but did not keep it. As far as the group goes, now every team has a chance of qualifying – so the home games for everybody will be important now.'

Benitez may have regretted making that statement just three weeks later on 19 October 2004, when his Liverpool side struggled badly yet again to break down a resolute Deportivo side in a frustrating game at Anfield.

If Liverpool really did need to win their home games in the group as Benitez had stated, then the manager could not have been happy when his team could conjure up no more than a 0–0 draw on home soil.

Failure to beat Deportivo at Anfield really put the pressure on Liverpool when they travelled to Spain two weeks later, knowing that if they lost the match, they could face an early exit from the competition.

Showing all the fight and spirit that would be needed if they were to succeed in Europe, Benitez's men put in an excellent rearguard display at Deportivo to take advantage of an early slice of luck when the home side scored an own goal after just thirteen minutes.

Taking the game to the Spaniards in the early minutes, Liverpool's pressure told when a wicked cross whipped in from the wing by Reds' left midfielder John Arne Riise was turned into his own net by Jorge Andrade under pressure from Baros. The early goal gave Liverpool the opportunity to sit back and attempt to catch Deportivo on the break, but they had a lot to thank their sound central defensive partnership of Jamie Carragher and

Sami Hyypia for keeping their opponents at bay in a vital 1–0 win, which opened up the opportunity that Liverpool could actually win the group.

However in keeping with the topsy-turvy nature of Liverpool's form in the competition, they spoiled all their good work in Spain by crashing to a 1–0 defeat in Monaco in another insipid display.

Monaco's victory meant Liverpool went into their final group game at Anfield against Olympiacos on 8 December 2004, knowing that only a win by two clear goals could guarantee them a place in the lucrative knock-out stages of Europe's premier club competition.

Such a scenario meant Anfield was heaving in anticipation of another one of those heroic European nights which had made the late 1970s and early 1980s such a special time for the club.

However the dogged Olympiacos, who were leading the group going into that final game, certainly hadn't read the script as they stunned Anfield by taking a first-half lead courtesy of an exquisite curling free kick from their Brazilian superstar Rivaldo. Going in a goal down at half-time and needing three without reply in the second half, Liverpool looked as good as dead and buried at a shell-shocked Anfield.

Whatever Benitez said during his half-time team talk to rally his troops appeared to work as he made an inspired substitution, replacing defender Djimi Traore with striker Florence Sinama Pongolle as Liverpool went in search of goals. The brave move took just two minutes of the second half to pay off as Pongolle gave his side a lifeline on forty-seven minutes when he side-footed home a cross from Harry Kewell.

Despite the renewed hope, Liverpool still laboured to find another way past the Olympiacos defence and as the game entered its final ten minutes it appeared their luck would be out.

However, Anfield was given renewed hope when another young substitute Neil Mellor smashed home a second goal with nine minutes to play before the old ground erupted in scenes of joy not experienced in over twenty years when talismanic captain Steven Gerrard cracked home an unstoppable twenty-yard strike five minutes later.

Somehow Benitez's Liverpool side had pulled off the great escape as they qualified for the last sixteen of the competition in second place in the group behind Monaco.

Stunned Olympiacos manager Dusan Bajevic said he just couldn't believe his team had their pockets picked so late on in the tie.

'When you are watching a game like that you do not believe you can lose in that way,' Bajevic said. 'But we brought the problems on ourselves, we did not create a chance from open play during the match. Liverpool were faster, stronger and better than us.'

Simply relieved to have made it into the last sixteen, Liverpool received a favourable enough knock-out tie when they were paired with German side Bayer Leverkusen. Liverpool had played Leverkusen in the quarter-finals of the competition in 2002 and were unlucky to lose 4–3 on aggregate on that occasion.

With revenge on their minds, the Reds tore into Leverkusen in the first leg game at Anfield on 22 February 2005. Playing with an intensity rarely seen under Benitez up until then, Liverpool caught their German opponents cold with a fantastic first-half performance which saw them take a 2–0 lead thanks to goals from Spanish winger Luis Garcia and John Arne Riise.

In one major scare for the Reds Steve Finnan had been lucky to survive a rare mistake when a poorly attempted back header from him had let Leverkusen striker Dimitar Berbatov through on goal when the score was just 1–0. Luckily for the Irishman, Berbatov put the ball wide when the whole ground expected him to score.

When midfielder Dietmar Hamann added to the Liverpool tally through a last-minute free kick, Anfield was in dreamland until a stoppage time howler from goalkeeper Jerzy Dudek allowed Leverkusen back into the tie.

With Liverpool already contemplating their quarter-final Champions League place, Dudek spilled a speculative long range shot from Berbatov which allowed his team-mate Franca to score an easy tap in for a crucial away goal.

Expecting an absolute onslaught from the home side in the second leg, Liverpool yet again confounded everybody by going to Germany and playing on the front foot.

With Steven Gerrard restored to the Liverpool midfield after missing the first leg through suspension, the Reds tore Leverkusen apart once again and had their tricky winger Luis Garcia to thank for finishing off the tie with two first-half goals that stunned Leverkusen.

Liverpool added a third through Milan Baros in the second half and not even a late goal for the Germans this time could deny Benitez a glorious win. The 6–2 aggregate score certainly set down a marker as Liverpool advanced to a quarter-final clash against the much vaunted Italians Juventus.

After two great displays against Leverkusen, Steve Finnan was confident the team could continue their run. 'Six goals in two legs against Leverkusen surely shows something about us,' Finnan said. 'That has been a tough test so there is no reason why we can't go all the way. We have the experience and the players at this level so hopefully we can do it and surprise people.'

Liverpool were certainly rank outsiders going in against a top-class Juventus side, who were top of the Italian league and had been beaten Champions League finalists just two years earlier.

Yet again Liverpool set about hitting Juventus hard from the start in the first leg at Anfield and stunned the Italians with two goals in the first twenty-five minutes. Centre-half Sami Hyypia sent Anfield into raptures with a stunning left foot volley from a corner after just nine minutes and the fans were in ecstasy when Luis Garcia belted an even better twenty-five-yard strike into the top corner sixteen minutes later.

Juventus had not become Italian champions repeatedly for nothing, however, and soaked up the Liverpool pressure before applying plenty of their own.

After a few major scares, Liverpool did eventually concede a goal midway through the second half when the Juventus defender Cannavaro was lucky to score with a weak header which the Liverpool goalkeeper Scott Carson, playing in place of the injured Jerzy Dudek, should have saved.

Juve's away goal turned the tie back in their favour as Liverpool travelled to Italy for a nerve-wracking second leg on 13 April.

Playing without the injured Steven Gerrard, manager Benitez decided to pack the Liverpool midfield with bodies and sit off Juventus in the hope of frustrating the home side. His tactics proved spot on as Juventus enjoyed plenty of possession but found it difficult to get past a blanket Liverpool defence, although the Reds did also carry a threat on the counter-attack through striker Milan Baros. In a true backs-to the-wall job, Liverpool remarkably survived their Italian test with a precious scoreless draw which sent them into a semi-final against new English powerhouse Chelsea.

Under the expert tutelage of Portuguese boss José Mourinho, who had won the previous year's Champions League title with unfancied Porto, Chelsea were dominating the Premier League and had already beaten Liverpool three times that season, including in the League Cup final.

That series of results meant Liverpool were the major underdogs again but just as they had done in Juventus, the Reds scrapped out a credible 0–0 draw away at Chelsea to bring the London side back to Anfield for what was set to be an explosive second leg on 3 May 2005.

Facing a wall of noise rarely equalled at Anfield, Chelsea were stunned after just four minutes when Luis Garcia scored another crucial Champions League goal to give Liverpool a dream lead.

Garcia had been the quickest in the box after Chelsea Peter Cech had appeared to have fouled the on-rushing Milan Baros to clip the ball home amid strong Chelsea protests that the ball hadn't crossed the line.

As a jam-packed Anfield roared them on, the Liverpool players ran themselves into the ground to keep Chelsea at bay and the away side rarely had a decent sight of goal as the Reds defended their early lead.

Unable to add a second to settle their nerves, Liverpool were forced to hang on right at the death when Chelsea forward Eidur Gudjohnsen wasted a glorious chance from inside the box when he shot wide as Steve Finnan just managed to avoid deflecting the ball into the net.

In a night of unbelievable joy at Anfield, Garcia's goal proved enough to send Liverpool into the Champions League final, where they would come up against crack Italian side AC Milan in Istanbul.

The Milan side, who had won the competition in 2003, was full of major international stars, including defenders Paolo Maldini and Jaap Stam, midfielders Andrea Pirlo and Kaka and sensational strikers Hernan Crespo and Andrei Shevchenko.

On the day of the final on 25 May, Steve Finnan revealed his pride at Liverpool making it so far against all the odds.

'Once or twice this season, we've looked as if we've been heading out of the competition but we've hung in and shown the character and determination we have as a squad. No one gave us much of a chance when we went a goal down to Olympiacos but we pulled through and we've been underdogs in every knockout round since the group stages. But we believed we were capable of beating Leverkusen, Juventus and Chelsea and so did the fans. We also believe we are capable of beating Milan.'

Later that night, Finnan took his place in a Liverpool defence alongside centre-backs Jamie Carragher and Sami Hyypia and left-back Djimi Troare.

In midfield, Benitez chose to start with Steven Gerrard and Xabi Alonso flanked by John Arne Riise and Luis Garcia, but his one surprise selection was Harry Kewell in a free role behind striker Milan Baros.

Finnan's time on the pitch proved to be a complete nightmare as a totally outplayed Liverpool were torn apart by a marauding Milan forward line of Brazilian Kaka and strikers Shevchenko and Crespo.

After falling behind in the very first minute to a goal from veteran Milan defender Paolo Maldini, Finnan and his fellow defenders just couldn't handle Kaka and Crespo as the latter added two more goals before half-time to leave the Reds trailing 3–0, apparently down and out.

To make matters worse, Finnan's game was ended at half-time by a troublesome thigh injury and he was replaced by German midfielder Dietmar Hamann as Benitez changed to a three-man defence for the second half.

It was a move which would alter the entire course of the match, as Hamann's introduction in midfield alongside Alonso freed Steve Gerrard to go and attack the Milan defence in the second half.

When Gerrard pulled a goal back for Liverpool with a well-placed header on fifty-four minutes, it appeared to be no more than a consolation but Benitez's men had other ideas as they went on the attack.

Within two minutes Vladimir Smicer, who had come on for the injured Harry Kewell, struck a second from just outside the box. Then, remarkably, Liverpool were level before the hour mark when Xabi Alonso rattled home a rebound from his own penalty, which had been awarded after Gerrard was fouled in the Milan box.

Back from the dead, Liverpool dragged the game into extra time and miraculously survived a late scare when keeper Dudek somehow managed to keep out a close range Shevchenko shot with his shoulder.

Ukranian Shevchenko was denied again by Dudek in the penalty shoot-out as the Liverpool goalkeeper proved the hero as the Reds captured the cup 3–2 on penalties.

Liverpool had managed to win their fifth European Cup crown in the most dramatic of fashion. And, as it was their fifth time winning the trophy, UEFA allowed Liverpool to keep it for good and it is stored with pride at the Anfield museum.

16

Where Next For Anfield's Irish?

When Liverpool were dominating English and European football from the early to late 1980s, no fewer than four home-grown Irish players were chosen to represent the club: Ronnie Whelan, Jim Beglin, Brian Mooney and Steve Staunton all made the step up from Irish clubs to the first team at Anfield.

Add to that the fact that another five British-born Republic of Ireland internationals made Anfield their home through that decade, there's no doubt that Liverpool relied heavily on its Irish contingent at that time.

However, the game has moved on substantially over the past two decades; by the beginning of the 2009–2010 Premier League season, manager Rafael Benitez had a staggering sixty professional players on the Liverpool books, yet not one of them was from Ireland.

It is a sign of the modern game that the vast majority of Liverpool's large squad of players come from much farther afield than Britain or Ireland, as the club now takes on teenagers from as far and wide as Spain, Hungary and Argentina.

The current Liverpool academy squad, made up of talented sixteen- to eighteen-years-olds, is also notable for the fact that it is short on any Irish representation.

With so many talented youngsters from each corner of the globe available to choose from, it begs the question as to whether Irish teenagers will ever again get the chance to come through the ranks at Liverpool.

The most recent to try was Cork-born full-back Shane O'Connor who, although impressing in the Liverpool academy team in the 2008–2009 season, has since been shipped out to join Roy Keane's Ipswich in the Championship.

Before O'Connor, talented Dublin striker Michael Collins spent two years at the academy before moving off to Italy to join second division club Triestina.

In the early part of the last decade, midfielder John Paul Kelly was tipped for great things after emerging through the academy to the Liverpool reserve team, but he returned to Ireland in 2005 having failed to make the final step up into the first team squad at Anfield.

A look at the underage international Republic of Ireland teams shows there is still an abundance of talent bursting to come through onto the professional football stage, yet it is equally noticeable that fewer players from these shores are making as big an impact at clubs such as Liverpool as they once did.

Fewer still are making the move to Anfield having already established themselves as a top player in a fellow Premier League club.

Ex-Reds midfielder Ray Houghton took almost ten years of hard graft before making his dream move to Merseyside in 1987. When Houghton signed on at Liverpool there were plenty of Irishmen dotted about the place and despite the obstacles facing young players in the modern game, he is confident that it can happen like that again.

'If the Irish players are good enough then I don't see any reason why it shouldn't happen,' he says. 'But there's no doubt that young players really have to work hard at their game and really love their football. What I always try to preach to young players nowadays is that it takes more than just the talent, you've got to really want to become the best professional you can be, especially now as there is so much competition from across the world.

'We can look back now and realise what a great player a guy like Ronnie Whelan was but the thing about players like Ronnie is how hard they worked to improve themselves and become great players. If Ronnie Whelan was a youngster at Liverpool now, he would still make it through the ranks to the first team because world-class quality like his, added to his ambition and hard work, will always shine through.'

When his playing days were long over, wing wizard Steve Heighway returned to Liverpool in 1989 to work as the head coach of the youth academy.

During an amazing nineteen-year stint as the director of the academy, Heighway was responsible for nurturing the careers of local talents Steven Gerrard, Jamie Carragher, Steve McManaman and Robbie Fowler, while winning three coveted FA Youth Cups along the way.

Dubliner Richie Partridge and Irish international midfielder Darren Potter also worked closely under Heighway on their paths to brief stints in the Liverpool first team.

Yet, in 2007, a disillusioned Heighway left his role at the club, citing a reduction in his control of the coaching of the youngsters as manager Rafael Benitez asserted his influence on the academy. For some ex-players, Heighway's banishment is a symptom of the complete control foreign managers now have on the Premier League clubs they manage.

Ian St John, the 1960s legend, laments the fact that so few young players from Britain or Ireland are getting the chance to come through at the club.

'When you look back to my playing days at Liverpool, almost all the lads were brought to the club from a lower level in England or Scotland and then later in the 1980s some fabulous players were brought through from Ireland.

'Jim Beglin is a player who springs to mind but he wasn't the only one; Ronnie Whelan was a particularly smashing player, one of the best to have played for Liverpool. We were digging these types of home-grown players up from everywhere and the Liverpool teams they played in won everything, including in Europe, so somebody at the club must have been doing something right.

'It hardly happens at all now. Steven Gerrard and Jamie Carragher are the last two local lads to really make it in the first team but you wonder after they are gone who will be next? And there's certainly not a lot of Scottish or Irish youngsters there now and you would fear that in the future, the way things are going, there may be none at all. I think the club needs a new Bill Shankly, a man who is prepared to work with home-grown talent and build them up into special players.'

In Ireland, a serious focus has now emerged on the quality of coaching available to young kids playing at all levels of the game.

Under its grassroots development programme, the Football Association of Ireland (FAI) is encouraging all coaches of schoolboy football teams across the country to part-take in coaching courses, right from a very basic level up to professional UEFA standards.

It is something which ex-Irish international Jason McAteer, who has been working towards getting his own professional coaching badges, says is really starting to bear fruit.

'I've spent a good bit of time in Ireland in recent years working on getting my coaching badges and there's no doubt that the coaching structures in the country are improving all the time. Everything is set up to bring the young players on and I firmly believe with the improvements made in this area, we can now look forward to producing not just one Robbie Keane but maybe four or five of them at the same time in the future.

'I know the League in Ireland has gone through a rough patch but the clubs there are always going to need to nurture young talent. But, to be honest, even if Ireland could become self-sufficient that way, there will still always be the lure of the Premier League in England, it's where all the best Irish players want to be really and with a bit of luck we will see another batch of them back at Liverpool.'

Where that future Liverpool will be operating out of is also still a matter of considerable concern for Reds' fans.

A move away from the iconic Anfield has been mooted for some years due to the fact the club has been unable to increase the capacity at the stadium from its current 44,000 to a scale similar to that at Old Trafford, where Manchester Utd can now attract a crowd of 75,000.

In 2003, Liverpool received planning permission for a new 60,000-seater stadium in Stanley Park.

Whilst nobody really wants to see the back of Anfield, the fact that rivals such as Man Utd get 30,000 extra fans through their gates per home game has made the move inevitable.

Even voice of Anfield George Sephton, the stadium ammouncer for the past three decades, agrees that the club has to move with the times.

'There's no doubt that to compete with the likes of Manchester Utd we are going to eventually have to get a bigger stadium,' George says. 'While I dread the day that Anfield will no longer be the club's home; certainly the last ever match there will be an extremely emotional occasion, I also look forward with some anticipation at what a new and much bigger stadium can do for the club. Anfield has been so fantastic and it will be a wrench to move away from all that history but if we want to be successful in the future we can't afford to be sentimental. And all of us who were lucky enough to experience all those great years at Anfield will still have the memories anyway.'

Despite gaining permission for the new stadium in 2003, Liverpool are still no nearer to actually moving out of Anfield as plans have consistently stalled.

Shortly after taking control of the club in 2007, Liverpool's present owners, US tycoons Tom Hicks and George Gillette, ordered a redesign of the new stadium and vowed that it would be built and ready for use by 2010. None of what Gillette or Hicks have promised with the new stadium has come to pass and the pair have become hate figures for Liverpool fans, angry at their broken promises and policy of loading debt onto the club.

In a bid to wrestle the club out of their hands, Liverpool fans are attempting to follow the lead set at Spanish giants Barcelona, where the club is effectively owned by 146,000 supporters who each have a vote on the make-up of the club's board.

In 2008, a Share Liverpool campaign was launched, with the hope of attracting 100,000 Reds fans to invest in the club, with each gaining a single share and vote similar to Barcelona.

The campaign naturally spread across to Ireland where Bernard O'Byrne has offered his expertise as former CEO of the FAI to become campaign director. Initially, the Share Liverpool campaign had hoped to raise a potential £500 million if each of the 100,000 fans it hoped to attract would invest £5,000 each.

Whilst Bernard O'Byrne now admits this probably isn't feasible – and Share Liverpool has changed its criteria to ask fans for just £500 each – he believes that greater involvement by fans in how the club is run is still the way forward.

'In all honesty you couldn't expect that the fans could come in and take over the running of the club from the off,' O'Byrne says. 'It would be a gradual process and there is no reason why they couldn't start with a 10 per cent share of the club and work at it from there. It's the policy not just at Barcelona but plenty of German clubs as well. I really hope it is a way Liverpool can move forward in the future because football is in crisis.

'There are players, managers and owners coming in to clubs from all over the world but they have very little attachment or emotional ties to the club and even less concern for the real grassroots of football in the area. Liverpool needs to get that attachment back through its fans.'

In another effort to mobilise Reds' fans into taking back their club, a supporters union, Spirit of Shankly (SOS), was established in 2008, urging Liverpool fans of all persuasions to come together as one in the interests of the club and its supporters.

Like the Share Liverpool campaign, the Spirit of Shankly has developed well beyond the confines of Merseyside and 10 per cent of its current membership hail from Ireland.

Ed Fitzsimons of the You'll Never Walk Alone Irish Reds supporters club says the Spirit of Shankly is conducting a very important campaign to save the club.

'I joined the SOS as I agree with how they are attempting to put the real interests of the club and its supporters first. That's what we need with Liverpool now. It's a club with such a fantastic history and of course we all want to see it doing well, but the supporters are as big a part of the history of Liverpool FC as anything else. All we want is that we will play just as big a part in the future.'

The Irish Reds: Half a Century Supporting LFC

17

The Fans Speak

The success lavished on Liverpool by Bill Shankly naturally ensured the club grew in popularity throughout the 1960s.

The Kop's terrace was regularly packed to the rafters as attendances at Anfield averaged 50,000. But it wasn't just on Merseyside that the interest around Anfield developed; the teams exploits didn't go unnoticed in Ireland, where a large and dedicated fan base, in awe of Shankly's team in red, began to grow.

Just as Matt Busby's Manchester Utd had done a decade earlier, Liverpool's successful attacking style captured the imaginations of Irish football supporters.

It also helped that the city of Liverpool was blessed with a huge Irish population (by the 1960s it was estimated that up to 20 per cent of the population of Liverpool was of Irish descent) and was only a short boat trip away from Dublin.

Television footage of English football was also becoming more accessible to the Irish public after the BBC launched its *Match of the Day* highlights programme in 1964.

The first ever game screened on the new show was a five-goal thriller at Anfield when star striker Roger Hunt scored the first goal in a 3–2 win for the Reds.

Not all fans were satisfied with brief glimpses of Shankly's team on television, however, and were only too happy to board the Friday night boat from either Dublin or Belfast to Liverpool and make it to Anfield in time for kick-off on Saturday afternoon. British & Irish Ferries (B&I) did a fair trade ferrying fans across the sea at a time long before low cost airlines arrived on the scene.

Dubliner Noel McQuaid, now a leading member of the You'll Never Walk Alone Irish Reds supporters club, was one fan who caught the bug after attending his first game at Anfield as a twelve-year-old in 1969.

'There was a time when the fans were getting the old cattle ship to Liverpool on a Friday night, until B&I brought in two new passenger ferries, the *Leinster* and the *Munster*, for the route in 1969,' Noel says. 'The routine for the fans was to meet up in town on the Friday night and head for the docks where the boat would leave for Liverpool at 10 p.m. and arrive the next morning at seven. Of course a lot of the older lads, including my brother, would have a few beers in the boat's Shamrock Bar on the way over and my job, since I was only twelve and obviously not drinking, was to get them all up in the morning and have their cups of tea ready for them.'

Noel still clearly remembers his first experience of the Kop in a vital league game against Leeds in 1969.

'It was an end-of-season game against Leeds and both teams were going for the league title at the time. Liverpool had kind of blown it a week before that when they only drew with Coventry and the game against Leeds actually finished in a 0–0 draw which went a long way to handing them the title ahead of Liverpool.

'But what amazed me that day was the reception the Liverpool fans gave the Leeds team at the end of the game. There were 28,000 Liverpool fans in the Kop that day and every one of them gave the Leeds team a huge round of applause even though we knew the result meant that they were going to win the league instead of our own team. That for me was very special and really summed up what Liverpool fans were all about.'

Graciousness in defeat was something which Bill Shankly had ingrained in his players and this noble trait trickled down to the fans. While supporting their own team with fervour and passion, Liverpool fans were equally capable of acknowledging the rare occasions when they were beaten by a better team.

Shankly was always proud of the Liverpool fans and while he was their hero, the manager also idolised the fans as Anfield became the envy of all other football grounds throughout the country for its atmosphere, humour and sense of sportsmanship.

Shankly's swashbuckling side was far from the only phenomenon hitting Liverpool in the 1960s however. Just as the football team made it back to the top in the First Division, the city was being put on the world map by four cheeky chaps with a musical rather than a footballing ability. The mop-topped Beatles were all the rage in the British charts as Liverpool enjoyed their first season back in English football's top flight.

Over the course of the decade, both the band and football club would enjoy meteoric rises and the thousands of Liverpool fans amassing on the Kop each week celebrated the success with passionate and humorous versions of the Fab Four's best hits.

Despite their superstardom, Shankly was typically nonplussed by Beatlemania, once memorably stating, 'Forget The Beatles and the other groups. The Kop is the real Liverpool sound. That's real singing.'

It wasn't only The Beatles' songs that had the fans in good voice – a tune from Gerry and the Pacemakers, another local group, really had the Liverpool supporters enraptured.

The 'Mersey Beat' group's version of stage song 'You'll Never Walk Alone' not only reached number one in the British charts for four weeks in 1963, but also the terraces and stands around Anfield where it quickly became a fans' favourite.

Traditionally sung by the fans before and after each game, the tune has taken on a life of its own over the years and is now so ingrained in the culture of the club that the song title is even part of the Liverpool football crest.

For Noel McQuaid, himself a promising young footballer who played in the League of Ireland for Thurles Town, Waterford Utd and

Shelbourne, the buzz of Anfield when songs such as 'You'll Never Walk Alone' were still relatively new on the Kop was something he found impossible to live without.

He used money saved up from a paper round and his work as a trainee fabricator to buy his first season ticket for the 1971–1972 season, at the princely sum of £11.

'The way it was for me back then was that almost all the money I had went on supporting Liverpool from the Kop. I was earning about £4 or £5 a week and used that for the season ticket, the ferry there and back, accommodation and whatever else you might need, I lived for Liverpool games. We would normally pack ourselves into the Kop about an hour-and-a-half before kick-off to start the songs and get the atmosphere really going inside the ground. The fans were really all part of the action on match day.'

When the action on the field had ended, Noel and his pals also knew the best spots in Liverpool to enjoy themselves.

'There was a place down by the Empire Theatre called the Sports Bar which was a good place to go for beers after the game on a Saturday night. What you'd do after the game was go for a few pints in the Park Bar near Anfield where you might even be lucky enough to bump into some of the players. When Phil Thompson came into the team in the early 1970s, he would often come into the Park Bar and throw his bag in the corner and enjoy a few pints.

'Later on in the night, we'd usually head back into town to the Sports Bar, it was where all the young crowd in Liverpool would go in those days. Other than that, you would head up to another place called the Beehive which, in the 1970s was, great, it was a Motown bar, the music was good in it, there would be a great buzz in there.'

However Noel admits it wasn't always just a barrel of laughs for the Irish fans threading over to Liverpool on a weekly basis back then. During the height of the Troubles in Northern Ireland in the 1970s, Liverpool fans from Dublin could often come into conflict with Protestant Liverpool fans from areas like the Shankill Road in Belfast.

'It would all kick off with a section of the lads from the North down by the pier in Liverpool early on Saturday mornings, that was a regular thing,' Noel says. 'You would get Dublin fans, not only of Liverpool but also Man Utd and Leeds, getting off the same boat in the morning and there would be lads from the Shankill waiting for us. The Dublin lads back then would stick together despite what team they actually followed. One week when we were changing our punts into sterling at a Woolworths in Liverpool, the trouble kicked off in a bad way, it was all over the newspapers later that day. Everywhere we went after that, people were asking what was the trouble between the lads from North and South, but that was just the way it was at the time.'

Although in his forty years travelling to Liverpool, Noel revealed that he has never witnessed any trouble between the Irish and the locals.

'I've honestly never had one single problem with a scouser in my entire life, even from those who support Everton. I suppose there is a strong connection between Ireland and Liverpool, due to the number of Irish who emigrated there over the decades. You could almost say it is an Irish city in a way, it's an Irish city with a scouse accent, that's it in a nutshell.'

Like many ardent Liverpool fans from the late 1960s and 1970s, Noel also has a great Bill Shankly tale to tell, after the iconic Reds' boss helped him into a derby game at Goodison Park.

It was March 1973 and Noel and a pal had made their weekly ferry trip to Liverpool in the vain hope that they might pick up a ticket for the crucial Merseyside derby.

'Because it was an away game, we just didn't have any tickets sorted but we took the chance of going over anyway,' Noel says. 'We got off the ferry at seven in the morning and headed straight for Anfield as we thought it might still be the best place to pick up a ticket. There was nobody at the ground when we arrived so we sat outside and actually fell asleep. After a while, we were woken up by none other than Bill Shankly himself, we couldn't believe it, we were just looking at each other saying, "It's Shankly". 'So he brought us into the ground, gave us a cup of tea and pulled out two match tickets. We had a good yap with him for half an hour before he sent us on our way chuffed to bits to have met him and also got tickets for the game. That was just Shankly all over. There was so much to admire about the man, he was just such an icon and an amazing character.'

Of course, it wasn't just in the main cities of Dublin and Belfast that Liverpool drew their Irish fans from; the club's popularity spread throughout the country.

Kieran Power, chairman of the Waterford branch of the Liverpool Supporters Club, recalls that, in the 1970s, Liverpool really were the team to support.

'Manchester Utd weren't having such a great time during the 1970s whereas Liverpool enjoyed lots of success and for many young lads growing up on the streets of Waterford, they became our team.'

Kieran's first opportunity to see the team play live in the flesh came at no less a place than Wembley in 1981, when the Reds defeated West Ham Utd 1–0 to win the season-opening Charity Shield.

When he made his first trip to Anfield seven years later, the Reds were again faced with West Ham and were already on the road to capturing yet another league title.

'It was nearing the end of the 1987–1988 season in which Liverpool had been absolutely phenomenal. John Barnes had just been signed that season and was running riot on the wing. The team was winning so many games that we all knew early on that the league would be ours. There were even scarves on sale around the ground and in the club shop proclaiming Liverpool as the 1988 league champions, that's how confident everyone was that the title was in the bag. The game against West Ham actually finished 0–0 but I was just hooked on the atmosphere from the Kop. It's never left me since and I've been there up to a hundred times since that first game.'

Being a Liverpool fan from Waterford, one player was always likely to stand out for Kieran during some of the great teams of the 1980s.

The Reds double-winning full-back from 1986 Jim Beglin hails from Waterford and gave Kieran and his pals an extra incentive to cheer on the Anfield men.

'There weren't too many Waterford lads playing at the top in England at the time so it was fantastic for us to see Jim in the Liverpool team and also doing so remarkably well,' Kieran says. 'Jim was a very consistent player, your typical sort of full-back who rarely made many mistakes and was obviously a big part in the team that won the league and FA Cup double in 1986.

'It was just such a shame that his career was pretty much ended just over a year later when he broke his leg as Jim would more than likely have been part of the Liverpool defence for up to a decade at least. But he still managed to play over a hundred games for Liverpool and is a worthy legend in my eyes.'

For Dubliner Gerry Farrell, the one player that stood out above all others when he travelled to Anfield as a young lad with his dad in the mid-1980s was Kenny Dalglish.

The Scottish international was a player of sublime skill and vision and is regarded now as the greatest ever player to don the red shirt. He is also remembered as one of the club's great managers after leading Liverpool to three league titles between 1985 and 1991.

'The first game I was ever at with my dad I was sitting in the Main Stand as Liverpool took on Ipswich in 1983,' Gerry says. 'The game finished in a draw but my one abiding memory from the night was watching Kenny Dalglish play, he was a massive hero for me then. We had been staying at the old Holiday Inn in the centre of Liverpool and the day after the match, I could hardly believe it when I saw Kenny Dalglish coming in to have his lunch there. He had no problem signing autographs and having a bit of a chat with us. It was great how accessible he was to the fans.'

Although Gerry admits there is one 'King Kenny' moment that he doesn't look back on all that fondly.

'There are always certain games that stand out for different reasons,' he says. I can remember the first match I went to see Liverpool play at Anfield after Kenny Dalglish had resigned as manager in 1991. We were playing QPR and we had tickets for the Anfield Road end, right beside the away QPR fans and they were singing at us, 'Where's your Kenny gone?'

'Kenny leaving was already a massive shock anyway but that just brought it home even more, it was like a death in the family.'

Dalglish's departure as Liverpool manager heralded in a period of uncertainty at the club, as the new man eventually brought in as his replacement, Graeme Souness, failed to spark a renewed upturn in the club's fortunes. Although a magnificent player and captain for Liverpool, Souness just didn't cut it as the club's manager, despite winning the FA Cup in first season in 1992.

But it was when the club hit this rocky patch in the early 1990s that well-known Irish Liverpool fan Ed Fitzsimons, chairman of the You'll Never Walk Alone Irish Reds Supporters Club, began to travel to Anfield more regularly.

'The club wasn't doing so well at that time, but I got tired of people writing them off and it was when I decided to start travelling more to games to give them my support,' Ed says. 'My first real interest in Liverpool was as a seven-year-old in the 1970s but I took more interest in listening to and watching their fans on the television as I did on the team itself. I was fascinated by the Kop and that continued with me right up to when I would travel over to support the teams in the 1990s.

'And it wasn't as if it was all bad back then. The right result against the right team would have Anfield in great voice and would make your week or month.'

For Ed, the one startling aspect of the city of Liverpool is how welcoming the locals are to Irish fans.

'I can even recall flying into Manchester airport on the way to a game at Anfield one weekend and I got talking to a scouse family who were just arriving back from their holidays. As soon as they heard I was going to the Liverpool game, they offered to put me up in their house even though I'd never even met them before. They say the Irish are a very welcoming race but I'm not sure you would even get that level of hospitality in Ireland.'

Gerry Farrell revealed that the friendships and bonds made in Liverpool have become just as a big a part of the Anfield experience as the football games themselves.

'As you start to grow up over the years of visiting Anfield, you grow out of wanting to chase after the players for pictures and autographs and start instead to embrace the city of Liverpool itself and its culture. The people in Liverpool are very welcoming and I've so many friends over there from all the years going to games. I think it is important that as Irish fans when we go over we should integrate as much as we can with the locals and show them respect.

'Unfortunately you do still see a lot of Irish Liverpool fans who treat the trip over as just an excuse to get drunk and not really get to know the city and its people. I'm proud of the fact that I have done that and have made many great friends for life. What I like about the local Liverpool fans is that they have seen and done it all supporting their team over the years – and they don't suffer fools gladly.'

Few Irish fans can claim to be as dedicated as ninety-six-year-old Maizie Flood, who has spent her entire life supporting the Reds and was even at full voice in the Kop in 2008 at the ripe old age of ninety-five.

Maizie, who counts Irish Kop legend John Aldridge as a friend, takes great pride in knowing the history and culture of the club while also keeping up to date with all the current players and what's happening around Anfield.

'The last game I made it to at Anfield was in 2008 when Liverpool beat Reading. I sat right in the Kop but the one thing that surprised me about some of the fans was that they didn't know the words to all of the songs. It is important to know all that, know about all the players and always remain in support of them no matter how the team is doing overall. What players need is confidence and if we can keep supporting them it makes it easier.'

That support is something which ex-Liverpool players say they have always received from Irish fans – even years after they have finished up playing for the club.

In October 2009, a Liverpool legends team, including ex-Irish international Phil Babb and 1980s stars Jan Molby and Ian Rush, came to Ireland to play in an exhibition match against Wicklow club Bray Wanderers at the Carlisle Grounds in Bray.

Even though it had been almost two decades since the height of their careers, players such as Rush were stunned to be mobbed by young Liverpool fans eager to get autographs and photos taken with their heroes.

Ex-Irish midfielder Ray Houghton says playing in front of the Liverpool fans was one of the deciding factors in signing for the club in 1987.

'It was just the thought of playing at Anfield in front of those fans who had seen their team do it all and wanting to give them even more special memories. Thankfully the Liverpool team I joined was one of the best and I'd like to think that we gave them those memories as they are great fans who deserved to see the team succeed.'

Of all the Liverpool success stories down through the years, few could match the unbelievable 2005 European Champions League final in Istanbul, when a Reds team that looked dead and buried at 3–0 down at half-time to AC Milan came back to win the trophy on penalties.

Waterford fan Kieran Power was in Turkey for every bit of the action and still finds it hard to believe it was real.

'The first thing that struck me was that the Ataturk stadium where the final was held was out in the middle of nowhere with almost nothing surrounding it, it may as well have been on the moon. That alone made it a surreal experience.

'Of course when the game itself kicked off, Milan scored almost straight away and took Liverpool apart in the first half to build up the 3–0 lead. All I was thinking for the second half was that we could score one goal, just even so we could a celebrate our team scoring a goal in the Champions League final. We all know now that they went much better than that by coming back to win and the feeling of elation was like we had just won the lottery.

'It's moments and finals like that which make it all worthwhile supporting a club like Liverpool. Okay we might not have won the league for far too long now but the team has still given us so much joy in various cup finals that the highs of being a Liverpool fan most definitely outweigh the lows.'

Remarkably, just a year after that incredible 3–3 Champions League final, Liverpool shared another six-goal thriller with West Ham in the FA Cup final.

Despite having a ticket for that epic game at Cardiff, Dubliner Ed Fitzsimons decided it would be more worthy to give it to someone else to enjoy the cup final experience.

'I brought my daughter over to that 2006 FA Cup final,' Ed says. 'Instead of going to the game, I actually gave her my ticket, which I couldn't even belief I did myself, as it meant I had to watch the game outside the Cardiff stadium on a big screen in a marquee. But it was very special for me to be able to do that for her as in years to come she will be able to look back at that game and say that she was there.'

For all the great games and moments that Irish Reds' fans have enjoyed throughout the decades, few can boast to actually sharing the same pitch as a Liverpool team.

That all changed for a group of amateur footballers from West Cork in August 2009, when Liverpool agreed to send a team over for a pre-season friendly game against tiny Dunmanway Town.

Dunmanway became the envy of every amateur soccer club across the country when a Liverpool reserve side decked out as their opposition – and they had their own player David Hall – who, believe it or not, is actually a Man Utd fan – for putting in the cheeky request.

Well-travelled Belfast doctor David, who spent some years playing football in England, had become friends with former Liverpool full-back Gary Ablett, manager of the Liverpool reserve team from 2006 to 2009.

When David suggested to Ablett that he should bring his team to Dunmanway for a game, little did he expect that the Premier League giants would actually agree. To the astonishment of team manager John Buckely, an ardent Liverpool fan, a letter from the club duly arrived in Cork in June 2009 stating that they were prepared to send a team over for a clash with a club who would normally boast no more than a handful of fans at their West Cork Premier Division games.

Even a change of reserve boss at Liverpool in the summer of 2009 couldn't scupper Dunmanway's dream game, as David explained. 'Originally as it was Gary Ablett who I spoke to about the reserve team coming over we got a bit nervous when he got sacked from that role. But thankfully when Liverpool appointed their new reserve manager John McMahon, who I also happen to know very well, he knew of our wish for a game and agreed to bring his team.'

Although David and his club soon found out just what it entailed to a host a megastar club like Liverpool in their own back-yard.

Firstly, Dunmanway had to move the game from their home pitch to a more suitable ground at Maria Immaculata Community College in Dunmanway, where they initially had expected to attract up to 3,000 fans.

However as news of the game spread outside of Cork, Dunmanway soon had to rethink their plans and with the help of the FAI, who issued a licence for the game, they installed temporary seating to accommodate 6,800 supporters.

The game was even attracting interest on Merseyside with over 200 Reds fans on that side of the water also seeking out tickets for the David v. Goliath clash.

David said, 'It soon became clear to us that staging the game was going to be a much bigger effort than we first thought and that it was going to cost a fortune. The stadium alone cost €150,000 and because of that we had to double the price of the tickets from €20 to €40, but all the locals fully understood this.'

With seven big Liverpool fans playing in the Dunmanway team, David Hall had naturally become the toast of the club for pulling off such a coup and his profile around the town as a whole had skyrocketed.

'I had so much attention on me in Dunmanway in the days leading up to the game this it was difficult to get anything done,' he said. 'There was obviously so much excitement at such a big club coming to our small town but it was amazing how much the whole community got behind the spirit of it; the entire town was decked out in the two team's colours.'

The Liverpool side that took to the pitch against Dunmanway was absent of any of its top stars such as Steven Gerrard but did still contain the promising reserve talents of Spanish forward Daniel Pacheco and Hungarian Christian Nemeth.

Despite falling a goal behind to a stunning Pacheco free kick after just ten minutes, Dunmanway more than held their own after that with the scoreline finishing a respectable 1–0.

'We could have even scored a few goals ourselves,' David says. 'One of our guys Stephen Donovan is a diehard Liverpool fan and he will be having nightmares for the rest of his life at a couple of great chances he missed to score against the club he loves.'

However, David said the experience of competing against Liverpool will live long in the memory. 'What stands out above everything else about the day was how Liverpool treated us with the utmost of professionalism. They took the game and everything surrounding it very seriously, as if we were their equals. They certainly weren't feeling sorry for us in any way or looked down on us.'

18

Hillsborough Horror: An Irish View

Saturday, 15 April 1989 is a date which sticks in the memory for more than one reason.

It was a particularly sunny day, not necessarily a scorcher but in the middle of April in Ireland a bright day was good enough for everyone.

The day had an added bit of interest for me as it was the Saturday my parents were taking me to all the fancy shops in the centre of Dublin to pick out my clobber for my upcoming confirmation.

The best thing about the day, though, was that my beloved Liverpool were getting set for an FA Cup semi-final clash with Brian Clough's Nottingham Forest. The game, taking place at Sheffield Wednesday's Hillsborough ground, was even being screened live on RTÉ so, with a bit of luck and a bit of harassment of my mother on my part, we'd have my confirmation gear bought well in time to make it back for the start of the match at three o'clock.

It was always going to be a tight call, though, as town was a good forty-minute journey away from our house in Shankill 12 miles south of Dublin city centre, and that was without taking into account waiting around for the DART train to arrive.

My sister came along for the jaunt into town and, after a few hours in and out of clothes, shirt and shoe shops, we managed to get me a black pair of chinos (all the rage in the late 1980s), smart white shirt, black suede shoes and a pseudo-leather jacket – well, we couldn't exactly afford the real thing but it looked good anyway.

I was sure I was going to look the business but to be honest as the day kept creeping closer to 3 p.m., I had more important things on my mind.

A quick stop off for a bite to eat in a café felt like forever and, despite my best efforts, it was after 2.30 p.m. as we headed for the train station to get the DART back out of town.

Reluctantly, I had to accept that I would miss the start of the match but, given that Forest versus Liverpool was always likely to be a tight game (the two teams had met in the semi-final the previous year which Liverpool won 2–1), the last hour of the clash would be the most interesting part of it anyway.

Even so, I can hardly recall another DART journey out of town that took as long it did that day. When it eventually hit Shankill, I was fit to sprint all the way home.

The game would have been little over twenty minutes old by that stage, leaving me with a fairly satisfactory seventy minutes to cheer on a Reds team containing plenty of my Irish heroes such as captain Ronnie Whelan, midfielder Ray Houghton, striker John Aldridge and young full-back Steve Staunton.

Little did I know then that the game had long since been halted.

The first signs that anything was wrong was on the walk back from the train station, when I spotted a young pal of mine who was possibly the biggest Liverpool fanatic I knew at the time out kicking a ball on the street.

Why wasn't he glued to the telly cheering on the Reds?

He told us the game had been cancelled after some Liverpool fans were crushed behind one of the goals.

It sounded serious enough although, even then, I hadn't fully comprehended that many Liverpool fans had at that stage already lost their lives in what was developing into English football's worst tragedy.

It wasn't until I finally got home and switched on the television that the harrowing images of fans crushed up against a terrace fence and later bodies strewn across the Hillsborough pitch began to hit home.

All the excitement that had been building up in me drained away like the colour in Liverpool manager Kenny Dalglish's face as the television pictures showed him watching in horror at the ensuing pandemonium.

As a pre-teen, I was still finding it somewhat difficult to compute the full enormity of the disaster unfolding at Hillsborough. Yet just over twenty years on from that dreadful day, the ninety-six Liverpool fans who lost their lives at Hillsborough, many of them almost as young as I was at that time, are even more in my thoughts now than they were back then.

Nevertheless that sunny day, trip into town and the horrific images of crushing on television have all been encapsulated into one defining memory of 15 April 1989, a day when, for once, football meant very little to this devout Liverpool fan.

It's a day which will also be forever etched in the mind of retired Dublin businessman James Bowen.

Just as it had for me and all Liverpool fans that morning, James' day started with a fair bit of excitement after his friend Tony Moloney had managed to nab a couple of tickets for the pair to go the semi-final game at Hillsborough.

James was thrilled, even more so as his two young sons, twelve-year-old Andrew and ten-year-old Simon were Liverpool fanatics, and had all the team posters and pictures all over the walls of their bedroom.

For the two lads, the knowledge their dad was heading over to the game made it even more special as they later sat down to watch it on the telly like thousands of other Liverpool fans dotted all over Ireland.

For James and Tony, the only snag that morning hit them at Dublin airport when their flight to Sheffield suffered a minor delay but they still managed to make it to Hillsborough with a good hour to spare before the game kicked off.

'It was a perfect day,' James recalls. 'The sun was shining, everybody was in the great spirits and the atmosphere outside the ground with half an hour to kick-off was electric. I can remember that as we headed towards the ground, Tony went off to buy something and I said I would wait for him close to the turnstiles from where we had to go in.

'Tony couldn't have been gone more than ten minutes but, in that time, the atmosphere began to change outside the ground as the game neared closer to kick-off time.

'There appeared to be quite a bit of confusion building up as the fans, trying to get into the Leppings Lane terrace end of the ground, weren't getting through the gates or turnstiles quickly enough. The only thing going through my mind at the time was that I thought they would have been able to solve such a problem without much hassle in a big ground like Hillsborough.'

Unbeknownst to James, however, this 'problem' he was witnessing at the Leppings Lane end would quickly turn into a deadly crush after a series of fatal errors by the police and ground authorities.

Firstly, with about eight minutes to kick-off the police ordered that a main exit gate at Leppings Lane be opened in a bid to alleviate the growing crush of fans still outside the ground trying to get in.

By the time they had opened this gate, the two middle pens of the Leppings Lane, which were numbered three and four and should have had a maximum capacity of just 1,600 people, already had over 2,000 Liverpool fans herded in for the game.

When the exit gate was opened, a further 5,000 fans rushed in, but there had been a failure to close off these middle pens and the Liverpool fans streaming in from the outside automatically rushed towards the central area leaving the 'outer' pens one, two and five, almost completely empty.

Meanwhile as his friend Tony arrived back, James gave the ensuing chaos building up outside the Leppings Lane gates little thought, as they headed off through their own turnstiles to the South Stand, which was to the right of the Leppings Lane terrace.

'We were almost right down by the touchline and had a perfect view of the pitch,' James recalls. 'Everything seemed as if it was ready for a great game as the two teams arrived out but with about five minutes to kick-off both myself and Tony were looking over at the Leppings Lane and you could see even then that things didn't appear quite right.'

Even so, James remembers that the game kicked off like a 'rocket' as the two sets of fans got ready to really cheer their team on.

'But things were seriously deteriorating by the second in that terrace, you could see that there was a massive surge and people were getting crushed up by the barriers. Even as the game was going on we knew that we were about to witness a great tragedy.'

The surge which James had witnessed happened after a crush barrier in the Leppings Lane gave way and fans began to fall on top of each other, exacerbating the stifling crush.

Those at the front who couldn't escape were having the life sucked out of them.

Out on the field, twenty-year-old Irish full-back Steve Staunton could hear the screams of the fans and goalkeeper Bruce Grobbelaar was also quickly realising that the supporters behind his goal were in real trouble.

Farther up field, Irish midfielder Ray Houghton was engrossed in the game and was at first startled to see a Liverpool fan run across the pitch with little over five minutes gone.

'I can remember centre-half Alan Hansen shouting at the fan to get off the pitch, that he would end up getting the club in trouble. But the fan was shouting back at us that there were people being crushed on the terrace, that was the first time that we as players knew something wasn't right.'

As more distraught Liverpool fans began to stream on to the pitch, match referee called a halt to proceedings and ordered the players of both teams back into their dressing rooms.

As the players trudged off the Hillsborough pitch, it became more and more apparent that a deadly crush was taking place in the Leppings Lane.

However, back in the dressing rooms, both teams were told to keep ready as the game was still likely to be restarted. 'We had no idea of the real magnitude of the situation at the time,' Ray Houghton said.

Although it soon became more apparent to captain Ronnie Whelan and his team-mates when fans with tears in their eyes came streaming past the dressing rooms shouting that people were dying.

For James Bowen, what he was witnessing from his vantage point on the South Stand was not just an unimaginable tragedy but also a serious injustice. 'You could see that fans were doing their best to either get over the barriers and onto the pitch or get lifted up into the stand above the terrace. It was obvious it was a crush but the police thought they were dealing with a riot when you could clearly see with your own eyes that it was a crush.

'All around people were passing out or being laid out onto the pitch, there were bodies piling up everywhere. I will never, for the rest of my life, forget seeing the bodies of two beautiful young teenage girls being laid on the grass in front of me.

'All we wanted to do was get out there and help somehow, but the police were seeing to it that that wouldn't happen.'

Whilst James and all the other stunned Liverpool fans around him expected to see ambulances and medics stream out onto the pitch, instead all they saw was a heavy cordon of police.

'They were just facing us with their backs turned to the chaos behind them. There must have been at least a hundred of them and all they were interested in doing was making sure that nobody from our end of the ground could get out on the pitch, even though all we wanted to do was help.'

Even as it became more apparent that a tragedy of epic proportions was unfolding, the authorities' response to the disaster was slow and badly co-ordinated.

Fire fighters with cutting gear had difficulty getting into the ground, and although dozens of ambulances lined up outside Hillsborough, access to the pitch was delayed because police were reporting what they described as 'crowd trouble'.

With little or no medical assistance, desperate fans were left to try CPR on their stricken friends and family members whilst others were forced to use the pitch side advertising hoardings as makeshift stretchers as they tried to get the injured out of the ground and to hospital.

Back in the dressing room, the Liverpool players soon realised that a serious situation with the fans was unfolding outside.

The game was officially called off at 4 p.m., by which time significant number of Liverpool fans had already perished.

In an interview with the *Irish Daily Star Sunday* sport's reporter Cathal Dervan in April 2009, Captain Ronnie Whelan remembers Kenny Dalglish leaving the dressing room to find out exactly what was happening out on the terrace.

'When he came back he didn't look the best and, before long, we knew that a major disaster was unfolding,' Whelan said. 'We only got the full picture when we went upstairs after the game was abandoned. Our wives and families were in the players' lounge and they were in bits. There were pictures on the television of the bodies lying on the advertising hoardings on the pitch.'

It was well after four o'clock by the time Dublin fans James Bowen and Tony Moroney got out of the ground, totally dazed and completely bewildered at the scenes that had just gone on before their eyes.

Mindful of the fact that his wife Mary and two sons were watching the game on television back in Ireland, James quickly tried to find a public phone box so that he could call and put their minds at ease.

'But, naturally, with everything that was happening every single phone box within the vicinity of the ground had queues of people lining up to use them, we couldn't find a free one anywhere. I can't recall for how long or how far we walked from the ground but eventually we got a taxi back into the main centre of Sheffield and it must have been close to 6.30 p.m. by the time I got to ring and you could imagine the relief from my family when they finally knew that I was safe.'

It was after 10 p.m. that evening when James and Tony arrived back into Dublin airport when a team of media and journalists were waiting to get reaction from Irish survivors of Hillsborough.

And James said he was surprised by the attitude still prevailing about the day's tragic events.

'There still seemed to be this belief amongst even the Irish what had happened earlier that day at Hillsborough was some sort of a riot. I know football in the 1980s had a bad reputation for trouble, but I had to try my best to insist to everyone that what happened was a crush and the worst effects of it could have been avoided had the police acted completely differently than the way they did.'

Back on Merseyside, the pain was really beginning to sink in.

The number of dead had reached ninety-four on the day of the disaster, later increasing to ninety-six, all innocent fans who had done little more than go to a game of football to cheer on their favourite team.

In the days and weeks after the tragedy, the Liverpool players and officials attended one funeral after another and the grief appeared to become harder to bear for some.

For Ronnie Whelan there was the pain of attending the funeral of eighteen-year-old Ian Whelan, an avid Liverpool fan whose nickname was 'Ronnie' as the Irishman was his favourite player.

But few were hit quite as hard as John Aldridge, a born and bred scouser who, if he hadn't have been playing for Liverpool at Hillsborough that day, was sure he would have been in the Leppings Lane terrace with all the other Reds' fans.

Less than a week after Hillsborough, an emotional Aldridge had announced in a newspaper interview that he didn't care if he never played professional football again. The comments were picked in both the national and international media as Aldridge's retirement warning caused a bit of a stir on this side of the Irish sea.

Just eleven days after the Hillsborough disaster, the Republic of Ireland football team were set to play a crucial World Cup qualifier against Spain at Lansdowne Road.

The four Irish players at Liverpool – Staunton, Whelan, Houghton and Aldridge – were called up to the Republic of Ireland squad for the game by national manager Jack Charlton.

All but Aldridge decided to make the trip to Dublin.

Aldo's absence from the Irish squad and his previous threat to quit the game came under closer scrutiny after a bizarre rant by Spain's manager Luis Suarez.

Arriving in Dublin ahead of the Lansdowne Road encounter, the Spanish boss said nothing would be achieved by Aldridge retiring.

'Aldridge has let his country down,' Suarez fumed. 'This decision is one I cannot accept as an international team manager. Aldridge's attitude won't get anyone anywhere. I can understand him being upset, but you don't solve anything by not playing football.'

However Suarez's uncaring approach was criticised by Aldo's international team-mates.

Defender Kevin Moran, at the time playing his trade in Spain with Sporting Gijon, said everybody in the Irish camp fully understood Aldridge's emotion.

'If Mr Suarez fully understood the depth of feeling that the

Hillsborough tragedy has provoked he might not have made those comments,' Moran said.

Despite their grief, Staunton, Houghton and Whelan all featured prominently in the Ireland team for the Spanish clash with the Boys in Green pulling off a famous 1–0 win, a result that went a long way to helping Ireland qualify, alongside Spain, for a first appearance at World Cup finals a year later.

Back in England, Liverpool were also soon forced back into action with an emotional league encounter against Everton on 3 May.

The eventual ending to the 1988–1989 season turned out to be one of the most riveting in the club's history, as the brave Liverpool side overcame the horror of Hillsborough by winning the FA Cup 3–2 after extra time against Everton but sadly lost the league title a week later to a last-minute Michael Thomas goal for Arsenal at Anfield.

Off the pitch, the families of those fans lost at Hillsborough were engaged in a battle for the truth behind the tragedy, a battle which, to this day, they are still unfortunately locked in.

In the initial aftermath, British Lord Justice Peter Taylor was appointed to conduct an inquiry into the tragedy which the families hoped might pinpoint the reasons and the mistakes made which lead to the deaths of their loved ones.

In his interim report on 4 August 1989, Lord Justice Taylor wrote that the key element of police control at fault was the failure to close off the tunnel at Leppings Lane which lead to the central pens where the crush subsequently happened. Taylor went on to criticise police for their failure to handle the build-up of fans outside the ground properly, and their slow reaction to the unfolding disaster.

Some of his strongest words were reserved for the police commander, Chief Superintendent David Duckenfield, for 'failing to take effective control', and South Yorkshire police, who attempted to blame supporters for the crush. Despite the Taylor report, which was also critical of Sheffield Wednesday Football Club and Sheffield City Council, on 14 August 1990, the Director of Public Prosecutions in Britain decided not to bring criminal charges against any individual, group or body on the grounds of insufficient evidence.

Inquests into the deaths of the victims returned a majority verdict of accidental death, but many families did not accept this and began to campaign for a fresh inquiry.

Despite the massive clamour for fresh investigations into the Hillsborough tragedy, Dublin fan James Bowen said he was never once questioned by anyone in authority about what he witnessed that day.

'I rang the British embassy here in Ireland and also got on the Home Secretary's office in the UK and said that I was more than prepared to act as a witness in any investigation into Hillsborough. However I never got a single call back from anybody and have never approached to give my account of what happened on that day.'

Seven years after Hillsborough, and only through a concerted public campaign by the families, British Home Secretary Jack Straw ordered a 'scrutiny of evidence' in 1996.

Lord Justice Stuart-Smith was appointed to review new evidence which had not been submitted to the inquiry or inquests and also dozens of police and witness statements, apparently critical of police, which had been altered.

Lord Justice Stuart-Smith's conclusion was that the fresh evidence did not add anything significant to the understanding of the disaster, and that while statements should not have been edited, this was simply an 'error of judgement'.

Jack Straw accepted the findings and ruled out a new inquiry, but, in August 1998, the Hillsborough Family Support group brought charges of manslaughter against David Duckenfield and his deputy, Superintendent Bernard Murray, in a private prosecution.

The case came to trial in 2000. After six weeks, the jury found Mr Murray not guilty of manslaughter, and said it could not reach a verdict on Mr Duckenfield.

The judge, Mr Justice Hooper, ruled out a majority verdict and refused a retrial on the grounds that Mr Duckenfield had faced public humiliation and a fair trial would be impossible.

Throughout all of this, the families have continued their quest for justice and, just four days after a highly charged and emotional twentieth anniversary commemoration at Anfield on 15 April 2009, the British

Home Secretary Jacqui Smith ordered that secret files on the Hillsborough disaster be made public.

The Bishop of Liverpool, the Right Reverend James Jones, has been appointed chairman of a five-person panel which will oversee the release of these files over the next two years.

Bishop Jones says he is well aware of the public anguish over Hillsborough. 'The wound is very deep still and longing to be healed. This will be very poignant for many families and will require sensitivity as families will be seeing documents that will make them relive those moments.'

Even with the passing of time, the pain hasn't eased for the players who witnessed Hillsborough.

'The thing is that every year there is another anniversary and it just brings all those painful memories flooding back,' Ray Houghton says. 'But what I do also recall is just how much the tragedy brought the city of Liverpool together. The way both the Liverpool and Everton fans reacted to Hillsborough was amazing and I will always have a strong affinity for the club and the city after what happened that day.'

However, Houghton fears the families may never get the proper justice they are still desperately seeking. 'I don't think we will ever see the day when either the police or the authorities in the ground that day will hold their hands up and say the tragedy was their fault. Whether that's out of a fear of being sued or that they cannot accept the truth, I'm not sure. But it is unlikely that there will ever be full closure in this.'

In his interview with the *Irish Daily Star Sunday*, Ronnie Whelan said he is also unsure the families of the victims will ever see proper justice served. 'They'll probably never see justice. It's been pushed under the carpet. I doubt they ever will and that's why there is still a lot of anger and hurt in Liverpool. The families do feel that somebody should be held accountable.'

For fan James Bowen, the real tragedy of Hillsborough was that so much of it could have been avoided.

'There is absolutely no doubt in my mind that the orders given to the police officers that day caused most of that tragedy,' James said. 'Had they even given themselves the chance to think that what was happening was a crush and not a riot a lot of lives could have been saved. That they weren't was definitely down to the police and there are certain individuals out there who should have served prison sentences for what happened at Hillsborough that day.'

The ninety-six victims of the Hillsborough Tragedy, 15 April 1989

John Alfred Anderson (62)
Colin Mark Ashcroft (19)
James Gary Aspinall (18)
Kester Roger Marcus Ball (16)
Gerard Bernard Patrick Baron (67)
Simon Bell (17)
Barry Sidney Bennett (26)
David John Benson (22)
David William Birtle (22)
Tony Bland (22)
Paul David Brady (21)
Andrew Mark Brookes (26)
Carl Brown (18)
David Steven Brown (25)
Henry Thomas Burke (47)
Peter Andrew Burkett (24)
Paul William Carlile (19)
Raymond Thomas Chapman (50)
Gary Christopher Church (19)
Joseph Clark (29)
Paul Clark (18)
Gary Collins (22)
Stephen Paul Copoc (20)
Tracey Elizabeth Cox (23)
James Philip Delaney (19)
Christopher Barry Devonside (18)
Christopher Edwards (29)
Vincent Michael Fitzsimmons (34)
Thomas Steven Fox (21)
Jon-Paul Gilhooley (10)
Barry Glover (27)

Ian Thomas Glover (20)
Derrick George Godwin (24)
Roy Harry Hamilton (34)
Philip Hammond (14)
Eric Hankin (33)
Gary Harrison (27)
Stephen Francis Harrison (31)
Peter Andrew Harrison (15)
David Hawley (39)
James Robert Hennessy (29)
Paul Anthony Hewitson (26)
Carl Darren Hewitt (17)
Nicholas Michael Hewitt (16)
Sarah Louise Hicks (19)
Victoria Jane Hicks (15)
Gordon Rodney Horn (20)
Arthur Horrocks (41)
Thomas Howard (39)
Thomas Anthony Howard (14)
Eric George Hughes (42)
Alan Johnston (29)
Christine Anne Jones (27)
Gary Philip Jones (18)
Richard Jones (25)
Nicholas Peter Joynes (27)
Anthony Peter Kelly (29)
Michael David Kelly (38)
Carl David Lewis (18)
David William Mather (19)
Brian Christopher Mathews (38)
Francis Joseph McAllister (27)
John McBrien (18)
Marion Hazel McCabe (21)

Joseph Daniel McCarthy (21)
Peter McDonnell (21)
Alan McGlone (28)
Keith McGrath (17)
Paul Brian Murray (14)
Lee Nicol (14)
Stephen Francis O'Neill (17)
Jonathon Owens (18)
William Roy Pemberton (23)
Carl William Rimmer (21)
David George Rimmer (38)
Graham John Roberts (24)
Steven Joseph Robinson (17)
Henry Charles Rogers (17)
Colin Andrew Hugh William Sefton (23)
Inger Shah (38)
Paula Ann Smith (26)
Adam Edward Spearritt (14)
Philip John Steele (15)
David Leonard Thomas (23)
Patrik John Thompson (35)
Peter Reuben Thompson (30)
Stuart Paul William Thompson (17)
Peter Francis Tootle (21)
Christopher James Traynor (26)
Martin Kevin Traynor (16)
Kevin Tyrrell (15)
Colin Wafer (19)
Ian David Whelan (19)
Martin Kenneth Wild (29)
Kevin Daniel Williams (15)
Graham John Wright (17)

19

Anfield: A Home from Home

For the many thousands of fans who make an almost weekly trek across the Irish Sea to cheer on their heroes in Red, Anfield has become like a second home. The songs, the banter and the games around Anfield Road have become just as vital a part to life for Irish Reds as food and oxygen.

Anfield is a truly unique experience, a ground so central to the great history of Liverpool Football Club, yet possessing an aura and intimate history all of its own. It can evoke memories of glory, heartache, passion and pride and is one of the most popular places of worship for Irish people outside of Ireland.

For one special night that very same Anfield became the home of thousands of non-Liverpool fans, not there to cheer on the men in red shirts, but they still cheered and sang in the spirit of the famous ground.

Fans of Manchester Utd, Arsenal, Celtic and even Everton threw away their allegiances on an emotional night when rousing renditions of 'You'll Never Walk Alone' rang out across the famous old stadium like they had done on hundreds of previous occasions. Yet never before had it been sung by so many at Anfield with so few scouse accents.

The date was 13 December 1995, and about 25,000 green-clad Irish fans had crammed into Anfield to cheer on their national team in a vital Euro 1996 play-off qualifier with the Netherlands.

With England set to host the European Championships in 1996, Liverpool's ground had been earmarked for the prestigious play-off which would provide the final qualifying spot for the sixteen-team tournament.

If truth be told, both the Irish and Dutch sides would have hoped to have avoided coming anywhere near Anfield for that December clash – as all it did was highlight the two country's failure to have already qualified for the tournament outright through their qualifying groups.

However, as Europe's two worst-placed runners-up from the group stage, Jack Charlton's Republic of Ireland and Guus Hiddink's Netherlands side had no choice but to clash with each other in the play-off at Anfield.

Whilst neither national manager would have been rubbing his hands with glee at the prospect of the game, officials around Anfield were chuffed that two such well-supported teams had been paired together for the high-profile clash.

Ireland and Holland had crossed swords at three of the previous four major international tournaments and the colourful sets of fans from both countries were set to make the match a pre-Christmas carnival on Merseyside.

Even before a ball had been kicked, the clash was being billed as a home game for the Irish. Thousands upon thousands of fans were expected to clamber aboard boats and planes in Dublin for the short trek to Liverpool and whilst the Dutch would also be well supported, the green of Ireland was still predicted to outnumber the orange of Netherlands by at least two to one in the stands.

Three of Jack Charlton's Irish squad – Phil Babb, Jason McAteer and Mark Kennedy – were Liverpool players who had made Anfield their home base on a weekly basis.

Charlton himself recognised the advantage of the game being played at Anfield.

Prior to the clash with a talented Dutch side made up mainly of Ajax

Amsterdam players, who were the reigning European Cup champions at the time, Charlton admitted Anfield was more likely to suit his players.

'I don't think the Dutch will be too pleased about having to play there as it will be almost a home game for our lads,' Charlton said. 'I'm glad the game isn't at another stadium such as Wembley. The Dutch have always viewed Wembley as a big-game venue and I think if it was being played there it would pump them up even more.'

As expected on the day of the game, Irish fans took up almost three quarters of the stadium and were in great voice as they got set to roar their team on, even though they were battling against the odds against a Dutch side hotly tipped to win the play-off.

Nevertheless the noise from the Irish fans was little short of deafening as kick-off time approached and veteran stadium announcer George Sephton, known as the 'voice of Anfield', said he could hardly recall an atmosphere like it in all his years working at the ground.

'It was exciting to know that Anfield was going to be hosting that Euro 1996 play-off and when it was confirmed that it would be between Ireland and Holland that just made the whole thing even better as they were two of the best and most passionate sets of supporters across Europe. And they were all certainly in great voice that night, Anfield was literally shaking. It was tremendous and there was absolutely no animosity between the Irish and the Dutch, we knew we weren't going to get any trouble at the ground that night.'

The only trouble the Irish did find themselves in was out on the pitch, where they were finding it difficult to match a classy Dutch side blessed with the talents of Edgar Davids, Clarence Seedorf, Denis Bergkamp and Patrick Kluivert.

In comparison to the young Dutch side, Ireland was an old team in reversal who had struggled through the latter part of their group, losing twice to an Austrian side they would have beaten easily a couple of years earlier.

Charlton was still relying on legendary players John Aldridge, Tony Cascarino, Andy Townsend and Paul McGrath, along with a flurry of fullbacks, but they were simply no match for the Dutch masters who passed them off the pitch.

The Dutch dominated possession for most of the night and were 1–0 up at half-time courtesy of a clinical strike from their teenage forward Patrick Kluivert.

Despite the fact their team was clearly behind on the pitch, the Irish in the stands around Anfield kept up the atmosphere, as George Sephton testifies.

'The Irish just kept on singing, it didn't matter that they were being beaten at the time,' he said.

And the Anfield announcer played his own role in keeping the signing ticking over during the half-time break by playing one of the Irish fans' favourite tunes over the tannoy.

'Somebody had passed me on a copy of the 'Fields of Athenry' and asked me if I would play it at Anfield for that Irish game,' George says. 'I was glad to do it and of course that went down exceptionally well with the Irish fans. However, for some reason, English fans at the game that night took it up as an Irish rebel song and were not too happy that it got played over the sound system at Anfield. I got a few letters of complaint about it. But the funny thing is that the song has since been taken up by Liverpool fans as the 'Field of Anfield Road' and as everyone knows that is now one of the most popular songs sung at Liverpool games these days.'

Although the singing continued well into the second half, the game didn't get much better for the Irish as Patrick Kluivert added a second for the Dutch late on to seal the Boys in Green's fate.

Afterwards, Jack Charlton admitted there had been no shame in losing to a Dutch side who played a passing game Bill Shankly would have been extremely proud of.

Whether he knew it at the time, the Dutch defeat at Anfield would also be Charlton's last match in charge of the Irish team after nine colourful years during which the country qualified for three major tournaments for the first time in its history.

Such was the emotion involved in the game that Charlton was forced to walk back out onto the Anfield pitch well after the game had finished as not one Irish fan had left the ground until they sang a proper farewell to Big Jack.

With tears in his eyes, Charlton stood in the centre of the pitch as the

Irish fans roared their hearts one last time for the popular Geordie who had put the Irish football team on the world map.

Former chief executive of the Football Association of Ireland (FAI), Bernard O'Byrne, admitted it was one of the most emotional nights he had ever been involved in with Irish football. Bernard, a keen Liverpool fan and regular visitor to Anfield, added that it was also the noisiest night he had ever experienced at the famous old ground.

'I'm sure there have been Liverpool games down through the years where the noise and excitement was every bit as good as that but I obviously just wasn't there for them,' Bernard says. 'It was just the sustained level of the support that night was phenomenal, the fans just never stopped singing from the first minute to the last. I think the Irish fans really knew our team was up against it and it spurred them on to get behind them even more but that Dutch side just proved to be far too good.'

Former Liverpool player Ray Houghton was an unused substitute for the Irish team that night and said he was also bowled over by the passion of the fans for the Anfield clash.

'It was obvious with Liverpool being so close to Ireland that thousands of our fans would make their way over on planes and boats and Anfield really did become our home ground of the night. Unfortunately for myself I wasn't picked by Jack to start the match against Holland and I watched it all from the bench. The atmosphere was brilliant as the Irish fans really got behind the team as always, but in all fairness the Dutch were the much better team and made us look like a very old side on the night.

'It was a sad way for it to end for Jack but at the same time he got a fitting send off from the fans and I can't think of a better ground that could have happened in England than Anfield.'

Following the Anfield play-off, it was suggested in certain sections of the media that Liverpool's ground could even have been used for Ireland home matches. Both the FAI and the Irish Rugby Football Association (IRFU) were keen to have the dilapidated old Lansdowne Road redeveloped, but Irish football desperately needed to find an alternative ground before this could happen.

The temporary move out of Lansdowne Road, which reopened in August 2010 as the new Aviva Stadium, only became possible after the

Gaelic Athletic Association (GAA) relaxed its rules to allow the other sports stage games at its 80,000-capacity Croke Park. However had Croke Park not become available, then Anfield may very well have been one of the only other alternatives for the FAI.

'I would have had mixed thoughts about that,' says Ray Houghton. 'Naturally I have an affinity for Anfield having played there in a great Liverpool side but I think it would always have been important for Ireland to play their games on home soil. I know the fans would always be loyal but I think it would have been asking too much of them to travel to Anfield for home games. It was much better that things worked out and Croke Park became available so that our home matches would remain in Dublin.'

TIMELINE

April 1892 — County Monaghan man John McKenna is appointed secretary of the newly established Liverpool Association Football Club.

October 1894 — County Down forward David Hannah becomes the first ever Irish-born player to sign for Liverpool FC.

May 1896 — Derry-born goalkeeper William Donaghy makes six appearances for Liverpool after signing from Scottish club Clyde.

February 1912 — County Wexford winger Bill Lacey moves to Liverpool from local Merseyside rivals Everton.

September 1912 — Belfast-born Elisha Scott begins his twenty-two-year tenure as a Liverpool goalkeeper.

May 1923 — Centre-back Billy McDevitt makes the move to Liverpool from his local club Belfast Utd.

October 1925 — Another Belfast boy David McMullan graces Anfield when he is signed from Distillery.

January 1928 — Forward Billy Millar, from Ballymena, becomes the latest Irish recruit at Liverpool after signing from Linfield.

August 1933 — Coleraine-born striker Sam English is signed up by Liverpool from Glasgow Rangers.

March 1937 — Defender William Hood swaps Cliftonville for a year-long stint at Liverpool.

December 1952 — Belfast-born striker Sammy Smyth joins Liverpool from Stoke City.

August 1970 — Dublin-born winger Steve Heighway makes his Liverpool debut against West Brom.

February 1981 — Left midfielder, and future Republic of Ireland international, Kevin Sheedy makes his Reds debut.

TIMELINE **221**

April 1981	Nineteen-year-old Dubliner Ronnie Whelan scores on his Liverpool debut in a 3–0 win over Stoke at Anfield.
August 1981	Irish international defender Mark Lawrenson is signed from Brighton for £900,000.
May 1983	Republic of Ireland forward Michael Robinson is signed from Brighton.
May 1983	County Waterford man Jim Beglin is iconic manager Bob Paisley's last signing for Liverpool in a £20,000 deal with Shamrock Rovers.
October 1986	Dublin-born defender Brian Mooney makes his one and only appearance for Liverpool in a League Cup clash with Fulham.
January 1987	Super striker John Aldridge is bought from Oxford Utd to replace Ian Rush.
October 1987	Irish international midfielder Ray Houghton is signed from Oxford Utd.
September 1988	Drogheda-born Steve Staunton makes his debut in a 1–1 draw with Tottenham.
September 1994	Irish international defender Phil Babb becomes the most expensive defender in English football after a £3.6 million move from Coventry to Liverpool.
March 1995	Dublin-born winger Mark Kennedy makes the switch from Millwall to Liverpool in a £1.5 million deal.
September 1995	Jason McAteer makes his Liverpool debut in a 3–0 win over Blackburn following his £4.5 million move from Bolton.
November 2000	Flying Dublin-born winger Richie Partridge stars for Liverpool in an 8–0 win over Stoke City in the League Cup.
July 2003	Limerick-born full-back Steve Finnan joins Liverpool in a £3.5 million move from London club Fulham.

August 2004 Liverpool-born Irish international midfielder Darren Potter plays his first game for the Reds in a Champions League qualifier against Austrian's Graz AZ.

July 2008 Boyhood Liverpool fan Robbie Keane makes his Reds debut in a Champions League qualifier following his £20 million switch from Tottenham.

PLAYER PROFILES

Name: David Hannah

Date of birth: 28 April 1867

Place of birth: Raffrey, County Down

Position: Forward

Years at Liverpool: 1894–1897

Games played: 33

Goals scored: 12

Other clubs: Sunderland, Dundee, Woolich Arsenal, Renton

County Down forward Davy Hannah signed for Liverpool from Sunderland in October 1894 as the team struggled to make an impact in their first season in the English First Division.

He was brought in to strengthen Liverpool's attacking options and became the first Irish-born player to sign for the club. He made his debut in a 3–1 defeat to Stoke City at the Victoria Ground on 11 October 1894, which was Liverpool's seventh defeat in thirteen games and saw the club plummet to the bottom of the First Division.

A week later, Hannah made his Anfield debut in a mammoth local derby with near neighbours Everton and the occasion could hardly have gone better for the forward. Liverpool had suffered a 3–0 defeat to Everton in their first competitive Merseyside league derby a month earlier, but thanks to the heroics of Hannah, they were not to be beaten for a second time. After falling a goal behind, Hannah equalised for Liverpool with a blistering shot that sent Anfield into raptures during an exciting game that eventually finished 2–2.

However, this was one of the few high points for Hannah and Liverpool, as they continued to struggle in the First Division throughout the 1894–1895 season.

Despite this, Hannah endeared himself to the Anfield faithful by notching up a few goals.

Just a week after his goal against Everton, Hannah was on the score sheet again, this time against his old club Sunderland but, unfortunately, Liverpool still fell to a 3–2 defeat. He had better luck with his next two goals which both came in two of Liverpool's best performances of the season, a 3–1 win over Small Heath (now Birmingham City) and 4–0 thrashing of West Brom. These two victories could not save Liverpool from relegation and even though Hannah scored in another two wins over Nottingham Forest and Derby County, Liverpool dropped back down to the Second Division for the 1895–1896 season.

During his second season, Hannah found himself down the pecking order behind fellow forwards Thomas Bradshaw, Frank Becton and the prolific Scottish marksman George Allan. He played in just eleven league games for Liverpool that season as they stormed back into the top flight by winning the Second Division on goal average from Manchester City. Hannah helped his team on their way to achieving this by scoring two goals in a 4–2 away win over Loughborough Town in September 1895 and another in a 5–1 home win over Port Vale.

When Liverpool returned to the First Division under new manager Tom Watson for the 1896–1897 season, Hannah remained at the club but made only three more league appearances in a Liverpool shirt.

Hannah's first game that season saw him score an impressive double against Sunderland at Anfield, but his time with Liverpool drew to a close when he played his last game for the club in a 0–0 draw away to Aston Villa in March 1897. Hannah was allowed to leave Liverpool on a free to join Dundee in Scotland, but he left the club with a decent strike rate of twelve goals in thirty-three league and cup games.

Name: Willie Donnelly

Date of birth: 1 January 1872

Place of birth: Magherafelt, County Down

Position: Goalkeeper

Years at Liverpool: 1896–1898

Games played: 6

Goals scored: 0

Other clubs: Hibernian, Clyde, Glasgow Celtic, Belfast Celtic

Goalkeeper Willie Donnelly became the second Irishman to wear the famous shirt of Liverpool when he signed for the club from Scottish side Clyde in May 1896.

Born in Derry but raised in Scotland, Donnelly had built a reputation as a very talented goalkeeper and shot-stopper during his time with Clyde. Unfortunately for Donnelly, Harry Storer was already installed as Liverpool's first-choice number one and Donnelly spent much of his time at Anfield as his understudy.

Donnelly had to wait until December 1896 before his debut for Liverpool which came in a 4–1 thumping at Burnley on St Stephen's Day.

He then kept his place in goals for Liverpool's trip to Bolton on New Year's Day 1897 and enjoyed a much better occasion as the Reds came out on top in an emphatic 4–1 win. He also played in the next six games for Liverpool in which they were undefeated for five, before he had to step aside to allow the fit again Storer to retake his position in goals.

The Derry man didn't feature again that season as Liverpool, under the guidance of new manager Tom Watson, finished fifth in just their second year in the English First Division. A year later, Liverpool finished ninth under Watson but Donnelly was unable to dislodge Storer and played no more games for the club.

Donnelly eventually left Anfield in June 1898 when he returned up north to Clyde.

Name: Bill Lacey

Date of birth: 24 September 1889

Place of birth: Wexford

Position: Winger

Years at Liverpool: 1912–1924

Games played: 259

Goals scored: 29

Honours: First Division Championship (1922, 1923)

Other clubs: Shelbourne, Everton, New Brighton, Cork Bohemians

If Liverpool's local rivals Everton were smarting at passing up the chance to sign legendary keeper Elisha Scott, they must have been equally kicking themselves at allowing pacey winger Bill Lacey to also end up at Anfield.

Wexford-man Lacey was part of a swap deal between the two Merseyside clubs in February 1912 which saw him replace his blue shirt of Everton with that of the red of Liverpool, with Harold Uren moving in the opposite direction.

Liverpool manager Tom Watson proved just how much of a shrewd operator he was with this deal as Lacey would go on to become one of the Reds' best players over the following decade. He also became a firm favourite with the Liverpool fans with his tricky wing play and a toughness which made him difficult to shake off the ball.

After signing up at Anfield, Lacey went straight into the Liverpool team and starred in their remaining eleven league matches that season, scoring one goal, as the club finished in a disappointing seventeenth position, narrowly avoiding relegation to the Second Division.

In his first full season at the club, Lacey really showed his class in the FA Cup where his goals helped Liverpool to comfortable 3–0 and 4–1 wins over Bristol City and Woolwich Arsenal. Despite another Lacey goal in a 1–1 third-round tie against Newcastle, Liverpool departed from the cup that season after losing 1–0 in the replay.

However, Lacey kept up his great goal-scoring form in the FA Cup a season later when his five goals brought Liverpool to their first final of the world's most prestigious club cup competition.

Lacey began Liverpool's exciting cup run that season with a goal in a 1–1 home draw with Barnsley in January 1914 and finally helped the Reds shake off their gritty opponents with a eighty-ninth-minute winner in the replay.

Lacey hit the back of the net again just a couple of weeks later when Liverpool brushed past Gillingham 2–0 at Anfield in the second round of the cup and he scored two more in a 5–1 rout of West Ham in a third-round replay.

The Wexford man also played his part in a magnificent semi-final performance by Liverpool when they beat hot favourites Aston Villa 2–0 but they were unable to repeat the heroics in the final, held at Crystal Palace, when they went down 1–0 to a tough Burnley side.

That was as good as it got for Lacey in the FA Cup during his Anfield career but he remained a very consistent performer for the club in the First Division, despite the interference of the First World War.

Lacey played in thirty-two out of Liverpool's thirty-eight league games during the 1914–1915 season but the team finished way off the pace back in thirteenth place as Merseyside rivals Everton grabbed league title glory.

Like all players of that time, Lacey's career was then interrupted for almost five years as the First World War led to the suspension of English football.

Then, when Lacey returned to competitive action for Liverpool in 1919, he went on to enjoy the best years of his career, helping Liverpool to back-to-back First Division titles in 1922 and 1923.

Alongside goalkeeper and fellow Irishman Elisha Scott, Lacey was an integral part of Liverpool's double championship-winning team.

He played in thirty-nine out of forty-two league games, scoring one goal, as Liverpool raced to the title a full six points clear of nearest rivals Tottenham in 1921–1922.

When Liverpool embarked on retaining the title a year later, Lacey played in thirty league games, again scoring just one goal, as the Reds won their fourth league championship by holding off the challenge of Sunderland and Huddersfield.

Despite this success, Lacey's career at Liverpool was nearing an end as he reached his mid-thirties.

He starred in just eight league games for Liverpool in 1923–1924 as the club relinquished their title to Huddersfield and Lacey was transferred to New Brighton in June 1924 after making his last appearance in a 4–1 defeat to Bolton in March of that year.

Had it not been for the interruption of the First World War, Lacey would no doubt have added countless more games to his total of 259 appearances for Liverpool and may even have won more silverware.

Even still, Bill Lacey's time at Anfield was packed full of achievement and he goes down in history as one of the most successful Irishmen to have ever played for the club.

Name: Billy McDevitt

Date of birth: 5 January 1898

Place of birth: Belfast

Position: Centre-half

Years at Liverpool: 1923–1925

Games played: 4

Goals scored: 0

Other clubs: Belfast United, Swansea Town, Exeter City

Belfast-born centre-half Billy McDevitt signed for Liverpool in the summer of 1923 from his hometown club Belfast Utd.

It was a massive move for the twenty-five-year-old defender as he was joining a successful club who had just completed back-to-back First Division league titles.

That success, coupled with the fact that Liverpool already had a very strong list of defenders including Scottish international Donald McKinlay and the commanding Walter Wadsworth, meant it was always going to be difficult for McDevitt to force his way into manager Matt McQueen's team.

He made his debut for Liverpool on 17 November 1923 in a 0–0 draw at Villa Park and remained in the team when Liverpool entertained Villa at Anfield just a week later.

This time, Villa won the game 1–0 and McDevitt didn't feature again in the Liverpool side until a 3–1 defeat to Arsenal at Highbury in March 1924 as the Reds finished the season twelfth in the league.

McDevitt remained at Liverpool for the 1924–1925 season but made just one more appearance for the first team in a 4–1 victory over Sheffield Utd at Anfield in October 1924.

With his chances to play in the Liverpool side limited, McDevitt made the move to Swansea Town in June 1925 before later going on to play for, and manage, Exeter City.

Name: David McMullan

Date of birth: 11 October 1901

Place of birth: Belfast

Position: Half-back

Years at Liverpool: 1925–1928

Games played: 35

Goals scored: 0

Other clubs: Forth River, Belfast Distillery, New York Giants, Belfast Celtic, Exeter United

Half-back David McMullan arrived at Liverpool in October 1925 as manager Matt McQueen desperately attempted to win back the league title Liverpool had last won in 1923.

McMullan was one of seven new signings made by Liverpool that season when he was snapped up from Belfast side Distillery as McQueen looked to improve on the team's fourth place finish the season before.

McMullan made his Anfield debut the same month he signed for the club as he helped Liverpool to a 2–1 win over Manchester City.

He didn't appear again for over a month until McQueen threw him back in his starting eleven for a 1–0 defeat to Bury and McMullan then remained in the side for the next eleven matches with Liverpool winning five of them including a FA Cup third-round replay win over Southampton at Anfield.

However, by the end of January 1926, Liverpool had been knocked out of the cup by Fulham and McMullan found himself out of favour and didn't appear in the side again that season as Liverpool finished back in seventh place in the league.

McMullan didn't fare much better in the 1926–1927 season when he appeared only twice for Liverpool, in a 3–0 win over The Wednesday at Anfield and a 3–2 defeat away to Leicester City.

The half-back's best run of games for Liverpool came the following season when he started in nineteen league matches.

Although Liverpool struggled to make any impact on the First Division

PLAYER PROFILES 237

that season, losing seven of the nineteen games McMullan played in, and finished a disappointing sixteenth in the league and were dumped out of the FA Cup in the fourth round by Cardiff City.

McMullan's last game for Liverpool was hardly a memorable one as they were thrashed 6–1 by Manchester Utd at Old Trafford in May 1928.

When McMullan left Liverpool in June 1928, he decided to cross the Atlantic to play his football by signing for the New York Giants.

Name: Billy Millar

Date of birth: 25 October 1906

Place of birth: Ballymena, County Antrim

Position: Forward

Years at Liverpool: 1928

Games played: 3

Goals scored: 2

Other clubs: Lochgelly United, LInfield, Barrow, Newport County, Carlisle United, Sligo Rovers, Cork City, Drumcondra

Talented Ballymena-born forward Billy Millar signed for Liverpool in January 1928, just at a time when the club was going through a difficult transition.

Not long after Millar arrived at Liverpool, the club replaced its Scottish manager Matt McQueen with Englishman George Patterson, who came into Liverpool for the final couple of months of the 1927–1928 season, though Millar didn't feature in any games that year.

Millar, who had been signed from top Irish league side Linfield, finally made his debut for Liverpool against Bury at Anfield on the opening day of the 1928–1929 season.

The forward wasted little time in making an impression when he slotted home a goal within the first minute and added to it with another later on in the game in an impressive 3–0 win for Liverpool.

Despite that brilliant start, Millar was never able to cement a place in the Liverpool team. He starred in just two more games for the Reds that season, when they lost 2–1 to Sheffield Utd at Anfield in September 1928 and beat Newcastle 2–1 a month later.

Unfortunately for Millar, his Liverpool career just never took off after this and he left Anfield just a few months later to sign for Barrow.

Name: Sam English

Date of birth: 18 August 1908

Place of birth: Coleraine, County Derry

Position: Forward

Years at Liverpool: 1933–1935

Games played: 50

Goals scored: 26

Other clubs: Rangers, Queen of the South, Hartlepool United

Former Glasgow Rangers sharp-shooter Sam English was brought to Anfield for £6,000 in August 1933 to bolster a Liverpool attack that had failed to drag the club above its mid-table status throughout the early part of the 1930s.

English had scored goals for fun in Scotland with Rangers, and Liverpool manager George Patterson hoped he could keep it up in the English league. Patterson wasn't to be disappointed as the prolific English settled well at Liverpool and began scoring in a red shirt almost straight away.

English made his Liverpool debut in a 3–2 defeat at Wolves and scored his first goal for the club in a 1–1 draw with Stoke at Anfield just four days later.

He was a big powerful centre-forward whose all-action bustling displays always kept opposition defenders on their toes. After his first goal against Stoke, English added another seven in his next seven games, including two in an impressive 3–0 win at Spurs and an eightieth minute winner in a 3–2 Merseyside derby win over Everton at Anfield.

But despite English's goals, Liverpool were struggling to keep clean sheets at the other end and were losing as many games as they were winning, hampering any chance they had for a challenge on the league title.

By January 1934, English had scored sixteen league goals and was the club's second highest scorer behind the prolific South African Gordon Hodgson, one of the club's greatest goal scorers of all time.

English added to his tally with two goals in a 3–1 fourth-round FA Cup win over Merseyside neighbours Tranmere but Liverpool eventually crashed out of the cup after a crushing 3–0 defeat to Bolton at Anfield in the fifth round. The Reds also finished the season in a disappointing eighteenth position in the league, but English had notched up a respectable twenty goals during the campaign.

In his second season at Anfield, English played in just nineteen league games for Liverpool as the club improved on their previous season to finish seventh in the league. English chipped in with six goals that season and despite the fact that Liverpool won five out of those six games, he was never able to reach the goal-scoring heights of his first season.

English's last goal for Liverpool came in a 3–2 defeat to Grimsby in February 1935 and he played his last game for the club in a 5–1 defeat to Spurs in April that year. English left Liverpool in July 1935 to return to Scotland, where he signed for Queen of the South.

Name: William Hood

Date of birth: 3 November 1914

Place of birth: Belfast

Position: Defender

Years at Liverpool: 1937–1938

Games played: 3

Goals scored: 0

Other clubs: Cliftonville, Derry City

Belfast defender William Hood came to Liverpool from Cliftonville in March 1937 as manager George Kay guided the team to seventeenth place in the First Division during his first season in charge.

As a new member of the squad, Hood didn't play any games that season and was not drafted into the Liverpool side until the following November when Liverpool were beaten 1–0 at Anfield by Huddersfield.

Full-back Hood never really got the chance to get an extended run in the team and played just two more matches as a replacement for the regular defender Tom Cooper.

Hood's second match was a 1–0 win for Liverpool over Blackpool but he was on the wrong end of a 4–3 defeat to Derby in his only other game in a red shirt.

Liverpool finished the 1937–1938 season in eleventh position in the league but Hood's time at the club was coming to a close.

He was allowed to leave Liverpool in the summer of 1938 and he returned to Ireland to play for Derry City.

Name: **Sammy Smyth**

Date of birth: 25 February 1925

Place of birth: Belfast

Position: Forward

Years at Liverpool: 1952–1954

Games played: 44

Goals scored: 20

Other clubs: Linfield, Dundela FC, Wolves, Stoke City, Bangor City

Striker Sammy Smyth was brought to Liverpool in December 1952 as the club desperately tried to avoid relegation to the Second Division.

Liverpool manager Don Welsh paid fellow strugglers Stoke City £12,000 to get Smyth on board and the Northern Ireland international proved his worth by banging in some important goals which helped keep the Reds afloat in the First Division that season.

Smyth, who famously scored for Wolves in the 1949 FA Cup final, found the back of the net seven times in eighteen games over the following five months, which helped the team gain four crucial wins as they avoided relegation by just two points at the expense of Smyth's old club Stoke.

Smyth made his debut for Liverpool against Stoke on 3 January 1953 just days after signing for the club but had to wait until his fourth match to score first goal which came in a vitally important 3–2 win away to Middlesbrough.

A week later, Smyth had his first goal at Anfield in an impressive 3–0 win over West Brom and made it three goals from three games with another in a 2–1 win at Newcastle as the Reds made the vital push necessary to keep themselves up that year.

It proved to be only a temporary reprieve, however, and despite Smyth's scoring heroics throughout the 1953–1954 season, Liverpool finished bottom of the league to finally drop into Division Two.

Smyth did his best to keep them up by scoring thirteen goals in twenty-six league games, making him the club's highest scorer for that ill-fated season.

Smyth shone in two of Liverpool's better performances in 1953 when he scored two goals in a 5–1 rout of Aston Villa at Anfield and added another two in a 3–0 home win over Sheffield Utd.

The Belfast-born striker added to his tally with another brace against Chelsea but couldn't help his team avoid going down to a 5–2 defeat on the day.

This defeat was the start of a harrowing twenty-game losing streak for Liverpool in which they only won one match, a 5–2 victory over Blackpool in which Smyth scored. He notched up another three in two wins over Middlesbrough as the season neared its end but it was too little to save Liverpool from inevitable relegation.

Smyth's last ever game for Liverpool ended in a 3–0 defeat away to Blackpool on 24 April 1954, and his last goals had come just a week earlier when he scored twice in a 4–1 win over Middlesbrough.

When the season ended, Liverpool did not renew Smyth's contract and he returned to Belfast to play for Bangor City. He left Anfield with a very respectable strike rate of twenty goals in forty-four games.

Name: Mark Lawrenson

Date of birth: 2 June 1957

Place of birth: Preston, England

Position: Defender

Years at Liverpool: 1981–1988

Games played: 356

Goals scored: 18

Honours: First Division Championship (1982, 1983, 1984, 1986, 1988); European Cup (1984); FA Cup (1986); League Cup (1982, 1983, 1984)

Other clubs: Preston North End, Brighton & Hove Albion, Barnet

Bob Paisley, Liverpool's most successful manager, had a knack of making incredibly astute signings and he added another one to his list when he snapped up defender Mark Lawrenson for £900,000 from Brighton in August 1981.

The transfer fee for Lawrenson was massive at the time but Paisley knew it would be money well spent on a player almost all of the big clubs in England wanted in their team. Liverpool had a tough battle on their hands to prise Lawro away from Brighton as fellow Division One giants Man Utd and Arsenal also showed a keen interest in signing him.

The Reds' determination to get their man was proven right as Lawrenson went on to enjoy a trophy-laden seven seasons at Anfield, forming an impenetrable central defensive partnership with the classy Scot Alan Hansen, and is now remembered as one of the club's best defenders.

Versatile Lawrenson actually began his Liverpool career playing at left back when he made his debut in a 1–0 defeat away to Wolves on 29 August 1981. Despite this early season blip for the reigning European champions, Liverpool went on to claim the First Division title that season, with Lawrenson playing everywhere across the defence and even in midfield.

He starred in thirty-nine of Liverpool's forty-two league games that season, scoring two goals in wins over Nottingham Forest and Tottenham, as Paisley's team pegged back plucky Ipswich to win the league by four points.

It was not the only winners' medal that Lawrenson would pick up in his debut season at Anfield as the Reds also embarked on a glorious run in the League Cup culminating with a 3–1 victory over Tottenham in the final at Wembley.

The only sore point for Lawro in the whole season came when he was red carded late on in extra time as Liverpool crashed out of the European Cup at the quarter-final stage to Bulgarian side CSKA Sofia.

Season two for Lawrenson at Anfield proved to be every bit as eventful as the team once again went on the glory trial. As in his first season, Lawrenson helped Liverpool back to Wembley for the League Cup final with victories over Ipswich, Rotherham Utd, Norwich and his old club Brighton, to set up a tantalising final against arch rivals Man Utd.

Lawrenson started the final in the centre of the Liverpool defence alongside Alan Hansen, as the Reds survived a Utd onslaught to win the game 2–1 in extra time in front of a crowd of 100,000.

Just weeks later, Lawrenson picked up his second Division One winners' medal as Liverpool coasted to the title with eleven points to spare over runners-up Watford.

The season also proved to be Lawrenson's most prolific in front of goal as he helped himself to seven goals, including a brace in a 5–0 win over Southampton at Anfield in September 1982.

But in almost a carbon copy of the previous season, Liverpool again crashed out of the European Cup in the quarter-finals to Eastern European opposition, when Poland's Videz Lodz beat them 4–3 on aggregate.

Despite these European heartbreaks, Lawrenson was not to be denied the following season when Liverpool remarkably again won the League Cup and First Division titles, but this time also added the European Cup.

Lawrenson played in all of Liverpool's forty-two league games in the 1983–1984 season as they pipped Southampton to the title by three points and he was also ever present during the team's successful League Cups and European Cup runs.

Liverpool needed twelve matches to win the League Cup including a replay in the final against their Merseyside rivals Everton, but it was their heroic win in the European Cup final over Roma in the Italian's own home ground that really stood out.

Lawrenson played his part during that famous night on 30 May 1984, as the whole Liverpool team stood firm to etch out a 1–1 draw with Roma, before winning the cup in a nerve wracking penalty shoot-out.

In all, Lawrenson played in an incredible sixty-six games for Liverpool in a season that still ranks as the club's greatest ever.

After all this success there was always likely to be a season where things would not go so well for Lawrenson and his Liverpool team-mates and it duly arrived in 1984–1985.

They had another strong showing in the league, in which Lawrenson played in thirty-three games, but Liverpool still surrendered their title to a resurgent Everton as they finished second. They also lost their first game in the League Cup in five years when Tottenham knocked them out 1–0 in a White Hart Lane encounter in October 1984.

However, Liverpool still made headway in the European Cup as Lawrenson helped them on to another final against Italian champion's Juventus.

Instead of enjoying another momentous occasion, Lawrenson had to endure the nightmare of playing that final even though thirty-nine people, mostly Juventus fans, had lost their lives due to crowd trouble.

Lawrenson was substituted early on in the game as Liverpool lost the final 1–0 but the result mattered little in the greater scheme of things.

After the final, Liverpool were handed a six-year ban from all European competitions, but, on the home front, the team got back to business on the pitch under new player/manager Kenny Dalglish.

Lawrenson played in thirty-eight of Liverpool's forty-two league games in 1985–1986 as the Reds just beat off the challenge of Everton to regain their title, the club's sixth that decade.

For once, Liverpool also made a run at the FA Cup by beating Norwich, Chelsea, York and Watford to set up a semi-final clash with Southampton.

Lawrenson wasn't in the Liverpool team that edged past Southampton 2–1 in that semi-final, but was back playing centre-half as Liverpool beat Everton 3–1 at Wembley to land their first ever double.

The 1986–1987 season proved not to be one of the best for Lawrenson. Although he played in all eight of Liverpool's games on their way to a

League Cup final clash with Arsenal, an injury meant he missed out on the big Wembley occasion.

Liverpool lost the game 2–1 and also missed out the on the league title to Everton as they finished runner-up to their local rivals for the second time in three seasons. The Liverpool side which started the 1987–1988 season had a dramatic new look to it as boss Kenny Dalglish freshened things up.

Lawrenson was still a big part of his plans, however, and he featured in most of Liverpool's games in the early part of the season as they racked up an incredible twenty-nine-game unbeaten start to the league.

But injuries were starting to take their toll on thirty-one-year-old Lawro and, by the turn of the year, he was struggling to remain fit.

Lawrenson made the last of his fourteen league appearances for Liverpool that season in a 2–0 win over Arsenal at Anfield on 16 January 1988, before a persistent Achilles injury ended his career.

He did pick up another league winners medal at the end of the season as he had played in more than the necessary ten games to warrant one.

Bowing out with an injury was a sad way for Lawrenson to finish his remarkable time at Liverpool as he no doubt had another two or three seasons in him to have achieved even more.

Still, Lawrenson had won five league titles during his time at Anfield and had helped the club to further success by winning a European Cup, three League cups and a FA Cup. Not a bad return for the £900,000 the club paid for him.

Name: Kevin Sheedy

Date of birth: 21 October 1959

Place of birth: Builth Wells, Wales

Position: Left-wing

Years at Liverpool: 1978–1982

Games played: 5

Goals scored: 2

Other clubs: Hereford, Everton, Newcastle United, Blackpool United

If Everton had cause to regret letting legendary keeper Elisha Scott and talented Wexford winger Bill Lacey slip through their grasp, then Liverpool may have been equally annoyed to have let classy winger Kevin Sheedy create a successful career at Goodison Park.

Born in Wales, Sheedy qualified to play for the Republic of Ireland through his parents and he was one of his country's star performers at their first appearance at a World Cup finals in 1990.

Long before then, the left-footed Sheedy was brought to Liverpool as a young nineteen-year-old from Hereford in 1978. The Reds coughed up £80,000 for the youngster but he was still a long way from making it into the Liverpool first team, considering the club had just won back-to-back European Cup crowns.

Instead, Sheedy had to bide his time playing in the reserves until he was eventually called up for his debut by manager Bob Paisley in February 1981.

Sheedy's first taste of Anfield action came in a 2–2 draw with Birmingham when he lined up alongside the likes of Liverpool legends Graeme Souness, Terry McDermott and Kenny Dalglish. Liverpool went on to snatch their third European Cup that year, but Sheedy only ever played in that one league game. He reappeared in the red shirt in October 1981 as an eighty-ninth minute substitute for forward David Johnson in another 2–2 draw, this time with Swansea City.

Sheedy got more time to impress in the Liverpool starting line-up later that month when he scored his first goal in a 6–0 romp over Exeter City in the second round of the League Cup. Sheedy kept his place in the team for a third-round clash with Middlesbrough at Anfield and scored again as Liverpool ran out easy 4–1 winners. The Reds actually went on to capture the League Cup that season with victory over Tottenham in the final, but Sheedy did not make any more appearances.

His only other game for Liverpool that season came as a sub in a 1–0 defeat to Brighton at Anfield in a league game in March 1982.

This was Sheedy's last appearance in a Liverpool shirt and, in May 1982, he was transferred across Stanley Park to Everton for £100,000.

It proved to be money well spent by the Toffees as Sheedy went on to help the club capture two league titles, an FA Cup and a European Cup Winners Cup during his time at Goodison Park.

Name: Michael Robinson

Date of birth: 12 July 1958

Place of birth: Leicester

Position: Forward

Years at Liverpool: 1983-84

Games played: 52

Goals scored: 13

Honours: First Division Championship (1984); European Cup (1984): League Cup (1984)

Other clubs: Preston North End, Man City, Brighton, Queen's Park Rangers, Osasuna

When forward Michael Robinson signed up to play for Liverpool in May 1983, little could he have imagined how dramatic a first season he would be involved in with the Reds. Leicester-born Robinson, who played for the Republic of Ireland, arrived at Anfield just at a time that Joe Fagan's men were embarking on one of their most successful ever seasons. With star striker Ian Rush forging an unstoppable partnership with Scottish sensation Kenny Dalglish up front, Robinson had been brought to Liverpool as back up. However, he did get an extended run in the team alongside Rush in the early part of the 1983–1984 season as Dalglish was used in a more withdrawn role.

Robinson made his debut in a Charity Shield clash with Manchester Utd at Wembley which the Reds unfortunately lost 2–0 to a brace of goals from England midfielder Brian Robson.

Despite this, Robinson kept his place in the team for Liverpool's opening league game a week later which finished in a 1–1 draw with Wolves.

Liverpool's new striker endured a barren spell in front of goal and failed to score in his first nine games for the team. His luck finally changed when he notched up two goals in a 5–0 European Cup romp over Danish side Odense in October 1983 and added to this with a League Cup goal against Brentford and a hat-trick in a league game against West Ham over the following month.

Robinson kept his scoring boots on for the visit of Everton to Anfield for the Merseyside derby in November when he netted in a 3–0 win.

In all Robinson scored six league goals that season in twenty-four games as Liverpool won the league by three points from the determined challenge of Southampton.

The league title wasn't the only bit of silverware Liverpool were chasing that season, as they also won the League Cup with victory over neighbours Everton in a replay.

Robinson had come on a substitute in the initial final with Everton which finished 0–0 but did not play any role when Liverpool won the replay 1–0.

Even more impressive by the Reds that year was their run in the European Cup as they made it all the way to their fourth final to take on Italian giants Roma in Rome.

Robinson played his part in helping Liverpool get there with victory over Odense in the first round, Spain's Athletic Bilbao in the second and Benfica of Portugal in the third round.

He was also a part of the squad as Liverpool edged past Dinamo Bucharest in the semi-final and came off the bench in the latter stages of the famous final in Rome as Liverpool won their fourth European Cup.

In all, Robinson played his part in forty-two games for Liverpool that season and while he was never prolific, he certainly did his bit to help Liverpool claim the treble. After such an exciting debut season, Robinson's next year at Liverpool was always likely to be something of anticlimax and that was how it turned out.

The tall striker started just two league games as Liverpool lost their title to Merseyside rivals Everton and made the bench for just two European Cup ties before Christmas 1984 as the Reds, once again, marched on to the final the following May, this time losing to Juventus.

However, Robinson had already departed the club by then after he was sold to QPR on 27 December 1984 for £100,000. His last goal for the Reds had come in a 2–0 League Cup win over Stockport County at Anfield on 9 October 1984.

Name: Jim Beglin

Date of birth: 29 July 1963

Place of birth: Waterford

Position: Left-back

Years at Liverpool: 1983–1987

Games played: 98

Goals scored: 3

Honours: First Division Championship (1986); FA Cup (1986)

Other clubs: Shamrock Rovers, Leeds United, Plymouth, Blackburn Rovers

Few players have enjoyed the amazing highs and suffered the terrible lows of professional football as much as talented left-back Jim Beglin.

The Waterford man enjoyed a whirlwind two years at Liverpool winning major trophies before his career was effectively ended by a cruel leg break.

Beglin began his career at Shamrock Rovers in the League of Ireland and had come to the attention of a number of top English teams before Liverpool manager Bob Paisley took a chance and brought him to Anfield on a month's loan in 1983. Suitably impressed by Beglin's ability and steel, Paisley made him his last ever signing when he paid Shamrock Rovers £20,000 in May 1983 to take him on permanently.

Like most new players who arrived at Liverpool back then, Beglin had to wait for his opportunities and mostly played second fiddle to established left-back Alan Kennedy for the first year he was at the club.

Beglin finally made his Liverpool debut on 10 November 1984 in a 1–1 league draw with Southampton at Anfield. He made another nine league starts for Liverpool that year but the Reds were unable to retain their title as they finished second to Everton.

Despite not being a regular during that league campaign, Beglin had forced himself into the Liverpool side for their vitally important European Cup semi-final clash with Panathinaikos in April 1985 and even managed to get on the score sheet with a header during a 4–0 win.

He kept his place in the team for the final against Juventus at the Heysel Stadium in Belgium but it was a night that will always be remembered for the awful things that happened off the pitch.

By the following season, Beglin was installed as the regular first-choice left-back by new boss Kenny Dalglish and Liverpool embarked on another glorious season.

Beglin started in thirty-four of Liverpool's forty-two league games in an exciting First Division campaign that went right down to the wire, with Liverpool just pipping neighbours Everton to the title by two points.

In the FA Cup, Beglin helped Liverpool to victories over Chelsea, York, Watford and Southampton as the Reds set up an unbelievable Wembley decider with Everton.

Beglin once again took his place on the left of the defence as Liverpool came from behind to beat Everton 3–1 to capture the club's first ever league and FA Cup double.

If it hadn't have been for defeat to QPR in the semi-final of the League Cup, Liverpool and Beglin may even have been celebrating an unique treble.

The 1986–1987 season looked to be business as usual for Beglin as he remained Liverpool's main left-back, starring in twenty league fixtures up to January 1927.

But Beglin's career as a footballer was effectively finished after a horrific leg break during a League Cup clash against Everton on 21 January 1987.

Beglin never played for Liverpool again after that and although he bravely tried to revive his career with Leeds Utd and Blackburn, he eventually had to retire early from the game. Had it not been for such cruel luck, Beglin would surely have enjoyed more glory with both Liverpool and the Republic of Ireland.

Name: Brian Mooney

Date of birth: 2 February 1966

Place of birth: Dublin

Position: Midfield

Years at Liverpool: 1983–1987

Games played: 1

Goals scored: 0

Other clubs: Home Farm, Wrexham, Preston North End, Sunderland, Burnley, Shelbourne United, Bohemians

Dubliner Brian Mooney made a dream move to Liverpool in August 1983 from his home-town club Home Farm.

Like legendary midfielder Ronnie Whelan before him, winger Mooney hoped to make the giant step up from Home Farm to the Liverpool first team, although he had a number of obstacles in front of him.

The Liverpool side Mooney joined in 1983 was the best in Europe at the time and already consisted of an array of top-class attacking and midfield options such as Kenny Dalglish, Craig Johnson, Ronnie Whelan and Ian Rush. While that Liverpool side went on to claim an incredible treble of league, League Cup and European Cup in the 1983–1984 season, Mooney had to make do with playing in the Liverpool reserve team.

As Liverpool continued to mop up trophies in the following seasons, Mooney's chance of a break in the first team just never materialised.

He eventually made his one and only appearance for Liverpool in a League Cup clash at Fulham in October 1986 when he replaced fellow Irishman Jim Beglin in a 3–2 win.

After this, Mooney spent a loan spell at Welsh side Wrexham and he secured a permanent move away from Anfield in an £80,000 deal with Preston in October 1987.

Name: John Aldridge

Date of birth: 18 September 1958

Place of birth: Liverpool

Position: Striker

Years at Liverpool: 1987–1989

Games played: 104

Goals scored: 63

Honours: First Division Championship (1988); FA Cup (1989)

Other clubs: Newport County, Oxford United, Real Sociedad, Tranmare Rovers

Liverpool-born striker John Aldridge finally realised a lifelong ambition when he signed for the club he supported as a boy in January 1987.

Reds' manager Kenny Dalglish brought twenty-eight-year-old Aldridge on board after he impressed at Oxford Utd where he had scored the goals that helped them lift the League Cup just a year earlier.

Dalglish also needed a replacement for ace goal scorer Ian Rush who was leaving for Juventus in the summer of 1987 and Aldridge was the man to fit the bill.

After his £700,000 move from Oxford, Aldo made his dream debut in a red shirt when he came on a second-half substitute for Craig Johnson in a 2–2 draw at Aston Villa on 21 February 1987.

A week later, Aldridge made his first start for Liverpool at Anfield and even helped himself to the only goal of the game in a 1–0 win over Southampton. Despite this, Aldridge had to wait until the final game of the season on 9 May for his next start when he again scored in an exciting 3–3 draw with Chelsea at Stamford Bridge.

Those two goals were just a glimmer of the goal-scoring potential Aldo possessed and, when he finally gained a regular first-team spot the following season, he was on fire. Aldridge managed to score in each of Liverpool's first nine games in the 1987–1988 season as the team remained unbeaten for the first twenty-nine league games, effectively wrapping the league title up with a few months to spare.

He got the ball rolling with a goal in the season's opener at Arsenal as Liverpool won 2–1 and followed it up with ten more strikes in the next eight games which included his first Anfield hat-trick in a 4–0 win over Derby County. Aldridge had struck up a lethal understanding with the Liverpool wingers John Barnes and Ray Houghton and fellow forward Peter Beardsley and Liverpool looked unstoppable throughout the season.

They didn't suffer a defeat in the league until Merseyside rivals Everton beat them 1–0 on 20 March 1988, a game in which Aldridge played no part.

The defeat to Everton mattered little, though, as Aldridge's twenty-six goals in thirty-six league games saw Liverpool win the First Division by eleven points over Manchester Utd.

Aldo was also in blistering form in the FA Cup, scoring the two goals which helped Liverpool to a vital 2–1 win over Nottingham Forest in the semi-finals. His luck didn't hold up in the final, however, when Aldridge surprisingly missed a penalty as Liverpool went down to a shock 1–0 defeat to Wimbledon, scuppering their chances of a second league and cup double in three seasons.

By the season's end, Aldridge had managed to notch up an impressive twenty-nine goals in forty-five appearances and there was even more to come from the striker in the following season. Remarkably that summer Dalglish decided to bring Ian Rush back to Liverpool but there was no way Aldridge was prepared to step aside just yet.

He made some kind of amends for his missed penalty against Wimbledon when he banged in two in the Charity Shield clash against them at Wembley in August 1988, and followed this with a perfect hat-trick in Liverpool's first league game away at Charlton a week later.

The goals just kept coming with Aldridge, so much so that it was often Rush who had to take a back seat, only scoring eleven goals compared to Aldo's thirty-one for the 1988–1989 season.

By early April 1989, Aldridge had raked up twenty-four league and cup goals as the Reds looked to be on their way to achieving the second double that had just eluded them twelve months earlier. But things changed forever for the club on 15 April 1989, when ninety-six Liverpool fans were crushed to death in harrowing scenes during the club's FA Cup semi-final clash with Nottingham Forest.

When football resumed for Liverpool following the tragedy, Aldridge somehow managed to muster the strength to keep on scoring.

During the highly emotional rearranged match with Nottingham Forest, Aldo bagged two goals in a brilliant 3–1 win for the Reds which set up a second famous all Merseyside FA Cup final with Everton.

Aldridge again took centre-stage when he rammed home a goal with his first shot of the final before Rush wrapped up an amazing 3–2 victory with two goals in extra time to claim the cup.

Just two days after that final, Liverpool were back in action in the league when Aldridge scored in a 5–1 win at Anfield that looked to have secured them the First Division title. All that remained was for Liverpool to avoid a 2–0 defeat to Arsenal four days later, but incredibly they somehow managed to lose by that scoreline as future Red Michael Thomas won the title with almost the last kick of the entire season.

Even still, Aldridge had finished the season with an even better scoring ratio than his previous by notching up thirty-one goals in forty-seven games.

It was difficult to imagine then but just a few months later, Aldridge would be waving goodbye to his beloved Anfield after Dalglish made the shock decision to sell him to Spanish side Real Sociedad.

Aldridge started the 1989–1990 season on the bench for Liverpool as the manager preferred to use Rush up front and he only made it onto the pitch for two substitute appearances before he was finally sold in September 1989.

His last appearance for Liverpool came in a fantastic 9–0 rout of Crystal Palace on 12 September 1989, when Aldridge came off the bench to score a penalty.

It was the last act of a man who had made his mark for the club he loved most and Aldridge left Anfield with a sensational scoring record of sixty-three goals in 104 games.

Name: Steve Staunton

Date of birth: Drogheda

Place of birth: 19 January 1969

Position: Left-back

Years at Liverpool: 1986–1991 & 1998–2000

Games played: 148

Goals scored: 7

Other clubs: Dundalk, Bradford City, Aston Villa, Crystal Palace, Coventry City, Walsall

A tradition of Liverpool's throughout the 1980s was to bring in some of the best young players from Ireland and the club continued this when full-back Steve Staunton joined the red ranks in a £20,000 deal with Dundalk in September 1986. Just like Ronnie Whelan and Jim Beglin before him, fearless Staunton came into a star-studded Liverpool side and never looked out of place.

Left-back Staunton made his Anfield debut as a first-half substitute during a 1–1 draw with Spurs in September 1988 and went on to become a regular feature in the team that season as Liverpool challenged for the league title and FA Cup. Staunton got his first start for Liverpool just three days after the Spurs outing in a clash with Arsenal in the English league's special Centenary Trophy tournament and even managed to get on the score sheet in a 2–1 defeat.

His versatility meant Staunton was equally as comfortable playing as a wide midfield man as in defence and it gave boss Kenny Dalglish more scope to use him in different positions to help the team.

Mostly Staunton shared the left-back duties with another young full-back David Burrows and, between them, they helped a multi-talented Liverpool launch a bid for a league and FA Cup double.

Staunton started in eighteen league games for Liverpool during that season and was on the pitch the night Liverpool agonisingly lost the title to Arsenal in a 2–0 defeat at Anfield.

But the pain felt that night bore no comparison to the tragedy which had occurred a Hillsborough just a month earlier. Staunton had managed to squeeze his way into the team in the latter stages of Liverpool's FA Cup run that year, playing left back as Liverpool hammered Brentford 4–0 in the quarter-finals.

He was in the Liverpool line up for their ill-fated semi-final clash with Nottingham Forest at Hillsborough, and was in the team that won 3–1 in the rearranged fixture almost a month later.

The Drogheda man got his first taste of a big Wembley occasion on 20 May 1989, as Liverpool defeated Everton 3–2 to claim the FA Cup and so give Staunton his first major winners medal.

It would not be last, however, as Kenny Dalglish's charges mounted a determined challenge to win back their league title from Arsenal in the 1989–1990 season. Staunton again shared the left-back position with Burrows and starred in twenty league games as Liverpool won the title for the eighteenth time.

Perhaps the highlight of his season, however, came in a remarkable League Cup game against Wigan in October 1989 when Staunton came off the bench to replace striker Ian Rush and went on to score a memorable hat-trick from his forward position.

To this day, Staunton remains the only Liverpool player to have scored a hat-trick after coming on as a substitute. For the third season running, Liverpool also came agonisingly close to snatching the league and cup double as Staunton helped them on to a FA Cup semi-final clash with Crystal Palace with wins over Swansea, Norwich and QPR.

Yet again, though, Liverpool and Staunton were left disappointed after Crystal Palace pulled off a shock 4–3 extra-time victory, leaving the Reds to have to settle for just their league triumph.

Liverpool began the 1990–1991 season as red-hot favourites to retain their title and Staunton was again in the thick of the action playing in twenty-four league games as they went toe-to-toe with old foes Arsenal.

The Gunners eventually prevailed that season but Liverpool were left stunned midway through it when Kenny Dalglish unexpectedly resigned as manager just a day after a scintillating 4–4 FA Cup draw with Everton in February 1991.

The Reds eventually finished that campaign empty handed, the first time Staunton had ended a season without a winners medal of some sort in his pocket.

When Liverpool returned for the following season under new boss Graeme Souness, Staunton found himself out of favour and was sold on to Aston Villa in a £1.1 million deal.

It was not the last that the Anfield faithful would see of him, though, as the loyal Staunton returned for a second stint in the Red shirt in 1998.

After seven excellent seasons at Villa Park, Staunton jumped at the chance to reignite his faltered Liverpool career when manager Roy Evans picked him up on a 'Bosman' free transfer in July 1998.

It looked a dream move for the player but it soon turned sour when Liverpool made the decision to appoint Frenchman Gerard Houllier as joint-manager with Evans. This arrangement failed badly and Evans found himself out of the manager's position, leaving Staunton to play for a new man who hadn't signed him.

Staunton did still manage to play in forty games for Liverpool during that 1998–1999 season but the team finished well off the pace in seventh place in the Premier League.

Inevitably Staunton's role within the Liverpool team lessened the following year as Houllier brought in his own players and he started just seven league games as they finished fourth.

Staunton's time at Anfield finally wound down midway through the 2000–2001 season when Houllier allowed him to go back to Aston Villa on a free transfer on 6 December 2000.

His final appearance for Liverpool came as substitute in a 2–2 draw away to Greek side Olympiacos in the UEFA Cup in October 2000. Liverpool went on to capture the UEFA Cup that season but, unfortunately for Staunton, he had already left the club by the time this was achieved.

During his two separate stints at Liverpool, Steve Staunton had managed to play in a total of 148 league and cup games and scored seven goals.

Name: Ray Houghton

Date of birth: 9 January 1962

Place of birth: Glasgow

Position: Midfield

Years at Liverpool: 1987–1992

Games played: 202

Goals scored: 38

Honours: First Division Championship (1988, 1990); FA Cup (1989, 1992)

Other clubs: West Ham, Fulham, Oxford United, Aston Villa, Crystal Palace

Industrious midfielder Ray Houghton became part of a fantastic Liverpool revolution when he signed up to play for Kenny Dalglish's all-star attacking team.

Bought from Oxford Utd for £800,000 in October 1987, Houghton proved to be another gem of a signing by the wily Scottish manager, making the right-midfield berth his own as Liverpool marched on to glory.

Just as Aldridge, Beardsley and Barnes had done in the few months before him, Houghton blended in seamlessly to this new Liverpool team and struck up a frightening attacking understanding with his team-mates that made them almost unbeatable.

As Barnes patrolled the left wing with his mesmerising trickery and pace, Houghton did the same on the right with his industry and vision.

Houghton made his Liverpool debut just five days after signing for the club as he helped them to a 1–0 win in a tricky away game at Luton Town.

His first goal arrived in his next match when Houghton came off the bench to score a crucial equaliser in a 1–1 draw at Wimbledon which extended Liverpool's unbeaten start to the season to twelve games.

Houghton proved to be actually pretty handy at pitching in with his fair share of goals, adding another three that season in impressive wins over Newcastle, Coventry and Nottingham Forest as Liverpool strolled to the league title.

He also scored the only goal of the game in a memorable FA Cup fifth-round win over Merseyside rivals Everton at Goodison Park and kicked off the scoring in a brilliant 4–0 rout of Man City in the quarter-finals. However Houghton had to settle for a runners-up medal as Liverpool lost 1–0 to Wimbledon in the final.

Rather than rest on his laurels, Houghton, in the traditional Liverpool way, actually upped his game another notch in his second season playing in all thirty-eight league matches and scoring two more goals than in the previous year.

He once again scored in a Merseyside derby as Liverpool had to settle for a 1–1 draw with Everton at Anfield while other goals of his helped the team to vital points in games against Aston Villa, Wimbledon and Sheffield Wednesday.

Like everyone at Anfield though, Houghton's season was effectively ended on 15 April 1989 by the Hillsborough Disaster.

Through enormous strength of character, he and his team-mates fought back from it to claim the FA Cup in an emotional 3–2 win over Everton at Wembley.

They eventually lost out on the league title to Arsenal despite the best efforts of Houghton whose two goals in a 5–1 win over West Ham in the penultimate league game looked to have secured the title until Liverpool's dramatic collapse in the final game of that season.

An injury problem curtailed Houghton's involvement in the early part of the following season for Liverpool but he emerged back to his best in the team by October as they once again made a strong challenge for the First Division crown.

Houghton played in nineteen league games that season as Liverpool were put under pressure by Aston Villa and Arsenal before they broke away to win the title with nine points to spare over Villa.

This was to be the last league winners medal Houghton would pick up in his career, but it was not the end of his glory trail with Liverpool.

Although the Reds finished without a trophy in the 1990–1991 season, which also saw the shock departure of Kenny Dalglish as manager, Houghton came back a year later to have one of his best seasons in a red shirt.

The diminutive midfielder excelled under new boss Graeme Souness and although Liverpool struggled in the league, finishing only sixth, they made it back to Wembley to secure the FA Cup with a 2–0 final win over Sunderland.

Houghton scored twelve goals throughout that campaign and had even been voted by Liverpool fans as the club's player of the year.

It came as a massive surprise then when in the summer of 1992 Souness decided to cash in on Houghton and sold him to Aston Villa for £825,000. Houghton's last league game for Liverpool, before the 1992 FA Cup final, had been in a 0–0 draw away to Sheffield Wednesday, with his last goal coming in a 3–2 FA Cup fifth-round victory over Ipswich Town.

Name: Phil Babb

Date of birth: 30 November 1970

Place of birth: Lambeth, England

Position: Defender

Years at Liverpool: 1994–2000

Games played: 170

Goals scored: 1

Honours: League Cup (1995)

Other clubs: Millwall, Bradford City, Coventry City, Tranmare Rovers, Sporting Lisbon, Sunderland

Phil Babb was signed by Liverpool in September 1994 as new manager Roy Evans shelled out £3.6 million to bring him to Anfield from Coventry City. Defender Babb had enjoyed an excellent World Cup finals with the Republic of Ireland earlier that summer, where his partnership with Paul McGrath helped the country to a famous 1–0 victory over Italy as they made it to the last sixteen of the tournament.

Babb, who was club captain at Coventry, arrived at Anfield just a day before another defender John Scales was signed for £3.5 million as Evans looked to radically change the Liverpool defence.

With Evans' preference for three central defenders flanked by two wing-backs, Babb and Scales took their places in the three-man defence alongside either Neil Ruddock or Mark Wright.

Babb made his Liverpool debut as a sub during a 2–0 defeat to Man Utd on 17 September 1994 and made his first start a week later in a 1–1 draw with Newcastle.

Babb was virtually a regular in the Liverpool defence after this playing in thirty-four league games as the team finished fourth in the league, conceding just thirty-seven goals, two less than the eventual champions Blackburn Rovers.

Liverpool enjoyed great cup success that season, however, as they marched on to the League Cup final with Babb helping them to victories over Stoke, Blackburn, Arsenal and Crystal Palace before starring in the

Liverpool defence in the 2–1 final win over Bolton Wanderers.

The League Cup winners medal Babb got that day proved to be the only silverware he would win at Anfield as Liverpool flattered to deceive in the years to come.

Babb played in twenty-eight league games for Liverpool in the 1995–1996 season as they improved on their league position by one place to finish third behind Newcastle and champions Man Utd.

Liverpool enjoyed a great FA Cup run that year too, as they marched on to an eagerly awaited final date with Man Utd at Wembley. Babb was part of a Liverpool team that failed to shine on the day and they were beaten 1–0 in a largely disappointing game.

Nevertheless, Liverpool started the following season with strong hopes of winning the league but, once again, they fell short.

Babb played in twenty-two league games that season and while Liverpool were leading the table for long periods, they fell off near the end and finished in a disappointing fourth spot.

Babb also had to endure the agony of losing a major semi-final that season, as Liverpool crashed out to Paris St Germain in the European Cup Winners Cup.

The 1996–1997 season was also notable for the fact that Babb scored his one and only Liverpool goal in a 1–0 win at Highfield Road against his former club Coventry.

The following season was much of the same for Liverpool as they finished another promising league campaign in third place with Babb playing in just nineteen league matches.

For the start of the 1998–1999 season, Liverpool brought in French coach Gerard Houllier to work alongside Roy Evans, but the co-manager double act was doomed to failure and Evans left the club a few months later after a poor start.

Babb remained in Houllier's plans for the remainder of that campaign, playing in twenty-five matches as Liverpool slipped back in the league to finish a lowly seventh.

Babb remained at the club for another year but failed to appear in any more matches before Houllier allowed him to leave the club on a free transfer to top Portuguese club Sporting Lisbon in July 2000.

Babb's last start for Liverpool was in a thrilling 2–2 draw with Man Utd at Anfield in which Liverpool came from two goals down to snatch a draw.

His last ever appearance in a red shirt was as a sub in a 3–0 victory over Wimbledon on 16 May 1999.

Name: Mark Kennedy

Date of birth: 15 May 1976

Place of birth: Dublin

Position: Winger

Years at Liverpool: 1995–1998

Games played: 21

Goals scored: 0

Other clubs: Millwall, QPR, Wimbledon, Manchester City, Queen's Park Rangers, Wolves, Crystal Palace

Winger Mark Kennedy became the most expensive teenager in English football when he joined Liverpool for £3.5 million from Millwall in March 1995.

Despite the large fee, and the fact that Kennedy had enormous natural ability to play either on the left or right wing, the youngster never lived up to his potential at Liverpool.

Kennedy struggled to establish himself in manager Roy Evans' team during the mid to late 1990s as Liverpool attempted to claim back their glory days from rivals Manchester Utd.

Kennedy made his debut for Liverpool just a month after signing when he came on as a substitute for Mark Walters in a 1–0 defeat to Leeds Utd at Anfield.

The Dubliner kept his place in the team for the remaining five league games that season, with Liverpool winning three of them to finish third in the Premier League.

With those games behind him, Kennedy was expected to go and stake a regular claim in the Liverpool side but, instead, he played in just six games the following season and started just one league match, a 1–1 draw with Southampton at Anfield in December 1995.

Liverpool made it all the way to the 1996 FA Cup final, which they lost 1–0 to Man Utd, but Kennedy never appeared throughout that entire campaign.

The following season proved to be much of the same for Kennedy, as he only appeared as a substitute in eight games for Liverpool as they finished fourth in the league.

Perhaps the biggest highlight for the winger that year was when he came on as substitute in Liverpool's dramatic European Cup Winners Cup semi-final second leg with Paris St Germain at Anfield.

Trailing 3–0 from the first leg, Liverpool managed to peg back two goals but just couldn't find a third to bring the tie into extra time in front of their own fans.

Kennedy played in just one more game for Liverpool after this when he came on as a substitute for striker Karl Heinze Riedle in a 2–1 win over Bolton in March 1998.

Resigned to the fact that he was unlikely to ever gain a regular first team slot at Liverpool, Kennedy departed Anfield for Wimbledon in a deal worth £1.75 million on 26 March 1998.

Name: Jason McAteer

Date of birth: 18 June 1971

Place of birth: Birkenhead

Position: Midfielder

Years at Liverpool: 1995–1999

Games played: 139

Goals scored: 6

Other clubs: Bolton Wanderers, Blackburn Rovers, Sunderland, Tranmere Rovers

Boyhood Reds' fan Jason McAteer was on the verge of signing for reigning Premier League champions Blackburn Rovers in 1995 when he received a last-minute call from Anfield that finally brought him to his beloved Liverpool.

Midfielder McAteer had been making a name for himself as the star player in the Bolton Wanderers side that gained promotion into the Premier League that year and a number of top clubs were after his signature.

McAteer even played against Liverpool in the 1995 League Cup final and had been impressing with the Ireland international team, so it was no surprise when Liverpool manager Roy Evans made his move for him.

Evans paid out £4.5 million for McAteer in September 1995 as he continued a rebuilding programme that he hoped would land Liverpool an elusive nineteenth league title. Liverpool certainly put in a number of title challenges during McAteer's four years at the club, but sadly they just fell short each time.

Full of energy and enthusiasm and plenty of running, McAteer fitted perfectly into Roy Evans plans as the right 'wing-back' in his 3–5–2 formation.

He made his debut for Liverpool as a late substitute for John Barnes in a comfortable 3–0 win at Anfield over Blackburn and got his first league start in a mammoth clash with Man Utd at Old Trafford which finished in an entertaining 2–2 draw.

McAteer played in twenty-nine league games in all for Liverpool during the 1995–1996 season as the Reds finished third in the Premier

League, their highest position since finishing runner-up to Arsenal in 1991.

Some of Liverpool's best performances that season had come in the FA Cup as they marched on to the final scoring nineteen goals and conceding just one.

McAteer played his part as his first three goals for Liverpool all came in the cup as he hit the back of the net in a 7–0 rout of Rochdale, a 4–0 away win over Shrewsbury Town and scored the final goal in an impressive 3–0 semi-final win over Aston Villa at Old Trafford.

Sadly for McAteer, he had to endure another disappointing day at Wembley, to add to his League Cup final defeat with Bolton a year earlier, when Liverpool lost the final 1–0 to Man Utd.

McAteer's first league goal for Liverpool came in a crucial 2–1 win over Arsenal at Highbury in March 1997 as they battled for the title with Man Utd and Newcastle.

The alert wing-back had reacted quickest after star striker Robbie Fowler's penalty was saved and he knocked the rebound in to keep Liverpool's title charge on course. It was the only goal McAteer would score that year as he played in all but one of Liverpool's league games and also helped them to the semi-finals of the European Cup Winners Cup.

Unfortunately, a poor end to the 1996–1997 season saw Liverpool pick up no silverware as they finished just fourth in the league and lost the Cup Winners Cup semi-final to Paris St Germain.

McAteer remained a key part of the Liverpool side the following season, playing in twenty-one league games, but the Reds were unable to make further progress under Roy Evans' finishing third in the league and losing out in a League Cup semi-final to Middlesbrough.

The 1998–1999 campaign proved to be McAteer's last at the club as the new, incoming French manager Gerard Houllier began to ring the changes.

McAteer played in just thirteen league games in that final season as Liverpool finished a disappointing seventh in the league. His last appearance for the Reds had been as a substitute on 24 January 1999 as they suffered an agonising 2–1 FA Cup defeat to Man Utd in which their fierce rivals scored two goals in the final two minutes to knock Liverpool out of the cup. McAteer was sold to Blackburn Rovers for £4 million just three days later, ending a lively but ultimately trophy-less time for him at Anfield.

Name: Darren Potter

Date of birth: 21 December 1984

Place of birth: Liverpool

Position: Midfielder

Years at Liverpool: 1999–2007

Games played: 17

Goals scored: 0

Other clubs: Southampton, Wolves, Sheffield Wednesday

Liverpool-born lad Darren Potter joined Liverpool in 1999 as a fifteen-year-old apprentice after initially been knocked back by fellow Merseyside giants Everton.

Midfielder Potter was eligible to play for Ireland through his parents and had, by 2010, played in four games for the Republic of Ireland.

Potter made it through the competitive youth system at Liverpool to make it onto the fringes of the Liverpool first team by the time new Spanish manager Rafael Benitez had come on board in the summer of 2004.

However, Potter was always going to find it difficult to dislodge Liverpool's top-class international trio of Steven Gerrard, Didi Hamann and Xabi Alonso.

Nevertheless, he did find himself in the Liverpool team for the start of their amazing European Champions League Cup run in 2004–2005.

Rafael Benitez threw Potter in at the deep end in Liverpool's crucial Champions League qualifier with Austrian side Graz AK, when he was brought on as a late substitute for fellow Irish international Steve Finnan in Austria as Liverpool ran out 2–0 winners.

He then started the second leg at Anfield on the right of the Liverpool midfield as the Reds endured a nervy night, losing the game 1–0 but progressing in the tie overall.

Potter's next appearance in a red shirt came in a 3–0 League Cup win over Millwall in October 2004 and he played a strong part in Liverpool's march to the final that season as he helped the team also overcome Middlesbrough, Tottenham and Watford.

Sadly for Potter, he did not feature in Liverpool's League Cup final squad as the Reds went down 3–2 to Chelsea in a thrilling game.

Apart from a start in Liverpool's disastrous 1–0 FA Cup defeat at Burnley in January 2005, Potter's only other appearances that season came as a sub in two Premier League games and he also made the bench for the club's incredible Champions League quarter-final victory over Italian giants Juventus.

However, Potter was not part of the cup final squad in Istanbul in May 2005 when Liverpool came from three goals down to beat AC Milan on penalties.

Potter did come back in to the Liverpool side for the beginning of their Champions League qualifiers the following year, helping the team back into the group stages with victories over Welsh side TNS, FBK Kaunas and CSKA Sofia.

Despite this, Potter's chances of regular first-team action remained limited and the only other game he started in the 2005–2006 season was a 2–1 defeat to Crystal Palace in the League Cup.

Potter's last game for Liverpool came as a substitute during a 0–0 with Spanish side Real Betis in the Champions League in November 2005.

He remained at the club for another season before being sold to Wolves for £500,000 in January 2007.

Name: Richie Partridge

Date of birth: 12 September 1980

Place of birth: Dublin

Position: Winger

Years at Liverpool: 2000–2005

Games played: 3

Goals scored: 0

Other clubs: Bristol Rovers, Coventry City, Sheffield Wednesday, Rotherham Utd, Chester City, Milton Keynes Dons

Flying winger Richie Partridge made a dream move to Liverpool in 2000 when he signed on as a trainee at the club. A tricky player with plenty of pace, a lot was expected of him at Liverpool but he sadly never got to realise his potential.

Despite impressing in the Liverpool youth and reserve teams, a series of injuries curtailed Partridge's chances of making it into the first team during his time at the club and he made just three appearances for Liverpool, all of them in the League Cup.

He made his full Liverpool debut during his first season at the club, when he started on the left wing during an 8–0 mauling of Stoke City in the fourth round of the League Cup in November 2000.

Liverpool, under French manager Gerard Houllier, went on to claim the League Cup that season as part of an incredible cup treble that also included the FA Cup and UEFA Cup but Partridge played no more part in any of this success.

In fact, it took another four long years before Partridge got another chance in the Liverpool first team, this time playing under new manager Rafael Benitez.

During this time, he had enjoyed a successful loan period with Coventry City but had remained a Liverpool player.

Partridge came on as a second half substitute in November 2004 as Liverpool beat Middlesbrough 2–0 in the fourth round of the League Cup and he appeared from the subs bench again a month later as Liverpool squeaked past Tottenham in a dramatic penalty shoot out.

Partridge was even brave enough to step up and take a penalty himself, smashing it home as Liverpool marched on to the final of the League Cup that season.

This successful penalty proved to be the last kick Partridge would ever make in a Liverpool shirt and he left Liverpool in July 2005 to resume his career with Sheffield Wednesday.

Name: Steve Finnan

Date of birth: 24 April 1976

Place of birth: Limerick

Position: Full-back

Years at Liverpool: 2003–2008

Games played: 217

Goals scored: 1

Honours: Champions League (2005); FA Cup (2006)

Other clubs: Birmingham, Notts County, Fulham, Espanyol, Portsmouth

All successful football clubs need a consistent full-back in their team and in Limerick man Steve Finnan Liverpool found one of the best.

Signed from London club Fulham for £3.5 million in July 2003, Finnan went on to help Liverpool re-establish themselves as a force in the European game in the five years he was at the club.

Used mainly as a right-back at Liverpool, Finnan was equally as comfortable playing on the left side of the defence or even on the wings and he was one of the best crossers of the ball at the club.

Finnan arrived at Anfield at the same time as flying Australian winger Harry Kewell as French boss Gerard Houllier continued his quest to land an elusive league title success.

Unfortunately, Finnan's first season at Anfield was curtailed by injury and he played in just twenty-two league games as the Reds finished fourth in the league.

Although the fourth place finish was enough to secure a vital European Champions League spot, Houllier was replaced by Spaniard Rafael Benitez as Liverpool manager and Finnan's Anfield career really took off.

He became the club's regular right-back under Benitez and although the team failed to make any improvement in the league in the 2004–2005 season, they embarked on a momentous Champions League run.

Finnan was in the team that squeezed past Austrian side Graz AK 2–1 on aggregate in the Champions League qualifier that sent them into the group stages and played his part in an unforgettable night at Anfield in December 2004 when Liverpool scored two late goals against Olympiacos to progress to the last sixteen of the tournament.

The consistent full-back kept his place in the team as Liverpool advanced past Bayer Leverkusen, Juventus and Chelsea to set up a mouth-watering final with AC Milan.

Finnan was again named in the team that night until an injury forced him off at half-time with Liverpool trailing Milan by three goals. Finnan's replacement Didi Hamann helped to shore up the Liverpool midfield as the team changed their system which led to the dramatic three-goal comeback that seen the Reds capture their fifth European Cup in the best final in the tournament's history.

With a Champions League winners medal in his back pocket, Finnan began the next season with renewed belief as Liverpool enjoyed one of their best league campaigns in a number of years.

Finnan played in thirty-three league games for the second season in a row as the Reds picked up as total of eighty-two points to finish third behind eventual champions Chelsea and Man Utd.

This was the highest number league points Liverpool had garnered since last winning their league title in 1990.

The Reds were also impressing in the FA Cup, with Finnan starring in the team as they edged past Luton Town 5–3 in an eight-goal thriller in the third round.

Finnan then helped Liverpool make it to the final the hard way that season, beating top Premier League opposition in Portsmouth, Man Utd, Birmingham and Chelsea to set up a Wembley date with West Ham.

Dependable Finnan was naturally one of the first names on Benitez's team sheet for that decider which remarkably also finished in a 3–3 draw with Liverpool capturing the cup after another dramatic penalty shoot-out.

Finnan was, once again, the regular right-back for the 2006–2007 season but, unfortunately, Liverpool were unable to make significant progress in the league table.

He played another thirty-three games but the team's form slipped back and they could finish no better than third but with fourteen points fewer then the previous season.

Thankfully, Liverpool had another unbelievable Champions League run to keep the fans entertained and Finnan was right in the thick of the action.

He was part of the team that put in a disciplined display in Spain to beat the reigning champions Barcelona 2–1 in their own back yard in the last sixteen and also starred in another joyous night at Anfield as Liverpool edged past Chelsea in a penalty shoot-out in the semi-final.

All this meant Finnan was playing in his second Champions League final in three seasons.

On a personal note, the 2007 final against old adversaries AC Milan in Athens was better for Finnan as he played in all but the last two minutes of the game, but Liverpool were unable to repeat their previous heroics and fell to a 2–1 defeat.

The 2006–2007 season also saw Finnan's place in the team challenged for the first time after Benitez brought in Spanish right full-back Alvaro Arbeloa to strengthen his defensive options.

Finnan played in just twenty-four league games in the 2007–2008 season, nine fewer than his three previous seasons, but the Reds had to settle yet again for little more than Champions League qualification after a fourth place finish in the table.

His participation in the Champions League was also limited, playing in just seven games, and he didn't feature at all as Liverpool lost to Chelsea in the semi-finals, the third such clash between the teams in four years.

Finnan's last ever game for Liverpool came in a 2–0 victory away to Tottenham on 11 May 2008 when he came on as a second-half substitute for Andriy Voronin.

His last start at Anfield came a week earlier as Liverpool beat Man City 1–0.

Finnan finally departed Anfield after an exciting five years when he signed for Spanish side Espanyol in August 2008.

Name: Robbie Keane

Date of birth: 8 July 1980

Place of birth: Dublin

Position: Striker

Years at Liverpool: 2008–2009

Games played: 28

Goals scored: 7

Other clubs: Coventry City, Inter Milan, Leeds United, Tottenham Hotspur, Celtic

Few players can have endured as bizarre a career at Anfield as Dublin-born striker Robbie Keane.

Brought to the club in a massive £19 million deal with Tottenham in the summer of 2008, Keane was hailed as the ideal partner for Spanish sensation Fernando Torres to finally help fire Liverpool to that elusive Premier League title.

Instead, Robbie spent just over half a season at the club before being shipped back out to Spurs after being deemed surplus to requirements by manager Rafael Benitez.

It was a cruel blow for Keane who had supported the club as a boy and never really got a fair chance to show what he could do in a red shirt.

After arriving at Anfield in July 2008, Keane made his competitive debut for Liverpool in a Champions League qualifying match away to Standard Liege which finished in a 0–0 draw.

Initially nervous in front of goal following his big money move, it took Keane eleven games before he registered his first strike for Liverpool which came in a 3–1 Champions League victory over PSV Eindhoven at Anfield.

He added another goal to his Champions League tally during Liverpool's 1–1 draw away to Atletico Madrid before notching up his first two goals in the Premier League in November 2008 with a first half brace in a 3–0 home win over West Brom.

Keane's best goal in a Liverpool shirt came a month later when he volleyed home a superb equaliser against Arsenal in a game at the Emirates which finished in a 1–1 draw.

The Dubliner followed this up with another couple of goals in his next match against Bolton as Liverpool marched to the top of the table with a 3–0 win.

Despite finding some good scoring form, Keane was bizarrely dropped for Liverpool's next league match at Newcastle and played just two more games in a red shirt, an FA Cup tie with Preston and a 1–1 derby draw with Everton at Anfield.

As Liverpool embarked on a battle with Manchester Utd for the Premier League title, Keane was sold back to Spurs before the end of the January transfer window in 2009, cutting short his Anfield career.

Statistics

TOP TEN EMERALD ANFIELD APPEARANCES
1. Ronnie Whelan: 493
2. Steve Heighway: 475
3. Elisha Scott: 468
4. Mark Lawrenson: 356
5. Bill Lacey: 259
6. Steve Finnan: 217
7. Ray Houghton: 202
8. Phil Babb: 170
9. Steve Staunton: 148
10. Jason McAteer: 139

TOP TEN EMERALD ANFIELD GOALSCORERS
1. Steve Heighway: 76
2. Ronnie Whelan: 73
3. John Aldridge: 63
4. Ray Houghton: 38
5. Bill Lacey: 29
6. Sam English: 26
7. Sammy Smyth: 20
8. Mark Lawrenson: 18
9. Michael Robinson: 13
10. David Hannah: 12

LIVERPOOL FA CUP FINAL WINS
1965
Liverpool 2–1 Leeds Utd (Hunt, St John)

1974
Liverpool 3–0 Newcastle Utd (Keegan (2), Heighway)

1986
Liverpool 3–1 Everton (Rush (2), Johnson)

1989
Liverpool 3–2 Everton (Aldridge, Rush (2))

1992
Liverpool 2–0 Sunderland (Thomas, Rush)

2001
Liverpool 2–1 Arsenal (Owen (2))

2006
Liverpool 3–3 West Ham (Cisse, Gerrard (2))
* Liverpool win 3–1 on penalties

LEAGUE CUP FINAL WINS
1981
Liverpool 2–1 West Ham (Dalglish, Hansen)

1982
Liverpool 3–1 Tottenham Hotspur (Whelan (2), Rush)

1983
Liverpool 2–1 Manchester Utd (Kennedy, Whelan)

1984
Liverpool 1–0 Everton (Souness)

1995
Liverpool 2–1 Bolton Wanderers (McManaman (2))

2001
Liverpool 1–1 Birmingham (Fowler)
* Liverpool win 5–4 on penalties

2003
Liverpool 2–0 Manchester Utd (Gerrard, Owen)

EUROPEAN CUP FINAL WINS
1977
Liverpool 3–1 Borussia Monchengladbach (McDermott, Smith, Neal)

1978
Liverpool 1–0 FC Bruges (Dalglish)

1981
Liverpool 1–0 Real Madrid (A. Kennedy)

1984
Liverpool 1–1 Roma (Neal)
* Liverpool win 4–2 on penalties

2005
Liverpool 3–3 AC Milan (Gerrard, Smicer, Alonso)
* Liverpool win 3–2 on penalties

UEFA CUP FINAL WINS
1973
Liverpool 3–2 Borussia Mönchengladbach (Keegan (2), Lloyd)
*Aggregate score

1976
Liverpool 4–3 FC Bruges (R. Kennedy, Case, Keegan) (Keegan)
*Aggregate score

2001
Liverpool 5–4 Alaves (Babbel, Gerrard, McAllister, Fowler, Geli (OG))

YEARS LIVERPOOL WON LEAGUE
1900–1901

	P	W	D	L	F	A	PTS
Liverpool	34	19	7	8	5	35	45
Sunderland	34	15	13	6	57	26	43
Notts County	34	18	4	12	54	46	40
Notts Forest	34	16	7	11	53	36	39
Bury	34	16	7	11	55	37	39
Newcastle	34	14	10	10	42	37	38
Everton	34	16	5	13	47	35	37
Wednesday	34	13	10	11	52	42	36
Blackburn	34	12	9	13	39	47	33
Bolton	34	13	7	14	39	55	33
Man City	34	13	6	15	48	58	32
Derby County	34	12	7	15	55	42	31
Wolves	34	9	13	12	39	55	31
Sheff Utd	34	12	7	15	35	51	31
Aston Villa	34	10	10	14	45	51	30
Stoke City	34	11	5	18	46	57	27
Preston	34	9	7	18	49	75	25
West Brom	34	7	8	19	35	62	22

1905–1906

	P	W	D	L	F	A	PTS
Liverpool	38	23	5	10	79	46	51
Preston	38	17	13	8	54	39	47
Wednesday	38	18	8	12	63	52	44
Newcastle	38	18	7	13	74	48	43
Man City	38	19	5	14	73	54	43
Bolton	38	17	7	14	81	67	41
Birmingham	38	17	7	14	65	59	41
Aston Villa	38	17	6	15	72	56	40
Blackburn	38	16	8	14	54	52	39
Stoke City	38	16	7	15	54	55	39
Everton	38	15	7	16	70	66	37
W. Arsenal	38	15	7	16	62	64	37
Sheff Utd	38	15	6	17	57	62	36
Sunderland	38	15	5	18	61	70	35
Derby County	38	14	7	17	39	58	35
Notts County	38	11	12	15	55	71	34
Bury	38	11	10	17	57	74	32
Middlesbro	38	10	11	17	56	71	31
Notts Forest	38	13	5	20	58	79	31
Wolves	38	8	7	23	58	99	23

1921–1922

	P	W	D	L	F	A	PTS
Liverpool	42	22	13	7	63	36	57
Tottenham	42	21	9	12	65	39	51
Burnley	42	22	5	15	62	41	49
Cardiff	42	19	10	13	61	53	48
Aston Villa	42	22	3	17	65	43	47
Bolton	42	20	7	15	68	59	47
Newcastle	42	18	10	14	59	45	46
Middlesbro	42	16	14	12	79	69	46
Chelsea	42	17	12	13	40	43	46
Man City	42	18	9	15	65	70	45
Sheff Utd	42	15	10	17	49	54	40
Sunderland	42	16	8	18	60	61	40
West Brom	42	15	10	17	51	63	40
Huddersfield	42	15	9	18	53	54	39
Blackburn	42	13	12	17	54	57	38
Preston	42	13	12	17	42	65	38
Arsenal	42	15	7	20	47	56	37
Birmingham	42	15	7	20	48	60	37
Oldham	42	13	11	18	38	40	37
Everton	42	12	12	18	57	55	36

Bradford City	42	11	10	21	48	72	32
Man Utd	42	8	12	22	41	73	28

1922–1923

	P	W	D	L	F	A	PTS
Liverpool	42	26	8	8	70	31	60
Sunderland	42	22	10	10	72	54	54
Huddersfield	42	21	11	10	60	32	53
Newcastle	42	18	12	12	45	37	48
Everton	42	20	7	15	63	59	47
Aston Villa	42	18	10	14	64	60	46
West Brom	42	17	11	14	58	49	45
Man City	42	17	11	14	50	49	45
Cardiff	42	18	7	17	73	59	43
Sheff Utd	42	16	10	16	68	64	42
Arsenal	42	16	10	16	61	62	42
Tottenham	42	17	7	18	50	50	41
Bolton	42	14	12	16	50	58	40
Blackburn	42	14	12	16	47	62	40
Burnley	42	16	6	20	58	59	38
Preston	42	13	11	18	60	64	37
Birmingham	42	13	11	18	41	57	37
Middlesbro	42	13	10	19	57	63	36
Chelsea	42	9	18	15	45	53	36
Notts Forest	42	13	8	21	41	70	34
Stoke City	42	10	10	22	47	67	30
Oldham	42	10	10	22	35	65	30

1946–1947

	P	W	D	L	F	A	PTS
Liverpool	42	25	7	10	84	52	57
Man Utd	42	22	12	8	95	54	56
Wolves	42	25	6 1	1	98	56	56
Stoke City	42	24	7	11	90	53	55
Blackpool	42	22	6	14	71	70	50
Sheff Utd	42	21	7	14	89	75	49
Preston	42	18	11	13	76	74	47
Aston Villa	42	18	9	15	67	53	45
Sunderland	42	18	8	16	65	66	44
Everton	42	17	9	16	62	67	43
Middlesbro	42	17	8	17	73	68	42
Portsmouth	42	16	9	17	66	60	41
Arsenal	42	16	9	17	72	70	41
Derby	42	18	5	19	73	79	41

STATISTICS

Chelsea	42	16	7	19	69	84	39
Grimsby	42	13	12	17	61	82	38
Blackburn	42	14	8	20	45	53	36
Bolton	42	13	8	21	57	69	34
Charlton	42	11	12	19	57	71	34
Huddersfield	42	13	7	22	53	79	33
Brentford	42	9	7	26	48	88	25
Leeds Utd	42	6	6	30	45	90	18

1963–1964

	P	W	D	L	F	A	PTS
Liverpool	42	26	5	11	92	45	57
Man Utd	42	23	7	12	90	62	53
Everton	42	21	10	11	84	64	52
Tottenham	42	22	7	13	97	81	51
Chelsea	42	20	10	10	72	56	50
Sheff Wed	42	19	11	12	84	67	49
Blackburn	42	18	10	14	89	65	46
Arsenal	42	17	11	14	90	82	45
Burnley	42	17	10	15	71	64	44
West Brom	42	16	11	15	70	61	43
Leicester	42	16	11	15	61	58	43
Sheff Utd	42	16	11	15	61	64	43
Notts Forest	42	16	9	17	64	68	41
West Ham	42	14	12	16	69	74	40
Fulham	42	13	13	16	58	65	39
Wolves	42	12	15	15	70	80	39
Stoke City	42	14	10	18	77	78	38
Blackpool	42	13	9	20	52	73	35
Aston Villa	42	11	12	19	62	71	34
Birmingham	42	11	7	24	54	92	29
Bolton	42	10	8	24	48	80	28
Ipswich	42	9	7	26	56	121	25

1965–1966

	P	W	D	L	F	A	PTS
Liverpool	42	26	9	7	79	34	61
Leeds Utd	42	23	9	10	79	38	55
Burnley	42	24	7	11	79	47	55
Man Utd	42	18	15	9	84	59	51
Chelsea	42	22	7	13	65	53	51
West Brom	42	19	12	11	91	69	50
Leicester City	42	21	7	14	80	65	49
Tottenham	42	16	12	14	75	66	44

	P	W	D	L	F	A	PTS
Sheff Utd	42	16	11	15	56	59	43
Stoke City	42	15	12	15	65	64	42
Everton	42	15	11	16	56	62	41
West Ham	42	15	9	18	70	83	39
Blackpool	42	14	9	19	55	65	37
Arsenal	42	12	13	17	62	75	37
Newcastle	42	14	9	19	50	63	37
Aston Villa	42	15	6	21	69	80	36
Sheff Wed	42	14	8	20	56	66	36
Notts Forest	42	14	8	20	56	72	36
Sunderland	42	14	8	20	51	72	6
Fulham	42	14	7	21	67	85	35
Northampton	42	10	13	19	55	92	33
Blackburn	42	8	4	30	57	88	20

1972–1973

	P	W	D	L	F	A	PTS
Liverpool	42	25	10	7	72	42	60
Arsenal	42	23	11	8	57	43	57
Leeds Utd	42	21	11	10	71	45	53
Ipswich	42	17	14	11	55	45	48
Wolves	42	18	11	13	66	54	47
West Ham	42	17	12	13	67	53	46
Derby County	42	19	8	15	56	54	46
Tottenham	42	16	13	13	58	48	45
Newcastle	42	16	13	13	60	51	45
Birmingham	42	15	12	15	53	54	42
Man City	42	15	11	16	57	60	41
Chelsea	42	13	14	15	49	51	40
Southampton	42	11	18	13	47	52	40
Sheff Utd	42	15	10	17	51	59	40
Stoke City	42	14	10	18	61	56	38
Leicester	42	10	17	15	40	46	37
Everton	42	13	11	18	41	49	37
Man Utd	42	12	13	17	44	60	37
Coventry	42	13	9	20	40	55	35
Norwich	42	11	10	21	36	63	32
Crystal Pal	42	9	12	21	41	58	30
West Brom	42	9	10	23	38	62	28

STATISTICS 297

1975–1976

	P	W	D	L	F	A	PTS
Liverpool	42	23	14	5	66	31	60
QPR	42	24	11	7	67	33	59
Man Utd	42	23	10	9	68	42	56
Derby County	42	21	11	10	75	58	53
Leeds Utd	42	21	9	12	65	46	51
Ipswich	42	16	14	12	54	48	46
Leicester	42	13	19	10	48	51	45
Man City	42	16	11	15	64	46	43
Tottenham	42	14	15	13	63	63	43
Norwich	42	16	10	16	58	58	42
Everton	42	15	12	15	60	66	42
Stoke City	42	15	11	16	48	50	41
Middlesbro	42	15	10	17	46	45	40
Coventry	42	13	14	15	47	57	40
Newcastle	42	15	9	18	71	62	39
Aston Villa	42	11	17	14	51	59	39
Arsenal	42	13	10	19	47	53	36
West Ham	42	13	10	19	48	71	36
Birmingham	42	13	7	22	57	75	33
Wolves	42	10	10	22	51	68	33
Burnley	42	9	10	23	43	66	28
Sheff Utd	42	6	10	26	33	82	22

1976–1977

	P	W	D	L	F	A	PTS
Liverpool	42	23	11	8	62	33	57
Man City	42	21	14	7	60	34	56
Ipswich	42	22	8	12	66	39	52
Aston Villa	42	22	7	13	76	50	51
Newcastle	42	18	13	11	64	49	49
Man Utd	42	18	11	13	71	62	47
West Brom	42	16	13	13	62	56	45
Arsenal	42	16	11	15	64	59	43
Everton	42	14	14	14	62	64	42
Leeds Utd	42	15	12	15	48	51	42
Leicester	42	12	18	12	47	60	42
Middlesbro	42	14	13	15	40	45	41
Birmingham	42	13	12	17	63	61	38
QPR	42	13	12	17	47	52	38
Derby County	42	9	19	14	50	55	37
Norwich	42	14	9	19	47	64	37

West Ham	42	11	14	17	46	65	36
Bristol City	42	11	13	18	38	48	35
Coventry	42	10	15	17	48	59	35
Sunderland	42	11	12	19	46	54	34
Stoke City	42	10	14	18	28	51	34
Tottenham	42	12	9	21	48	72	33

1978–1979

	P	W	D	L	F	A	PTS
Liverpool	42	30	8	4	86	17	98
West Brom	42	24	11	7	72	35	83
Notts Forest	42	19	18	5	57	30	75
Ipswich	42	20	9	13	63	49	69
Everton	42	17	17	8	52	40	68
Leeds Utd	42	17	15	10	67	51	66
Arsenal	42	17	14	11	61	48	65
Aston Villa	42	15	16	11	59	49	61
Man Utd	42	15	15	12	60	63	60
Coventry	42	14	17	11	59	66	59
Middlesbro	42	15	11	16	56	47	56
Bristol City	42	15	10	17	47	51	55
Tottenham	42	13	15	14	48	61	54
Man City	42	13	13	16	60	57	52
Southampton	42	12	16	14	47	53	52
Bolton	42	12	11	19	54	74	47
Wolves	42	13	8	21	45	69	47
Norwich	42	7	23	12	50	56	44
Derby	42	10	11	21	44	71	41
Birmingham	42	7	11	24	39	62	32
QPR	42	6	13	23	43	72	31
Chelsea	42	5	10	27	44	92	25

1979–1980

	P	W	D	L	F	A	PTS
Liverpool	42	25	10	7	81	30	85
Man Utd	42	24	10	8	65	35	82
Ipswich	42	22	9	11	68	39	75
Arsenal	42	18	16	8	52	36	70
Notts Forest	42	20	8	14	63	43	68
Wolves	42	19	9	14	58	47	66
Southmpton	42	18	9	15	65	53	63
Aston Villa	42	16	14	12	51	50	62
Middlesbro	42	16	12	14	50	44	60
Tottenham	42	15	10	17	52	62	55
Coventry	42	16	6	20	55	67	54
Leeds	42	13	14	15	46	50	53
Norwich	42	13	14	15	58	66	53
West Brom	42	11	19	12	54	50	52
Crystal Palace	42	12	16	14	41	50	52
Man City	42	13	13	16	45	64	52
Brighton	42	12	14	16	48	56	50
Stoke City	42	13	10	19	44	58	49
Everton	42	9	17	16	43	51	44
Bristol City	42	9	13	20	37	66	40
Derby County	42	10	8	24	45	69	38
Bolton	42	5	15	22	38	73	30

1981–1982

	P	W	D	L	F	A	PTS
Liverpool	42	26	9	7	80	32	87
Ipswich	42	26	5	11	75	53	83
Man Utd	42	22	12	9	59	30	78
Tottenham	42	20	11	11	67	48	71
Arsenal	42	20	11	11	48	37	71
Swansea	42	21	6	15	58	51	69
Southampton	42	20	9	14	73	67	69
Everton	42	17	13	12	56	50	64
West Ham	42	14	16	12	66	57	58
Man City	42	15	13	14	49	50	58
Aston Villa	42	15	12	15	55	53	57
Notts Forest	42	15	12	15	42	48	57
Brighton	42	13	13	16	43	52	52
Coventry	42	13	11	18	56	52	50
Notts County	42	13	8	21	61	69	47
Birmingham	42	10	14	18	53	61	44
West Brom	42	11	11	20	46	57	44

300 EMERALD ANFIELD

Stoke City	42	12	8	22	44	63	44
Sunderland	42	11	11	20	38	58	44
Leeds Utd	42	10	12	20	39	61	42
Wolves	42	10	10	22	32	63	40
Middlesbro	42	8	15	19	34	52	39

1982–1983

	P	W	D	L	F	A	PTS
Liverpool	42	24	10	8	87	37	82
Watford	42	22	5	15	74	57	71
Man Utd	42	19	13	10	56	38	70
Tottenham	42	20	9	13	65	50	69
Notts Forest	42	20	9	13	62	50	69
Aston Villa	42	21	5	16	62	50	68
Everton	42	18	10	14	66	48	64
West Ham	42	20	4	18	68	62	64
Ipswich	42	15	13	14	64	50	58
Arsenal	42	16	10	16	58	56	58
West Brom	42	15	12	15	51	49	57
Southampton	42	15	12	15	54	58	57
Stoke City	42	16	9	17	53	64	57
Norwich	42	14	12	16	52	58	54
Notts County	42	15	7	20	55	71	52
Sunderland	42	12	14	16	48	61	50
Birmingham	42	12	14	16	40	55	50
Luton Town	42	12	13	17	65	84	49
Coventry	42	13	9	20	48	59	48
Man City	42	13	8	21	47	70	47
Swansea	42	10	11	21	51	69	41
Brighton	42	9	13	20	38	68	40

1983–1984

	P	W	D	L	F	A	PTS
Liverpool	42	22	14	6	73	32	80
Southampton	42	22	11	9	66	38	77
Notts Forest	42	22	8	12	76	45	74
Man Utd	42	20	14	8	71	41	74
QPR	42	22	7	13	67	37	73
Arsenal	42	18	9	15	74	60	63
Everton	42	16	14	12	44	42	62
Tottenham	42	17	10	15	64	65	61
West Ham	42	17	9	16	60	55	60
Aston Villa	42	17	9	16	59	61	60
Watford	42	16	9	17	68	77	57

STATISTICS **301**

Ipswich	42	15	8	19	55	57	53
Sunderland	42	13	13	16	42	53	52
Norwich	42	12	15	15	48	49	51
Leicester	42	13	12	17	65	68	51
Luton	42	14	9	19	53	66	51
West Brom	42	14	9	19	48	62	51
Stoke City	42	13	11	18	44	63	50
Coventry	42	13	11	18	57	77	50
Birmingham	42	12	12	18	39	50	48
Notts County	42	10	11	21	50	72	41
Wolves	42	6	11	25	27	80	29

1985–1986

	P	W	D	L	F	A	PTS
Liverpool	42	26	10	6	89	37	88
Everton	42	26	8	8	87	41	86
West Ham	42	26	6	10	74	40	84
Man Utd	42	22	10	10	70	36	76
Sheff Wed	42	21	10	11	63	54	73
Chelsea	42	20	11	11	57	56	71
Arsenal	42	20	9	13	49	47	69
Notts Forest	42	19	11	12	69	53	68
Luton	42	18	12	12	61	44	66
Tottenham	42	19	8	15	74	52	65
Newcastle	42	17	12	13	67	72	63
Watford	42	16	11	15	69	62	59
QPR	42	15	7	20	53	64	52
Southampton	42	12	10	20	51	62	46
Man City	42	11	12	19	43	57	45
Aston Villa	42	10	14	18	51	67	44
Coventry	42	11	10	21	48	71	43
Oxford	42	10	12	20	60	80	42
Leicester	42	10	12	20	56	76	42
Ipswich	42	11	8	23	32	55	41
Birmingham	42	8	5	29	30	73	29
West Brom	42	4	12	26	35	89	24

1987–1988

	P	W	D	L	F	A	PTS
Liverpool	40	26	12	2	87	24	90
Man Utd	40	23	12	5	71	38	81
Notts Forest	40	20	13	7	67	39	73
Everton	40	19	13	8	53	27	70

QPR	40	19	10	11	48	38	67
Arsenal	40	18	12	10	58	39	66
Wimbledon	40	14	15	11	58	47	57
Newcastle	40	14	14	12	55	53	56
Luton	40	14	11	15	57	58	53
Coventry	40	13	14	13	46	53	53
Sheff Wed	40	15	8	17	52	66	53
Southampton	40	12	14	14	49	53	50
Tottenham	40	12	11	17	38	48	47
Norwich	40	12	9	19	40	52	45
Derby County	40	10	13	17	35	45	43
West Ham	40	9	15	16	40	52	42
Charlton	40	9	15	16	38	52	42
Chelsea	40	9	15	16	50	68	42
Portsmouth	40	7	14	19	36	66	35
Watford	40	7	11	22	27	51	32
Oxford	40	6	13	21	44	80	31

1989–1990

	P	W	D	L	F	A	PTS
Liverpool	38	23	10	5	78	37	79
Aston Villa	38	21	7	10	57	38	70
Tottenham	38	19	6	13	59	47	63
Arsenal	38	18	8	12	54	38	62
Chelsea	38	16	12	10	58	50	60
Everton	38	17	8	13	57	46	59
Southampton	38	15	10	13	71	63	55
Wimbledon	38	13	16	9	47	40	55
Notts Forest	38	15	9	14	55	47	54
Norwich	38	13	14	11	44	42	53
QPR	38	13	11	14	45	44	50
Coventry	38	14	7	17	39	59	49
Man Utd	38	13	9	16	46	47	48
Man City	38	12	12	14	43	52	48
Crystal Palace	38	13	9	16	42	66	48
Derby County	38	13	7	18	43	40	46
Luton	38	10	13	15	43	57	43
Sheff Wed	38	11	10	17	35	51	43
Charlton	38	7	9	22	31	57	30
Millwall	38	5	11	22	39	65	26

Acknowledgements

I would like to thank the following for all their help and support in putting this book together: Ciara Doorley, Claire Rourke, Ed Fitzsimons, Nicky Allt, Alison O'Reilly, Willie Miller, Malcolm Brodie, Padraig Coyle (Belfast Celtic Society), John Keith, Stephen Done, Niall Wallace, the staff at Liverpool Record Office, Nicola Hassan (Derry City), Derek Falkiner, my dad Noel Falkiner, partner Yvonne McWeeney and daughter Aoibheann.